A People's History of American Higher Education

D1474418

This essential history of American higher education brings a fresh perspective to the field, challenging the accepted ways of thinking historically about colleges and universities. Organized thematically, this book builds from the ground up, shedding light on the full, diverse range of institutions—including small liberal arts schools, junior and community colleges, black and white women's colleges, black colleges, and state colleges—that have been instrumental in creating the higher education system we know today. *A People's History of American Higher Education* focuses on those participants who may not have been members of elite groups, yet who helped push elite institutions and the country as a whole. This pathbreaking textbook addresses key issues that have often been condemned to exceptions and footnotes—if not ignored completely—in historical considerations of U.S. higher education; particularly race, ethnicity, gender, and class.

Hutcheson introduces readers to both social and intellectual history, providing invaluable perspectives and methodologies for graduate students and faculty members alike. *A People's History of American Higher Education* surveys the varied characteristics of the diverse populations constituting or striving for the middle class through educational attainment, providing a narrative that unites often divergent historical fields. The author engages readers in a powerful, revised understanding of what institutions and participants beyond the oft-cited elite groups have done for American higher education.

Philo A. Hutcheson is Professor of Higher Education at the University of Alabama.

Core Concepts in Higher Education is a textbook series for the education of new professionals, covering the core areas of study in the field of higher education and student affairs. This timely and dependable series provides the necessary tools to ensure practice is informed by theory and research. The books in this series invite students to think critically about the field to discover what has been left out and what needs to be learned, and also provides frameworks and constructs for addressing challenges facing higher education. The Core Concepts in Higher Education series moves thought, action, and scholarship forward by valuing, reconstructing, and building on the foundations of the field. Through a rich combination of research, theory, and practice, this series aims to move the field into a new generation of scholarship to better prepare students for authentic leadership of our colleges, universities, and academic communities.

Series Editors: Marybeth Gasman, Stella Flores, and Edward P. St. John

Student Development Theory in Higher Education
A Social Psychological Approach
Terrell L. Strayhorn

Law and Social Justice in Higher Education
Crystal Renee Chambers

Qualitative Inquiry in Higher Education Organization and Policy Research
Penny Pasque and Vicente Lechuga

American Higher Education
Issues and Institutions
John R. Thelin

Contemporary Issues in Higher Education
Edited by Marybeth Gasman and Andrés Castro Samayoa

A People's History of American Higher Education
Philo A. Hutcheson

A People's History of American Higher Education

Philo A. Hutcheson

Routledge
Taylor & Francis Group

NEW YORK AND LONDON

First published 2020
by Routledge
52 Vanderbilt Avenue, New York, NY 10017

and by Routledge
2 Park Square, Milton Park, Abingdon, Oxon, OX14 4RN

Routledge is an imprint of the Taylor & Francis Group, an informa business

© 2020 Taylor & Francis

Library of Congress Cataloging-in-Publication Data
A catalog record for this title has been requested

ISBN: 978-0-415-89469-2 (hbk)
ISBN: 978-0-415-89470-8 (pbk)
ISBN: 978-0-203-81306-5 (ebk)

Typeset in Minion Pro
by Swales & Willis Ltd, Exeter, Devon, UK

CONTENTS

Brittany Smotherson

Series Editor's Introduction   vii
Preface   viii

Chapter 1   Introduction: History as Inquiry   1

Chapter 2   From the Beginning: Leadership, Exclusion, and Stratification
             in the Colonizing Colleges and the Early Republic   19

Chapter 3   A Century of Destiny Built on Developing Traditions: Higher
             Education Expands   44

Chapter 4   The Progressive Era and Its Enduring Impact on Higher
             Education: Efficient, Rational Solutions to Moral and
             Social Problems   74

Chapter 5   War: Meanings of Patriotism in Higher Education   100

Chapter 6   Sex and Love! Beer! Football! And Other Important
             Student Activities   130

Chapter 7   The Research University, Revised   159

Chapter 8   From the Colonial Colleges to the Colleges and Universities
             of Today: Processes of Exclusion and Stratification   183

Chapter 9   An Epilogue on This History of U.S. Higher Education:
             Historical Dimensions of Meritocracy   200

Index   216

SERIES EDITOR'S INTRODUCTION

It is a pleasure to serve as an editor for the *Core Concepts in Higher Education* series, which is published by Routledge Press. Along with my co-editors, Edward St. John and Stella Flores, I am thrilled to have Philo Hutcheson's new book *A People's History of American Higher Education* in our series.

For years, I have been telling Philo, whom I have known since I was a new assistant professor at Georgia State University, to write a history of American higher education that engaged underrepresented individuals—across students, faculty, and administration—more fully. When we conceptualized this series, I asked him to write a book that would be inclusive, that would have his witty humor, and that would challenge students to think beyond the traditional ways of thinking about the history of colleges and universities.

For readers unfamiliar with Philo's voice, it is confident, funny, and thorough in tone and impact. Readers will enjoy the way that he walks one through the complicated nature of our past and pushes us to consider and reconsider various individuals, groups, and institutions.

Students in higher education programs and those taking history of higher education classes will benefit from this book's addition to the syllabus as it provides a view unlike any other available at this moment. It challenges others writing surveys of the history of American higher education and complements them in the same breath.

Enjoy this read as it will enlighten you and offer fresh perspectives.

Marybeth Gasman
Judy & Howard Berkowitz Professor, University of Pennsylvania
Series Co-Editor, *Core Concepts in Higher Education*

PREFACE

Broad histories of U.S. higher education typically begin with either an account of European medieval universities or the establishment of the first college in the Massachusetts Bay Colony in 1636 because there is a chronological reason to begin with the earliest events in recounting a history. This is an understandable approach, yet it forces the author (or authors) as well as the reader to specific comprehensions of higher education, in particular a focus on the old institutions, institutions that have often become elite, and how they have shaped higher education. While this book of course forces me as well as readers to specific comprehensions, I hope I have turned the comprehensions to a more challenging view. In this regard, Routledge Press chose to title this book as *A People's History of American Higher Education*; the author of *A People's History of the United States*, Howard Zinn, was a towering activist historian who demanded that we see our history from the perspectives of those typically excluded, marginalized, or brutalized from the centers of power in this nation. (A brief but important explanation is necessary. The book title uses the term American, which I can and do use for the discussion of the colonies, but throughout the text I use U.S. or United States because I am very wary of the idea that "America" solely refers to the "United States"—that usage leaves out the many countries across North and South America.) In view of the fact that by and large U.S. institutions of higher education have excluded students for a variety of reasons—gender, race and ethnicity, economic status, sexual identity, physical access, for example—this book cannot truly be a people's history. The people in the context of this book have privilege because they attend institutions of higher education, but many of them are too often not integral to the story in broad histories of higher education, missing the meanings of the histories of their exclusion or marginalization or both in the broad context of higher education. I accepted the challenge because it is important in teaching the history of U.S. higher education to think differently about higher education; what I write about is not what the elite institutions have done as the central focus, but rather what people of everyday standing have experienced in higher education as the central focus. The term "elite" is deliberate, in order to highlight a theme developed in this book, that we began segmenting society in terms of higher education institutions and their different roles in regard to building the nation in the early 1800s, a process that consistently accelerated in the 1900s and, it seems now, is firmly in a place as a means to determine who is most likely to receive what sorts of benefits from a higher education. To be clear, often the elite institutions' accomplishments are recognized globally, and indeed as a product of elite institutions, I am part of that elite status. Nevertheless, the book begins with those institutions as colonizing (more commonly called colonial, as I will do at times) colleges, and so I quickly challenge the general assumptions about those institutions' early years. In contrast to elites and their likely national status, most of the students and graduates of the vast majority of colleges and universities in this country are those who are leaders within their immediate communities, their states, and their regions, with consequences for the nation. Why not, I think, ask who they are and what they have done.

I have written this book for two reasons. First, it is a teaching text, asking readers to think historically and to challenge accepted ways of thinking historically about colleges and universities. I am struck by the differences between a teaching text and a scholarly text. While they are necessarily linked, in the case of teaching the history of higher education in this country, I draw more upon present perspectives than in my scholarly approaches, in great part because I know that my colleagues in the field are also well-read and that our shared knowledge is built upon a range of knowledge—including experience—that allows for interpretations formed as challenges to previous interpretations, a historical approach known as revisionism. Later, in the Introduction, I address presentism as well as revisionism, both of which are important issues in studying and teaching history. Second, I am deeply indebted to the many graduate students in my history of higher education courses—which I first taught 25 years before completing this manuscript. However much I enjoy my historical scholarship, and it is a passion that began in my doctoral program, it is the classroom where I feel most vibrant. And particularly in the history of higher education courses I have felt energy and grace, driving me toward more careful interpretations of our history while recognizing the differences, the similarities, the challenges, and the successes, of millions of people. Much of that response has come when students have asked me questions, and while I often know the answer, knowing how to frame the answer has always been a matter of great pleasure. Or as a colleague said to a student who told him she was in my history of higher education course, "That is Philo." As a result of all those years of teaching the history of higher education as well as encouraging students, regardless of their career aspirations, to write a dissertation on some aspect of the history of higher education or with a substantial section addressing history (as of the end of 2018, I had chaired 25 dissertations in the history of education or history of higher education), I have come to see the history of U.S. higher education through a much broader perspective than when I started, a reminder that a classroom or a campus is an educative process and not merely a place where a teacher dumps information into empty vessels. Students, and especially students with marginalized or oppressed experiences (an African American woman who never had an instructor recognize her when she raised her hand until my class), have taught me how to think about this topic. While I tend toward quips, as in the case when in response to a student's question about the difference between sociology and history, I said after a pause, "In general, historians are correct," I also ask myself and students to think deeply about our history. In affirmation of that approach, throughout the endnotes are dissertations that I have chaired or served on the committee.

So, in contrast to some or great degree with some of the histories I will briefly discuss in the Introduction and in the final chapter, I have written this book in order to convince readers of the importance of thinking historically in order to understand how we have created higher education in the United States from the ground up. Elements of our past have changed our present, even at those times when we do not know the specifics of historical events; the history of the decisions of college and university faculties to require this course or that one or none may not be written about in academic catalogues, but the effects are real. As William Faulkner noted in *Requiem for a Nun*, "The past is never dead. It is not even past." I want to convince readers about the importance of thinking historically in part because I would want to know whose history I ought to know, and more so because I am convinced that thinking historically allows us to engage the human experience, and if done with care, to have a better understanding of the human experience today. History does not, cannot, predict the present or the future, if only for the fact that whatever we know about history immediately reshapes our present. And the future, I think, is somewhat impervious to the present and past, events and people moving in both expected and unexpected ways. (Not once, as a doctoral student impatiently using a typewriter did I anticipate the power and weakness of today's electronic forms of writing. Or, while today's technology might seem inevitable, so too was educational television in the 1950s. How television educates today is a far cry from the presumptions of seemingly visionary articles and books about educational television back in the 1950s.) That said, history can teach us, if for no other reason than to know the events we can celebrate and the events that ought to haunt us, but can too easily remain hidden under the guise of a social construction that does not remind us that people and peoples participate in the life of the nation—or in the case of this book, specific types of institutions—in very different ways. Thinking of a white male college that remained all male until the 1970s or even the 1980s may lay a veil across the countering voices of gender and race and ethnicity if we are not careful.

The initial organizing approach for this book occurred to me when I was preparing to give a speech at Indiana University in the spring of 2011 at the invitation of Andrea Walton, a speech in which I offered broad themes while keeping the idea of challenging traditional centers of historical argument at the forefront of my inquiry. I asked, what would occur by starting this history from the middle, the middle of the country and the middle of the history of U.S. higher education? As a statement of researcher bias, such a popular statement nowadays, in 1969 I graduated from a New England prep school and got out of town, landing in Waukesha, Wisconsin, to attend Carroll College (now Carroll University). It was far from New England, it was small, coeducational, and offered a liberal arts curriculum. While my four years there may not have been as intense as my four days at Woodstock in 1969, it was a terrific experience, and I spent three years in admissions there before moving to an admissions position at Beloit College in Wisconsin. Beloit College, in fact, is the starting point of the history of higher education in the 1800s in Chapter 3. And so, I have a certain affection for higher education in the Midwest. Ah, then, that necessary artifact, the scholar's passion.[1] Eventually I returned to a baseline of chronology yet with a substantial and explicit use of themes rather than starting with the middle chronologically (the 1800s) and geographically (the Midwest), so that readers have the easy route of history, i.e., from the beginning until the chapter on war and the succeeding chapters, where theme is the narrative approach.

WHAT TO EXPECT IN THIS BOOK

All of these arguments explain the organization of this book. I always tell my graduate students preparing to write a paper or thesis or dissertation about some historical aspect of education that it is a good idea to organize the work in a chronological order of events. That approach has its uses, and for someone just beginning a com-prehension of historical events, such a straightforward organization is informative. In contrast, as an experienced historian of higher education, I can and will take risks (thanks to the trust of the series editors, Marybeth Gasman and Edward St. John, as well as the Routledge editor, Heather Jarrow). I am organizing this book in part through historical themes, and each theme has its chronological dimensions and necessarily exhibits interactions with other themes, driving home the point that we experience higher education in both chronological and thematic form. While the book proceeds from the earliest years of higher education in the colonies (which were at the same time colonizing forces in very real contemporary senses of that term) to the mid-1900s, a his-torian, Hayden White, who has written some highly insightful historiographical work, observes that a chronological approach nevertheless reflects a theory of narrative, the thematic approaches of each historian, and hence, one historian will write a history that emphasizes certain themes, another emphasizing other themes. So one history reads as "A, b, c, d, e, . . . z" while another historian's account of the same events reads "a, B, c, d, e, . . . z" and so on.[2] Many years ago a rising scholar of higher education said to me that he thought it would be interesting to write a thematic history of higher education—I was baffled, since I have long known history (not the trivia of game shows, but history as pursued by academics) to be deeply thematic. In the case of this book, I break away from the chronology in the context of themes. As a reminder, how individuals perceive colleges and universities often have thematic contexts in chronological form. On any given day someone on a campus may be focused on the university's football program, and on the next day be focused on the chemistry department. Hence, within the themes I tend to use chronology, and at the risk of confusing readers, I use chronology loosely, as many historians do. For example, historians may easily speak of the 1960s student protests on campus, but also easily argue that the period really begins somewhere in the late 1950s as the civil rights movement gains momentum among African Americans and Whites, and it ends in May 1970, with the killings at Kent State University and Jackson State University. The decade in historical terms does not begin with January 1, 1960 and end with December 31, 1969. As an important note, the killings at those two institutions are a telling example about my arguments regarding a social history with intellectual history at its core (a matter I discuss in greater detail in the Introduction). All too often we have defined May 1970 as the death of four young white people at Kent State University, ignoring the death of two black students at Jackson State University only a few days after the killings at the Kent State.

So rather than arguing from Cambridge, Massachusetts, westward—which is a reminder of an old *New Yorker* magazine cover of a New Yorker's westward view of the nation, pretty much nothing except a couple of dots on the horizon that are Chicago and San Francisco after the Hudson River—I am offering arguments about U.S. colleges and universities that focus on the people and institutions that reflect such national expectations as access, the college experience, and building communities, but at the local, state, and regional levels. Possibilities included starting with black colleges or women's colleges (the latter are better called, when referring to their histories, as white women's colleges and black women's colleges); I have chosen a broader approach, which I hope helps the reader to think of those and other institutions that are not broadly used as examples. Centering those who have not been at centers of power is an important approach because it reminds the writer and the readers that centers are often challenged in human affairs.

I would be unable to write this book if it were not for the remarkable outpouring of contributions to the history of U.S. higher education since the early 1990s, contributions challenging the traditional ways of interpreting the history of higher education.[3] I am deeply thankful to the many and varied historians who have made this effort possible. So many fellow historians of education have enriched my work with their comments and questions about my work and their own important contributions, it is impossible to list them all, but it is an important protocol to highlight several. In no particular order because I stand on all their shoulders: Harold Wechsler, Wayne Urban, Linda Eisenmann, Jana Nidiffer, Les Goodchild (who decades ago alerted me to the fact that more than anything, I am an intellectual historian), Mary Ann Dzuback, Kate Rousmaniere, Jackie Blount, James Anderson, Marybeth Gasman, Chris Ogren, Andrea Walton, Katherine Chaddock, John Thelin, Roger Geiger, Bruce Leslie, Caroline Eick, Linda Perkins, Tim Cain, John Rury, and more. I know that I missed aspects of higher education that they examined, and I look forward to their critiques. In addition, thanks to my higher education program colleagues at the University of Alabama and my former ones at Georgia State University for their support of the study of the history of higher education, offering far more than mere lip service to the foundational aspects of history for the study of higher education.

I also thank Dr. John Miller, Dr. Edward Carraway, and Dr. Amit Shah of Tuscaloosa, Alabama and Dr. Jose Osario of Birmingham, Alabama. Without their medical expertise and the care provided by them and their staff members, I would not have lived to write this book.

Without a doubt, the greatest enrichment in my life has come from my daughter, Monica Dyann Hutcheson. I will always be indebted to her for her support and love as well as her patience for my bad jokes.

I dedicate this book to Willow.

NOTES

1   Max Weber, "Science as a Vocation," in *From Max Weber: Essays in Sociology*, trans. and ed. H.H. Gerth and C. Wright Mills (New York: Oxford University Press, 1958), 129–156.

2   Hayden White, "Historical Text as Literary Artifact," in *Tropics of Discourse: Essays in Cultural Criticism* (Baltimore: Johns Hopkins University Press, 1978), 92.

3   In this regard, then, I am not attempting a history of U.S. higher education based on the very sort of work that the historians I thank, as well as their predecessors (without whom we would have no texts to challenge). Historical inquiry entails the careful use and reflection upon documents of all sorts and when life permits, oral history interviews, thereby producing a secondary source interpreting those documents and interviews. Citation upon citation in this book draws upon such secondary source materials, and the verve and vigor with which colleagues have conducted their research makes our field all the richer.

1

INTRODUCTION

History as Inquiry

Part of thinking historically is to understand how we think historically, what historians call "historiography." For a long time, Microsoft Word did not recognize the words "historiographical" or "historiography." Each time I had a Windows upgrade, I had to add those two words to the dictionary. It is indeed telling that the dominant form of creating a manuscript in today's world, Microsoft Word, did not know that we have different ways of thinking historically. It is all too easy to see history as a simple recounting of facts, of names, dates, and places (what I none too fondly refer to as name-date-place crap). While such an approach may earn you a winner's spot in a trivia game, it is not historical inquiry. If you or I want to think historically, we have to think about who did what when and where in terms of how and why. And, thanks to the post-World War II movements toward challenging glorious renditions of the past, the hows and whys of history are now far more complicated than they were even a generation ago, much less two or three generations ago. We create our historical narratives, and the purpose of this introduction is to be explicit about how I have attempted to create this history.

One way of thinking historically is to consider how the writer raises issues or addresses concerns that are not primary to the argument but are important; there are plenty of details and arguments in history and measuring which are more important than others is an important way of choosing how to present the historical narrative, as I noted in the Preface. The Turabian style manual, with the use of footnotes or endnotes as the primary form of citation in historical writing, allows the writer to offer secondary content, in comment on the primary content of the text, in addition to specific citations to tell readers where the information comes from. There are some of those notes in this book, and readers need to consider taking the time to read the content endnotes, rather than taking them as a way to reduce the amount of text that you have to read. Other endnotes will be simply reference notes, offering you, the reader, the opportunity to pursue the issues raised in the text by going to the original source and developing an informed way of thinking historically.

Writing a history of U.S. higher education is a daunting task of thinking historically for a number of reasons. First, the sweep of the centuries requires attention across multiple meanings of higher education, across multiple groups involved with higher education, across the rise and fall of multiple types of higher education institutions. Second, there are several strong histories of U.S. higher education, both in terms of sweeping interpretations as well as well-focused works on important aspects of meanings, people, or institutions. For the moment, I want to highlight six books that offer important and sweeping portraits of the history of U.S. higher education, starting with Frederick Rudolph, *The American College and University: A History*. Rudolph completed the massive task of reading dozens upon dozens of institutional histories (having read some, I am not going to recommend that effort unless you are very dedicated to sifting through presidencies, celebrations, and some glossing over of uncomfortable events), and his work starts with the beginning, Harvard's foundation in 1636, and ends in the 1950s. Notable given its first publication in 1962, Rudolph addresses women (mostly white women) and African Americans, groups all too often ignored well into the 1970s. Rudolph reminds readers that academic drift is highly characteristic of higher education in this country. There is also John S. Brubacher and Willis Rudy, *Higher Education in Transition; A History of American Colleges And Universities, 1636–1968*, an analysis of changes in U.S. higher education, with careful attention to such matters as the curriculum, professional education, and student life. Laurence Veysey wrote a very long dissertation (over 1,200 pages according to the legend), and his book, *The Emergence of the American University*, is the result. It addresses four meanings of higher education—discipline and piety, utility, research, and liberal culture—arguing that in the end, although discipline and piety had almost dissipated by the early 1900s, the other three meanings entered into an uneasy but oddly effective blend that established the American university. A fourth book, by John Thelin, *A History of American Higher Education*, in one sense furthers Rudolph's interpretations but in other important ways offers nuances about the complexity of the history and provides a direct challenge to practitioners to understand history in order to improve their practice, a long-standing interest of his. Fifth, Roger Geiger's book, *The History of American Higher Education: Learning and Culture from the Founding to World War II*, reflects his long-standing and successful inquiries into research universities and the colleges that support them, highlighting culture (of the intellectual sort) and reason. Finally, Barbara Solomon wrote *In the Company of Educated Women*, the first overview of women in higher education and a reminder that we are seriously remiss if we do not attend to all who attend higher education and experience its effects. Because of these books for the most part I have written this book built on articles even though historians of higher education know that a good book is the goal of a good historian, for the easy reason that broad interpretations of books find little hold in a brief article, so I do not wrestle directly with the well-informed and highly informative book-length efforts of these and other scholars that offer broad interpretations, although I rely on their work on more than one occasion.

The third reason why this effort is a daunting task is because there has been remarkable growth of the field in two associations, the Association for the Study of Higher Education and the History of Education Society, a growth from the late 1980s of a few (if any) presentations at the organizations' annual meetings to, at times in the case of the History of Education Society, a majority of the articles in its *History of Education Quarterly* addressing higher education. Long ago I arranged for a breakfast of historians of higher education at ASHE, the beginning of HASHE—historians at ASHE—and the increasing range of interests as more scholars enter the field over the years has been invigorating. Many talented scholars are now in the field, and any book attempting to address all the centuries, all the meanings, all the participants, all the institutional types will receive careful scrutiny.

THREE WAYS OF THINKING HISTORICALLY

Hence, I write this book as I teach the history of higher education, explaining my historical approach and then focusing on a broad range of people and institutions (with occasionally smart-aleck remarks, or as one of my African American students once said to me, "Philo, you are a piece of work"). At the beginning of each semester when teaching the history of higher education, I begin with a brief and perhaps unmerciful discussion of three types of history. The first is name-date-place crap. We inflict this understanding of history on ourselves and, most unfortunately, on generations of students. It is important to know when the first Morrill Land Grant Act passed (1862), but unless we also know its immediate context (the Civil War, hence the often-overlooked inclusion of military instruction) and the social power of its successor, the 1890 Morrill Land Grant Act (it authorized government monies for segregated white and black colleges and universities), it is merely a number. As another example, we know that Oberlin College was the first institution to admit white women and African American men and women. Yet the story of how that admission policy came about, and its consequences over the next several decades, is much more complex than the simple declaration that Oberlin College began admitting white women in 1833 and African Americans in 1835.[1] Understanding the ways that white female students and African American students experienced their higher education begins to shape a deeper understanding of the college experience.

Simple recounting of apparent facts can also drive a highly traditional, if not hidebound, approach to history. After all, given that white males were those who had the social, political, economic, and legal power to start organizations, not surprisingly, they usually founded colleges that reflected white male values and norms, and in fact, were typically reserved for white males. There are important differences, however, as the chapters highlight. It is inescapable that writing a history of higher education from the beginning nearly requires the writer to argue about white men. For now, suffice it to say that while I have to name in order to write a history, how I name, whom I will name, will be a central condition of this text. For example, I pay careful attention to how we name institutions of higher education. It is most curious that a careful reading of the quite famous Yale Report of 1828 reveals that such a venerable institution of higher education admitted boys by policy at the age of 14 at that time, and there were even exceptions to that age. Yale was a college, proud in its 1828 Report to point out that it was a college. Academies flourished at the same time, and these were institutions that often had many women students; shortly thereafter, in the 1820s and 1830s, normal schools began, and their enrollments were initially dominated by women. In both cases women in their teens were admitted. How is it that Yale is a college but academies and normal schools are not? Is it the curriculum—as if the classical curriculum of Yale, precursor to the modern liberal arts curriculum of today, is the only curriculum requiring higher thought? What, then, is an institution of higher education in the Early Republic? And what does that mean for today? Whom or what we name, and how and why, are deeply important problems, and by reflecting on those acts of naming, we can revisit how we think about those names and how we exercise power in the act of naming. The problem of naming is more than what name a community might prefer, as it includes even the opportunity to name a community. This book admittedly has a focus on white women and African Americans because there is a preponderance of scholarship on those groups, and I offer discussion of other groups as possible with the hope that such scholarship will continue to advance. There is sparse but growing scholarship in terms of many communities (such as Latinx, gender and sex identity, Asian), and I have made a decided effort to include rather than exclude even where the literature is at a nascent stage (here follows an endnote with both reference and content information, as an example of my arguments at the beginning of this chapter).[2]

The second is more complicated, what I call amateur history (with none of the connotation that "amateur" is not as good as "professional," as I mean by amateur that it is volunteer-supported). Amateur history tends to find its representation in such locations as local historical societies directed by volunteers, where displays of Marquis de Lafayette's gloves from the Revolutionary War inform viewers. These places are amateur in the sense that the gloves are interesting but even with a placard describing the time when the Marquis wore the gloves, there is no interpretive meaning—who wore such gloves and why? What social forces resulted in gloves for some and not for others? Who made the gloves and with what, if any, profit? What is very interesting about amateur history is that it has been a noticeable gendered participation in contrast to professional history (the third category). For a very long time, women rather than men were more likely to oversee these museums, as if it were acceptable for them to inform us historically in volunteer settings rather than in the classroom or at conferences, where monetarily rewarded (professional) historians did their work.[3] Creating a history that recognizes how protest develops among marginalized and oppressed groups tells us a great deal about how society and the polity change and don't change, and a gendered view of history is one way of addressing such recognition, a perspective that began among some paid historians in the late 1960s and early 1970s, which leads discussion of the third form of history, professional (i.e., paid) history, the world of academics, where three forms of evidence create history: the footnote or endnote, the archive, the oral history. Professional historians want readers to know where the evidence came from, so that information occurs in the footnote or the endnote. And the evidence lies either in archives or in oral histories, or in both. Archives have traditionally preserved written documents, and it is amazing what people have written and left behind. Oral histories are fairly recent forms of Western evidence, an indication of how we in the European world, especially the formally educated European world, awkwardly value the written word as truth while the spoken word is deemed ephemeral, as if no college president has ever written a memorandum or report that presents only part of the information about the institution in an effort to get more money. In the early 1970s scholars such as Jan Vansina argued that memory in either written or spoken form is a form of evidence, and slowly such arguments have met less resistance and received more acceptance, perhaps in part because the face of professional history has literally changed into a reflection of more diversity.[4]

So, this book embarks on professional history, and if I am going to teach history through this effort, I have to engage readers in thinking historically. What are appropriate sources of historical evidence, and why—who creates the distinction of appropriate and who created the sources? While drawing upon the same body of literature, or rather, the same body extended into the present from the early 1960s as other historians of higher education who have attempted to discuss, writ large, these meanings of events, people, and institutions, I argue for different emphases, which means arguing for a different interpretation. I would not presume to have the remarkable sense of activism and academic mind that Howard Zinn showed. Nevertheless, I must admit that I have long been deeply concerned about the ease with which we interpret higher education from the perspective of the elite, whether that is in terms of institutions (for example, research universities) or their participants (highly selective admissions for undergraduates and intense expectations of faculty members in regard to their research and scholarship). As best as I can determine, all groups with some sort of engagement in higher education too quickly turn to what they deem as the best—the best institutions, the most qualified students, the most productive faculty members—even in their sector of higher education. There are wonderful exceptions, as in the case of Willie and Edmonds' strong response to Jencks and Riesman's claim that black colleges were academic backwaters.[5] As the authors in Willie and Edmonds' edited volume note, black colleges face myriad challenges and address varied needs; one might well wonder why Jencks and Riesman, faculty members at an elite university at the time, did not recognize that white elite research universities faced a breadth of challenges and needs resting on the foundation of exclusion (at the time of their claim, their university did not admit women), albeit within an arena of huge amounts of money and social power.

In setting out to write a history of higher education from the ground up, this book does not start with the foundation of Harvard in 1636 by a group of admittedly hardy white men at the edge of what they knew and valued as civilization but with their use of Native Americans not only through genocide in acquiring land and wealth but also enrollment in their college. Nor does the book end with the wonder of highly selective colleges and universities leading the way for a stunning range of institutions and participants. In fact, throughout the book I cast a very critical eye upon selectivity and prestige and their outcomes.

COLLEGES AND THEIR COMMUNITIES IN HISTORICAL MEANING

As is often the case with scholarship, it took a long time to realize what I was writing here. (Students new to their graduate experience need to understand that rigorous research and scholarship results from reflection upon reflection, not simply finding evidence and writing about it.) One place kept coming back to haunt me, the dead college. It has been subjected to bad research with claims past and present that large numbers of colleges have died or are about to die, and then has had important revisions, and in the latter case, the clear conclusion that it is quite hard for a college to die.[6] Pundits have warned us for a very long time about these deaths, and report after report has warned us about them, but in actuality, colleges survive. They change, adapting enough to maintain some of their pasts while conforming to contemporary pressures. And even those that die often have lingering deaths of years and years, regardless of accreditation, financing, enrollments, etc. Why would it take so long for a college, facing all of those and more challenges, to die?

In a phrase, a socioeconomic contract. Here I do not mean the social contract that Jean Jacques Rousseau argues for, as a paraphrase, that we are all born free and into chains, even though it is a great phrase to consider and remember. Nor do I mean a social contract as other historians of higher education have suggested, as I am emphasizing the socioeconomic class structure and its relation to different institutions. When I was early in my career as an admissions representative, I watched a small college in the state where I was working die one of those lingering deaths. I even remember our vice president for financial affairs visiting its campus after it closed, hoping to find some good equipment, or office or classroom furniture at a low price, only to return saying that everything was in unbelievably poor shape. And I could not figure out why anyone would want to work at such an institution or attend it, a place where when a prospective student filled out an interest card, the admission office would send a letter of acceptance. The answer over the years has become clear to me, that institutions of higher education have what is often an unspoken and powerful socioeconomic contract with the people even vaguely connected to them. I could speak to this contract in global terms, but that is beyond the purview of this book; instead, I write about it in terms of the United States: colleges and universities have a socioeconomic contract to create and sustain the middle class and to further the interests of the upper class. They don't necessarily do that well, or consistently, or in obvious terms, but from a variety of perspectives that the socioeconomic contract obtains. So the problem of dying colleges is that they continue to offer a spirit that both compels and constrains people and institutions, leading to some important questions. Does the institution consistently meet the needs of its various constituencies well enough to survive, and most important, which constituencies want their needs met with what resources? Or does that institution falter, even fail? Or if it is a private institution, is it replaced by a public one? What about the institutions of higher education that primarily serve local, state, or regional constituencies? What about colleges and universities that primarily serve black or white women, or African Americans or Native Americans or Hispanics? A study of three dead colleges, "Not Harvard, Not Holyoke, Not Howard," highlights many of those issues and frames one last question.[7] How and why do we sustain elite colleges and universities over the centuries?

Who can define how we define the intellect and influential ideas has a highly powerful effect on who participates in society at what level of socioeconomic class in terms of gender and race and ethnicity. Thus, I have written a social history in which intellectual history is central. (Many scholars have complicated the arguments about class, gender, and race and ethnicity in such areas as disability studies and sexual identities. To some degree I will address those complications, although in all honesty, the now burgeoning field of the history of higher education has not seen many works in those areas, all of which leads to more possibilities of historical revisionism.) As a social history, I look at a number of groups (or as I have stated, communities) of people who have struggled to establish an institution that would advance their interests, and for many of those groups, in different ways at different points of time, in the face of powerful resistance to expanding the middle class, much less the upper class. The range of participants, as I have already suggested, is remarkable. More important, the breadth and depth of the resistance, often in subtle and enduring form, speaks to the formation of class in the United States. At the core of these considerations is the formation and maintenance of ideas about higher education, its intellectual history.

As a quick take on this perspective, consider the long-standing arguments about whether a college education ought to be useful or ought to be centered on the liberal arts. Why not ask, instead, who benefits, and who can benefit, in social, political, and economic terms from a lifetime based on a liberal arts education? In many cases, are not those who pursue a liberal arts education simply delaying the useful outcomes of formal education, whether in terms of a liberal arts education as precursor to professional education or as a form of intellect that opens social, economic, and political contacts? The idea of the liberal arts has powerful implications for a variety of groups.

In anticipation of the eighth chapter and the discussion of exclusion and stratification, it is unfortunate that there is not a deeper discussion of socioeconomic class issues in U.S. higher education, particularly in historical terms. Since we have long declined to recognize the power of socioeconomic class in this country, instead phrasing opportunity as being able to pull oneself up by one's bootstraps (as someone who actually dated a cattle rancher for a long time, I can assure all readers that if you attempt to pull yourself up by your bootstraps, you will fall over), the characteristic of socioeconomic class is often hidden from view historically. We can see gender in women's colleges both black and white, we can see gender as well as race and ethnicity in black colleges, tribal colleges, Hispanic-serving colleges. What is more powerful, as Mary Ann Dzuback reminded historians of education in a remarkable essay, is that gender occupies men's colleges and men's groups as well as coeducational ones; so too race and ethnicity occupy primarily white colleges and universities. What is unspoken or unseen is nonetheless present.[8] Socioeconomic class is not so visible and hardly at all measured or analyzed. Gender matters, race and ethnicity matters, many differences matter. I am convinced, however, that the most hidden force is a highly powerful one: socioeconomic class. There are attempts to bring socioeconomic class to the forefront in this work, but our use of the social sciences in this country tends to bury that characteristic, focusing on race and ethnicity, later on gender, more recently on a range of differences. Curiously, it seems that the quantitative researchers, particularly in economics and sociology, have more to say about socioeconomic class than those in other disciplines and fields and in different methodologies.

HISTORICAL INQUIRY AND SOME CLEVER TRAPS

Beyond the power of thinking historically to expand our capacity to see how social groups create means for thinking about each other, historical inquiry also challenges us not to commit the trap of presentism. Historians cannot simply escape the present, and indeed the present will inform what historical questions get asked by whom.[9] We would not have known to ask deeper and broader questions about the enslavement of Africans and others without the civil rights movement of the 1960s and its impact on opening doors of educational institutions, although still today the openings occur unevenly. What were literacy rates among enslaved Africans? What was the role of the

Bible in both literacy and spiritual life, and what was the role of African traditions in shaping literacy and responses to the Bible? How did such efforts reinforce the desire to establish black colleges? Nor would we understand the complicated lives of women on campuses without the rise of feminist arguments in the 1960s, arguments slowly broadening in their inclusion of different communities of women. Yet presentism can drive uncritical perspectives, so that as a result we understand the history of higher education in its present form. A fine example is an article on the early years of the land grant institutions, discussed in more detail later.[10] Today, although the land grant designation may not be obvious, we most certainly know these institutions. They are almost all huge, with tens of thousands of students and thousands of faculty and staff members. They receive a lot of media attention and are often the centerpiece of higher education for a state. Not so in the 1860s, 1870s, 1880s, even the 1890s. More than one opened and then closed or subsisted on an enrollment of as few as a dozen students. And while today there is the great ice cream debate (in many history of higher education classes, graduates of land grant universities are quick and vehement in their declaration that their alma mater produces the best ice cream), it is important to know that good ice cream doesn't come straight from the cow but requires rigorous practical science built on rigorous pure science, and neither of those forms of science existed on more than just a very few college and university campuses in the nineteenth century. And, in what may or may not be a statement of the obvious, big-time college sports did not exist in the 1800s. In fact, the expression of physical ability on many campuses focused on the men, who typically by class (sophomores versus freshmen was a favorite approach) beat each other badly, leaving victors and losers with bloodied, swollen faces.[11] So understanding that beginnings are not the same as contemporary versions, and beginnings don't always lead to certain contemporary versions without struggle, even failure, is an important historical perspective. Thinking within the time period under examination, while knowing the present, enables historical thought.

That story of violent physical activity offers another theme in this book, one that is also a trap in some historical approaches: the concept of the good old days.[12] Beating each other bloody is not good. Nor was the unabashed, and often faculty-encouraged, harassment of women on campus. Nor were skits with white fraternity members in blackface. And that theme leads to another theme. It is the historian's role to remind readers that humans have strengths and frailties, held together by the context of the moment. Our colleges and universities reflect those strengths, those frailties, the complexities of the context.

Historians, much like other scholars in the social sciences and humanities as well as natural and physical scientists, must practice revisionism. Theories about human behavior, animal behavior, plant behavior, planet behavior (poor Pluto), etc. are not permanent. As we learn more about different types and forms of behavior, we have to change how we describe those behaviors, what those behaviors mean, and what are the consequences of those behaviors. As a powerful example, until the 1972 Olympics, women were not allowed to run the 1500-meter race (much less the marathon) for the widely accepted reason—at least among men—that women would literally expire if they ran that far. Now, of course, the steady slap-slap of women's feet as they run the demanding 26.2 miles of the marathon is heard throughout much of the world. Higher education long practiced a version of this argument, as in the now infamous case of Edward Clarke, a Harvard University medical professor, who argued in 1872 that if women were allowed to pursue rigorous study, their blood would go to their brain and drain from their ovaries; as a result, they would not be able to reproduce, thereby increasing the chances of what people of the time called race suicide, the loss of the white race to other races with higher birth rates.[13] So, this history is a revision of previous works, works that are careful and accurate representations of the history of U.S. higher education, but works that start from a point that I choose to contest by naming all sorts of people and institutions from, as best as I can accomplish, their perspectives (obviously I write from the outside in). This book would not be possible if it were not for the remarkable outpouring of revisionist contributions to the history of U.S. higher education since the early 1990s, and I am deeply thankful to the many historians who have made this effort possible. Thus, as much as possible, this book is an attempt to avoid add-on histories of any marginalized group at any given point in time, instead showing how this deeply revisionist perspective can show all participants and institutions as a complicated reality where center meets the resistance of the periphery even while the center continues to pursue centrality.

WHY STUDY THE HISTORY OF INSTITUTIONS OF HIGHER EDUCATION?

This book is an effort to convince readers of the importance of thinking historically in order to understand how we have created higher education in the United States. That is not the same as knowing history, and indeed, I eschew the quip that those who do not know history are condemned to repeat it. We cannot repeat it, even in ignorance. I want to convince readers about the importance of thinking historically in part because I would want to know whose history I ought to know, and more so because I am convinced that thinking historically allows us to engage the human experience, and if done with care, to have a better understanding of the human experience today. History does not, cannot, predict the present or the future, if only for the fact that whatever we know about history immediately reshapes our present; furthermore, the future is somewhat impervious to the present and past, events and people moving in both expected and unexpected ways. History can teach us, if for no other reason than to know the events we can celebrate and the events that ought to haunt us. Otherwise those events can too easily remain hidden under the guise of a social construction that does not remind us that people and peoples participate in the life of the nation—or in the case of this book, specific types of institutions—in very different ways.

Having dismissed axioms about the importance of knowing history, it is appropriate to close this part of the introduction by briefly explaining why the history of higher education is important. What follows is a broad overview of historical thinking and then a compelling reason for placing history of higher education at the center of graduate programs of higher education as well as, in ancillary terms, why historians outside the broad field of history of education ought to place far more attention on schools, colleges, and universities. I return to this discussion in the final chapter.

First, history haunts us. We are not able to escape our history, or better phrased, our histories. The relations among racial and ethnic groups is as old as the first human social separations, and in the United States, blackening the Irish immigrants in the late 1800s, as Thomas Nast did in his political cartoons in order to critique both the Irish and the Roman Catholic Church, highlights the issue of color. Changing the definitions of color and ethnicity among central and eastern European immigrants during the 1900s both reaffirmed expanding notions of citizenship and belonging while simultaneously continuing to exclude African Americans.[14] The widespread distrust of the Roman Catholic Church continued well into the post-World War II period as exemplified by the concern during the 1960 presidential election about John F. Kennedy (of Irish descent) and the possibilities of control by the Vatican. And the dual role of Hispanics in education today, bilingual and bicultural, often finds voice more in bilingual education rather than bicultural (or more appropriately, given the variety of Latin American cultures, multicultural) education; hence, in over a century of second-language immigrant populations attempting to balance their cultures with their newfound cultures we still lose sight of that apparently essential duality so adroitly analyzed by W.E.B. Du Bois as double consciousness.[15] We are all born at least twice in this country, even albeit with what is a cruel irony, including Native Americans. They are the natives, the First Settlers, but they face the Westernized version of culture we celebrate on July 4. Nevertheless, of all the hyphenated or modified racial and ethnic groups (Italian American, Jewish American, the list is remarkably long), references to British Americans are exceedingly rare. It is worth reflecting what that means in terms of our intellectual definition of our social history: who defines who we are and what institutions of higher education do is critical to understanding the history of higher education as well as its present.

Second, this nation began at a most curious time in history; what is now in the early 2000s a dulled sense of difference was in the late 1600s and the 1700s both acute and radical. Leaders in the British colonies were products of an intellectually and philosophically radical set of arguments called the Enlightenment. Scottish and English philosophers in particular, although philosophers in other countries participated, argued against an age-old comprehension of humanity. No longer were people born to their station in life as ordained by the Christian god, Protestant or Catholic or Anglican. Instead these philosophers argued that humans were fully capable of rational thought that would lead to both reform and progress. What, then, better institution to develop and advance rational thought in humans in order to implement reform and progress than an educational institution? One of the key Enlightenment philosophers, John Locke, wrote an extended thesis focusing on the powers of education to change and improve life, *On Education*. He argued that education was the key to shaping the individual.

As such, then, formal educational institutions in the United States occupy central roles in the creation of citizens in social, political, and economic terms. For over a century each student who attends an institution of higher education has spent thousands of hours in school and college. Professors and staff members develop complex processes to shape students as members of social communities, as political participants, and as economic beings. No other institution has as much time with people as educational institutions, being at about age 5 or 6 and ending often enough in the early 20s but, then again, often enough lasting well into middle age. Historians would do well to attend more often to such a formative institution.

HOW THIS BOOK IS ORGANIZED

Thus, this book endeavors to examine who participated in what ways at which U.S. institutions of higher education over time. The chapters and their themes are as follows (there are times when I begin exploration of a theme before the chapter that fully explores those ideas, both to note the importance of certain events, institutions, or individuals as well as to establish a chronological foundation for the ensuing theme). The next, second, chapter attends to the colleges of the colonial era and the Early Republic, highlighting both the search for appropriate citizen and leader qualities as well as who constituted a citizen or leader, and in what ways. The third chapter focuses on the middle and the outside, addressing the 1800s and focusing on midwestern colleges and universities with discussion of southern and western institutions of higher education. This chapter continues the theme of contesting the centrality of elite institutions, a theme raised in the second chapter. Writing from the middle provides the analytical perspectives of women and African Americans in higher education, of the first and second Morrill Acts, of state colleges, of denominational institutions, and of the creation of an educated middle class with local, state, regional, and national characteristics. I also include a brief discussion of the beginnings of university administration as well as student affairs, in the latter case providing a clear argument against the prevailing notion that faculty members got interested in research in the late 1800s and so there became a need for student services administrators to take over the former professorial responsibilities for students' lives outside the classroom. The themes of the second and third chapters also allow me to write from the colonial era to the 1800s beyond the simplistic who came first and with the reminder that from the beginning, exclusion was part and parcel of U.S. higher education. The fourth chapter examines Progressivism, a movement of the late 1800s and early 1900s. While historians of education who examine public schools are deeply interested in the Progressive Era, which was approximately from the 1880s to the 1920s, historians of higher education do always not evidence such interest. The fourth chapter is an attempt to address that gap and begin to close it, in great part because universities are places where such key Progressive ideas as expert knowledge, decision-making based on expert knowledge, and planning for the reform of social and moral behaviors are central to academic inquiry in the social sciences and progress. Just as important, Progressivism was also a social movement that implemented lasting means for social sorting of classes, gender, and races and ethnicities as well as increased access; that tension between sorting and access is a highly important historical lesson. The discussion of sorting has institutional characteristics and it includes an examination of junior colleges, which contrary to common claims, was less of a sorting institution in its early decades than often thought. With the next, fifth, chapter, the book moves away from chronology, beginning the development of themes evident in the previous chapters. That chapter's theme is war, a theme still understudied in regard to higher education. It focuses on the Civil War, World War I, World War II, the Vietnam conflict, and the current war on terror (which is getting old enough to have historical connotations) to raise key issues about how institutions of higher education and three of their constituencies—administrators, faculty members, and students—respond to war. Topics in this theme range from gender to the development of research for national service to academic freedom. The college and university role in society is especially important here, as is how the government views higher education. Notably, the topic of war allows for the examination of federal financial aid and its meanings in terms of access to higher education given that war has heightened the national need for an educated citizenry and leadership. It is critical to understand the importance of war and its impact on U.S. higher education, particularly in how the federal government finds ways to serve its purposes by using higher education. World War II established the two main streams of activity for colleges and universities, the beginnings of massive research efforts and mass higher education, and the next chapter addresses students, titled "Sex and Love! Beer! Football! And Other Student Activities." Student informal extracurricular activity is as old as higher education in the Western world, and early on U.S. colleges and universities had highly successful extracurricular activities (often initiated by students) that often had unanticipated results. Descriptions of such activity in such settings as the European medieval university remind us that in some ways, some things never change, as students in their late teens and early 20s today write home to ask for money, having spent their dollars on beer and other enriching activities, just as some students did in the Middle Ages.[16] Yet historians know that change is real, and through this theme I show how colleges and universities have worked to influence directly the lives of students, even given the legal demise of *in loco parentis*, while students continue to resist such management. The seventh chapter focuses on the research university, particularly from the late 1940s to the early 2000s. The flow of federal dollars to support research at universities after World War II is well documented by a number of historians of higher education as well as other scholars of higher education, and the spread of research universities reflects that national goal. It is an unavoidable topic. This theme establishes how the federal government has transformed institutions of higher education, at times at amazing speed, and very much in its own interests. Many southeastern universities were quiet regional institutions at the end of the 1950s, representing college life more than a research ethos. While they continue in many cases to continue to represent college life, the research ethos has taken firm hold. Two troubling questions arise here, partially answered in the literature; first, to what extent does the rise of national visibility contribute to the racial desegregation of these institutions? And second, whose purposes are served by preserving traditions of college life? The overarching theme in the eighth chapter is exclusion and stratification. It's not just who gets into college, it is who gets into which colleges and with what college experiences. That sentence sounds simple, but there are complexities well worth considering. How different groups of individuals and different types of institutions experience and enact exclusion and stratification are at the heart and soul of higher education. I can only write a people's history of higher education by clarifying how all of the people are not fully participatory, which still defines even those who are fully participatory.[17]

Finally, there is the Epilogue, with some discussion of sources and their meanings, as well as issues of theory. It starts with fairly recent considerations of some of the scholarly and research literature on higher education and discuss how those works have influenced how I think historically about higher education. It's not a conclusion but is in fact more reminiscent of how Ralph Ellison structures his monumental novel, *Invisible Man*, with an epilogue that rightfully takes the reader back to the prologue. The final chapter also addresses an immeasurably complex problem for historians, the role of theory. Historians have long argued about theory and history, on the one hand suggesting the virtues of theory in providing deep explanations about causes and effects while on the other hand noting a central vice of any theory, that it is an abstraction that requires the exclusion of what can be described as inconvenient facts, those pieces or moments of evidence that do not fit the demands of the theoretical explanation. History is about inconvenient facts, a reminder that almost every single one of us leads a messy life with contradictions as well as consistencies; theory reminds us that there are powerful abstract explanations for our values, expectations, and behaviors. Although not a theoretical discussion, the Epilogue also examines in detail the meritocracy.

Understanding how we have reformed ourselves and our institutions in order to effect progress tells us a great deal about who is progressing in what ways because our machine of reform and progress is the educational institution. This is a first attempt at a deeply revisionist overview of the history of U.S. higher education, based on a fundamental understanding: Our history matters. Our histories matter.

NOTES

1   Jill K. Conway, "Perspectives on the History of Women's Education in the United States," *History of Education Quarterly* 14, no. 2 (Spring, 1974): 1–12 and Cally L. Waite, "The Segregation of Black Students at Oberlin College After Reconstruction," *History of Education Quarterly* 41, no. 3 (Autumn 2001): 344–364.

2   Philo Hutcheson, "Shall I Compare Thee? Reflections on Naming and Power," in *Understanding Minority Serving Institutions*, ed. Marybeth Gasman, Benjamin Baez, and Caroline Turner (Albany: State University of New York Press, 2008), 43–54. Another naming challenge, often raised by students embarking on a

paper in my history of higher education courses, is what are appropriate historical names for African Americans. I have long argued that using a name in quoting a historical text, unless it is a racial slur, is thinking historically, especially when the name of the time, for example, "Negro," was in fact an act of resistance and power. Nevertheless, unless I am trying to highlight that act, I use African American more often than not—explaining my usage in the first instance.

3 See Gerda Lerner, *Why History Matters* (New York: Oxford University Press, 1997), for a remarkable reflection of creating space for women historians in the U.S. historical profession. Lerner was a, if not the, groundbreaker when it came to changing the gendered face of professional history.

4 Peter Novick, *That Noble Dream: The "Objectivity Question" and the American Historical Profession* (New York: Cambridge University Press, 1988).

5 Charles V. Willie and Ronald R. Edmonds, eds., *Black Colleges in America: Challenge, Development, Survival* (New York: Teachers College Press, 1978).

6 James Axtell, "The Death of the Liberal Arts College," *History of Education Quarterly* 11, no. 4 (Winter 1971): 339–352. Axtell is responding to Donald G. Tewksbury, *The Founding of American Colleges and Universities Before the Civil War, with Particular Reference to the Religious Influences Bearing Upon the College Movement* (New York: Teachers College, Columbia University, 1932), in a pointed way, drawing upon the work of historians who had shown with meticulous effort that Tewksbury's numbers of closed colleges (seemingly alarmingly high) were wide of the mark.

7 Linda Buchanan, "Not Harvard, Not Holyoke, Not Howard: A Study of the Life and Death of Three Small Colleges" (Ph.D. dissertation, Georgia State University, 1997).

8 Mary Ann Dzuback, "Gender and the Politics of Knowledge," *History of Education Quarterly* 43, no. 2 (Summer 2003): 171–195. Mary Ann, with one exception, only used women authors as her references.

9 Philo Hutcheson, "Writing Through the Past: Federal Higher Education Policy," in *The History of United States Higher Education: Methods for Understanding the Past*, ed. Marybeth Gasman (New York: Routledge, 2010), 172–186.

10 Eldon L. Johnson, "Misconceptions About the Early Land-Grant Colleges," *Journal of Higher Education* 52, no. 4 (July–August 1981): 333–351.

11 Helen Lefkowitz Horowitz, *Campus Life: Undergraduate Culture from the End of the Eighteenth Century to the Present* (Chicago: University of Chicago Press, 1987). See page 44 for a photograph of three badly bloodied and swollen Princeton freshmen of the class of 1895.

12 W.P. Leonard, *History and Directory of Posey County: Containing an Account of the Early Settlement and Organization of the County of Posey, Ind., with References to the Formation of the North West Territory, Indiana Territory, and the State of Indiana; Also Numerous Incidents, Tragical and Otherwise, Which Occurred in the County; Also a Complete List of the Tax-Payers, the Post-Office Addresses and Places of Residence, Together with a Business Directory of Mt. Vernon and New Harmony, Besides Local & General Information of Peculiar Interest, Also Biographical Sketches of Prominent Citizens of the County* (Evansville, IN: A.C. Isaacs, Book Printer & Binder, 1882). Leonard declares in the preface, with glee and enthusiasm, that the point of history is to celebrate our achievements, a sentiment long held by both amateur and professional historians. See Peter Novick, *That Noble Dream: The "Objectivity Question" and the American Historical Profession* (New York: Cambridge University Press, 1988) for an analysis of such celebrations; even today's elementary and secondary history textbooks typically offer such celebrations.

13 Sue Zschoce, "Dr. Clarke Revisited: Science, True Womanhood, and Female Collegiate Education," *History of Education Quarterly* 29, no. 4 (Winter 1989): 545–569. See also Barbara M. Solomon, *In the Company of Educated Women: A History of Women and Higher Education in America* (New Haven, CT: Yale University Press, 1985).

14 See, for example, Benjamin Justice, "Thomas Nast and the Public School of the 1870s," *History of Education Quarterly* 45, no. 2 (June 2005): 171–206; Zöe Burkholder, "From 'Wops and Dagoes and Hunkies' to 'Caucasian': Changing Racial Discourse in American Classrooms During World War II," *History of Education Quarterly* 50, no. 3 (August 2010): 324–358. James D. Anderson, "Race, Meritocracy, and the American Academy During the Immediate Post-World War II Era," *History of Education Quarterly* 33 (Summer 1993): 151–175.

15 See Michael R. Olneck, "What Have Immigrants Wanted from American Schools? What Do They Want Now? Historical and Contemporary Perspectives on Immigrants, Language, and American Schooling," *American Journal of Education* 115, no. 4 (May 2009): 379–406 and W.E.B. Du Bois, *The Souls of Black Folk* (introduction by David Levering Lewis) (New York: Modern Library, 2003). Please note that Du Bois (yes, it is two words, and pronounced with the "s" according to the eminent biographer, David Levering Lewis) published his volume in 1903. Sometimes name-date-place crap matters.

16 Charles Homer Haskins, *The Rise of Universities* (Ithaca, NY: Cornell University Press, 1923).

17 Mary Ann Dzuback, "Gender and the Politics of Knowledge," *History of Education Quarterly* 43, no. 2 (Summer 2003): 171–195. Dzuback argues that the absence of women in U.S. higher education at so many institutions for so long necessarily entails the meanings of genders even in the absence of one (and one can add today, or more than one gender).

2

FROM THE BEGINNING

*Leadership, Exclusion, and Stratification in the
Colonizing Colleges and the Early Republic*

Elite colleges and universities often represent important dimensions of U.S. higher education, not the least of which is their efforts to create and sustain a meritocracy of intertwined intellectual and social traditions; in addition, they are often models for other institutions of higher education within the United States and internationally, although the modeling too often unreflectively mirrors the problematic nature of meritocracy. Meritocracy, a term made popular in the late 1950s by Michael Young in his insightful and acerbic work, *The Rise of the Meritocracy*, refers to a set of ideals and values that laud those with talent yet also ensures that those who have that talent based on standardized measurements control much of our lives; the idea of meritocracy reflects arguments as old as the colonies, articulated in different forms by such early leaders as Thomas Jefferson. It was Jefferson who advocated for raking the rubbish for talent (to use his words) as well as drawing upon those segments of society (the middle and upper classes) where talent, according to him, was more evident. These arguments reflect two issues addressed throughout this book, exclusion and stratification. To understand the historical nature of higher education in the United States, it is key to recognize the complexities of exclusion—once the institution has opened a door, such as Harvard establishing the Harvard Annex in 1879 that allowed women to take Harvard courses although without a degree, a very common result is in changes in the nature of exclusion. In this case, the Harvard Annex was chartered as Radcliffe

College (a women's college) in 1894, and in 1977 Harvard became coeducational on its diploma. As for stratification, although the early story of the colonial colleges, with their minuscule student enrollments in contemporary terms (often no more than 15 to 20 students) is one more of exclusion than stratification, as higher education grew during the years of the Early Republic, institutions added the process of stratification, as will be clear in the discussion of the Yale Report of 1828, colleges, and academies and seminaries.

Nonetheless, these processes, developed from Enlightenment philosophers such as John Locke and Adam Smith, were based on revolutionary arguments even as they served meritocratic purposes. Their philosophies were not simply reconceptions of centuries of social, political, and economic orders but rather an understanding of the individual as capable of reason leading to improvement of the self and society, i.e., progress and reform. Happiness was within reach regardless of one's station of life, disruptive words indeed for Western European polities based on arguments that God's will determined one's position and that families passed that inheritance—whether it was noble or peasant or some other life—onto the next generations. What, then, better institution to advance rational thought in order to implement reform and progress than an educational institution? One of the key Enlightenment philosophers, John Locke, wrote an extended thesis focusing on the powers of education to change and improve life, *Some Thoughts Concerning Education*. He argued that education was the key to shaping the individual, although despite those basic principles of the Enlightenment, he specifically identified his work as addressing the education of gentlemen and not all citizens. The identification of the male illustrates a historical fact for the early decades of the nation, in that institutions as broad as the Constitution and as specific as any college offering the baccalaureate degree excluded women; in the case of the former they had no right to vote in federal elections until 1920 with the ratification of the 20th Amendment and in the case of the latter, they could not be students at degree-granting colleges. Furthermore, it was by and large a white male definition. The nation's leaders did not view African Americans by using Enlightenment principles; for the sake of population counts for voting, slaves were counted as three-fifths of a person in the Constitution (an estimated 450,000 slaves were in all 13 colonies at the start of the Revolutionary War, when the total population was about 2.5 million).

It is remarkably difficult to discuss the people (in the way Zinn interpreted U.S. history) and higher education because by its very design, most types of institutions of higher education are meant to keep some people out. Nevertheless, especially in an achievement-oriented society such as the United States, the efforts to gain credentials in order to advance are often powerful, as individuals work to advance personal goals. Nor can elites ever fully shut out access, as Pierre Bourdieu, a sociologist of class structures, has noted.[1] Hence the tension between the demands and expectations for access to higher education and the efforts to sustain exclusivity, writ large (no women admitted) or in subtle form (Native Americans are admitted, but their experiences are markedly different from those of white students) is a defining characteristic in the years of the colonies and Early Republic for higher education, even though the Enlightenment had a widespread impact on the development of the Early Republic. For example, regardless of their widespread exclusion from higher education, African Americans sought means to organize, read, debate, and develop speeches and written statements as a means to articulate "full citizenship and equal participation in the life of the republic." Free African Americans in northern cities formed literary societies starting in the late 1700s; by the 1830s, African American women were also establishing similar groups—thus, also challenging the meanings of public roles for men and women.[2]

The oldest colleges began in great part or whole with Enlightenment ideas, and while the philosophies of the Enlightenment addressed new concepts for humanity, the implementation of the ideas was consistently for white males. Given that several of the current elite colleges are among the oldest, founded in the colonial period (more accurately, the colonial and colonialization period in that while indeed those coming from Europe were often fleeing religious persecution, their institutions in the colonies colonized and even eradicated indigenous populations), they carry a sense of tradition of the importance of a college education where reason was a powerful instrument for the individual and society, a means for improvement of the individual and society. Women increasingly articulated their rights and abilities during and after the Revolutionary War, but the colleges remained all-male. African American and Native American men on occasion entered and even graduated from colleges at this time, although in comparatively small numbers.

After the American Revolution, in the period often called the Early Republic (roughly, from after the Revolution to 1830), state legislatures saw themselves as central to the means and needs of the nation, as in the case of the southern and then midwestern state universities established with such enthusiasm in the early decades of the Republic (a matter addressed in more detail later in this chapter and in the next chapter). It is highly important to remember, for both reasons of understanding the nation and more specifically to understand the role of colleges and, eventually, universities, in the ongoing development of the United States that the nation was an experiment, at the time a revolution of thought about human roles, capacities, and potentials. These ideas challenged the rulers of Europe, both civil and ecclesiastical, and most certainly led to the drafting of the Declaration of Independence and the Constitution. Expansion of higher education was important for a variety of reasons in the Early Republic.

Although there was interest at the federal level in the establishment of a national university, in great part to avoid sending the sons of the nation to Europe for a higher education (and George Washington even left land to the government for a campus), the idea never came to fruition. States were already establishing universities, a process that would continue throughout the following centuries. William Davie of North Carolina, followed by Abraham Baldwin of Georgia, exemplified the commitment to a new higher education with new ideals, thereby furthering the creation of a new nation. Davie, a graduate of the College of New Jersey (now Princeton), fought in the American Revolution, and was a criminal lawyer. He was a member of the North Carolina elite, a patrician, who as a member of the state legislature introduced the bill to establish the University of North Carolina; upon establishment of the institution, which began instruction in 1795, he was a remarkably active trustee, donating books to the library, attending to a variety of institutional issues such as student conduct, and engaging in the search for a president and professors. Most important, he advocated for an institution that would serve students and the state under the aegis of Enlightenment principles, with a curriculum that included what were considered modern subjects, including agriculture, chemistry, and English as well as a curriculum with electives. In Georgia, with a charter of 1785, Abraham Baldwin was the leader in the development of the institution. Markedly different from Davie, Baldwin was a graduate of Yale (where he had studied for the ministry and likely was as an instructor, called a tutor) who served as a chaplain in the American Revolution. He was a member of the U.S. House of Representatives and then was elected senator in 1799; prior to that he was a member of the Georgia state legislature, where he was very likely the sponsor of the bill to establish the University of Georgia as part of a system of education with the University at the pinnacle. Although appointed president by the governing board (which he chaired) of the institution, the board did not meet for over a decade after that. Finally, in 1799 he was able to reinvigorate the institution, which had sufficient funding from land grants (the sale of government land to fund the enterprise) to begin. In contrast to Davie, Baldwin preferred the Yale model of the classical curriculum (discussed later in this chapter), although the Georgia model did not include religious studies in recognition of the separation of church and state. Eventually, however, the modern curriculum of Virginia supplanted the classical curriculum at Georgia, but nevertheless, like Davie, Baldwin too saw the new university as a means to develop citizens and leaders in the new nation. Nation-building, then, was an early goal in U.S. higher education.[3]

In fact, state legislators eyed not only the possibilities of new state universities, but also private institutions. In New Hampshire, state legislators viewed Dartmouth College, a private institution, as a means to advancing state interests, and in 1815 they officially took over the institution. The trustees of Dartmouth responded with a lawsuit, one that eventually found its way to the fledgling U.S. Supreme Court. In an 1819 landmark decision perhaps influenced by a statement that still resonates today, the Court ruled that once granted, state charters of private institutions were inviolable. Supposedly, the Court was influenced by Daniel Webster when he uttered, "It is, Sir, as I have said, a small college, and yet, there are those who love it." More telling, he argued that the college was a private charitable institution chartered by and serving the government, and the trustees—not the state legislature—had responsibility for the institution. To this day, U.S. private institutions (which include business corporations as well as private colleges and universities) are well protected from unrestrained government takeover, no minor matter in the development and continuation of this society, as a result of this decision. This protection affords private colleges and universities a high level of autonomy even while they serve the state as they understand their role and the role of the state.

Students, too, at Dartmouth, engaged the issues surrounding the takeover. (It is very difficult to get to the lives of students in historical records, often a more piecemeal than comprehensive effort. Yearbooks and student newspapers can provide some form of information, but the astute historian knows that those publications have their own biases, if they are placed into archives at all, if the institution even maintains archives. At times, historians are able to find such documents as letters and diaries; while less systematic than newspapers, they often reach deeper into the individual experiences.) Many of the students at Dartmouth College (the standing private college) organized against the faculty group that formed Dartmouth University (the state legislature institution), to such an extent that in response to the faculty group's attempt to stop the students from taking the books from a literary society library (by the mid-1700s these were already popular on many college campuses, and they would continue to be throughout much of the 1800s) by breaking down the library door with an axe, the students responded with their own weapons (clubs, stones, etc.) and successfully stopped the faculty raid on their books. The students represented one of the important goals of the Early Republic, identifying meanings of leadership and educating toward those meanings, although the students were also very interested in maintaining their identity as youths with a decided level of exuberance, a tension of the college student desire for adulthood and youth that certainly seems to obtain today.[4] The goal of educating for leadership, thereby establishing a new political identity in the new nation, was complicated and important.

Elite institutions are also historically important because so many of them are private, safeguarded by the Dartmouth case and, thus, acting as autonomous or semi-autonomous agents. In a very real sense they represent the sorts of voluntary associations so admired by Alexis de Tocqueville in his 1830 visit to the United States, exercising some degree of freedom from government influence or control, although such freedom has faced considerable restraints in the post-World War II era. It is important to note, however, that the notion of a private college or university is highly ambiguous, given state (in earlier times, even colony) support for those institutions over the centuries. In like manner (and increasingly so today), public institutions of higher education have long enjoyed private funding. Nevertheless, the distinction between the two types is sufficiently substantial that knowing that an institution's relationship to a particular religion or to a community of graduates and supporters well beyond the boundaries of a state can provide meaning. State flagship universities as well as other public colleges and universities have ties to their states that demarcate them from private institutions of higher education that are more beholden to their graduates' and institutional leaders' notions of what a college or university should do. Nevertheless, for private institutions as well as public ones, advancing various means and goals of the state is a constant across the centuries.

Given the importance of institutions of higher education in the United States in terms of their role in the interests of the state (i.e., both the states and the nation), this chapter examines the medieval universities of northern Europe, the early years of higher education in the colonies that became the United States, and then extends that consideration to the Early Republic.[5] These foundations endure.

MEDIEVAL UNIVERSITIES AND THE COLONIAL COLLEGES

The Enlightenment is the philosophical beginning of higher education for the United States, to articulate through graduates (and non-graduates) the possibilities of progress and reform. In actuality, it is only the philosophical beginning, because many key roots of U.S. higher education institutions stretch back to the Middle Ages.

And, again showing the complexity of historical thinking, quite arguably the institutional form of higher education in the colonies did not begin until 1745 when the College of New Jersey—now Princeton University—established a governing board with representatives from the government, business, and denominations, more than a century after the establishment of Harvard College. That form of governance persists today, easily recognizable among public and private colleges and universities. The administrative organization of higher education institutions differed, however, from European versions; Harvard marks a substantial shift from the European universities because from the beginning, that college had a president (known in its beginning as a headmaster), as discussed in greater detail shortly.

What marks higher education as distinct from a term as engaging as higher learning is that it is a corporation, a matter perhaps too often overlooked. Specifically, it has means to reproduce itself that characterize it as different from places where people are able to gain more knowledge—examples of the latter are the library societies formed by African Americans as well as juntos formed by the impetus of Benjamin Franklin, learning societies based on book knowledge and discussion, providing a higher learning relative to the overall educational level of the population at the time. In regard to higher education as a term, the corporate (i.e., formal institutional) means of reproduction is the diploma, a certificate of attendance and achievement, and the colonial colleges of course offered diplomas. European medieval universities offered diplomas, called in Latin (the scholarly language of the time), among other titles, *ius ubique docendi*, which means the right to teach anywhere. That title is telling because, after all, what better way to reproduce an organization based on instruction than to offer a diploma indicating the teaching degree? The reasoning is almost tautological, and most certainly powerful, for it ensured that those who taught were licensed by the very medieval institutions where they could teach or teach young men (and a few young women) before entrance to the university.

Furthermore, the European medieval universities had a specific curriculum leading to the degree (here is a moment of name-date-place crap; readers ought to remember the following details because of their foundation, which supports higher education even in the present); again in Latin, the *trivium* and the *quadrivium*, often called the seven liberal arts. They are somewhat recognizable in current form. The *trivium* had three components: grammar, rhetoric, and logic. One might well hear echoes of what every college graduate needs in those three components, the lasting demand that college graduates write and speak clearly and convincingly with a definite underlying rationale for the arguments. The *quadrivium* lends itself less clearly to current form except in consideration of the development of breadth: arithmetic, geometry, music, and astronomy. Held together, the seven liberal arts evidence the sort of foundation and breadth of knowledge that likely characterizes a great many introductions to college and university catalog statements then and now that begin with wording such as "We expect our graduates to understand . . ." Of course, there are often other expectations in those statements, particularly the more recent explicit desire to supply the workforce or specifically the global workforce; the rise of practical education in the nineteenth century, discussed in the next chapter, is illustrative of the various ways that U.S. colleges and universities determined ways to serve the state in economic forms.

It would be an error to point only at white European males as the source of the curriculum. There is substantial evidence that during the Dark Ages, Irish monks and the Moors preserved some traditions of learning, particularly in the liberal arts; it would be too easy to claim that Irish monks were white European males, as the English indeed thought of the Irish as being colored. The roots of the seven liberal arts actually have some diversity to them, although as Mary Ann Dzuback notes, women were excluded from higher education until well into the 1600s.[6] Not until the 1730s did a woman, Laura Bassi, earn a doctorate, at the University of Bologna, where she later held an honorary professorship; since she could not teach at a university (a sustained theme until the late 1800s at coeducational and men's colleges and universities in the United States), she taught courses at home.

The medieval universities of Europe also evidenced two forms of organizational control; for the most part, northern European universities had faculty control and southern European universities had student control. While control is a somewhat ambiguous notion given the possibilities of student resistance at the former and faculty resistance at the latter, the extent to which these groups indeed ran the universities was remarkable. In northern Europe, professors formed guilds (or faculties), generally according to subject matter such as theology, canon law, medicine, and philosophy. These guilds controlled access to teaching and the university while defining the curriculum of the faculty. (In the South, students determined such matters as how many hours a teacher would have to teach each term as well as penalties for instructors who missed class.) Faculty temperaments were at times contentious, as one scholar noted that in meetings when disputes between the nations erupted (faculty members divided by their nations of origin within guilds), the meetings usually ended in fistfights.[7]

Institutionally, the heritage of the U.S. institution of higher education is based on the northern European university in terms of corporate form, curriculum, diplomas, and faculty organization and impetus toward organizational control, and the lineage is quite direct. In what would now probably be a very popular faculty choice at times, in the Middle Ages one common faculty response to disagreement with another group of faculty members at a university was to migrate to another location and form a new university. A group of faculty members left the University of Paris (probably in the eleventh century), crossed the Channel, and started Oxford University. In the early 1200s faculty members at Oxford left (although they were fleeing angry local residents) and founded the University of Cambridge. The only Puritan college at either Oxford or Cambridge was Emmanuel College (founded in 1584) at Cambridge, and graduates of the College were among those who left England for what we now know as Massachusetts and Maine, the Massachusetts Bay Colony. Those Emmanuel College graduates were instrumental in the establishment of Harvard College in 1636. Harvard is named for an early benefactor, John Harvard, recognized in the chapel of Emmanuel College with a stained-glass window, although neither the stained glass nor the very formal attire he is pictured wearing seem to be Puritan. (Nor is the statue of John Harvard on the Harvard campus a representation of him, since there were no pictures available of him. Institutions of higher education have long celebrated history in ways markedly different from history itself.) Curiously, in some ways without necessarily including faculty members, there were college migrations in the colonies, from the decision of the founders of Yale College to separate from Harvard—perhaps already moving toward its Godless state, to the myriad religious college founders who saw establishing colleges as a means to spread their denominations' word as well as establish civilization in the 1800s, discussed in the next chapter.

Surprisingly, given that northern Europeans were the largest group of colonialists in those colonies that became the United States, as noted the nine colonial colleges had one important, very different, and enduring characteristic, the president. Northern European universities did not have a man (the gender designation here is deliberate) who was administratively the head of the institution, legally buttressed by a governing board of various names; rather, their faculties elected a rector (or by another title) from the faculty who held a leadership position for a limited number of years. While the college president of the 1600s, 1700s, and 1800s typically also taught, and until the late 1800s at even the larger institutions by and large conducted most if not all administrative affairs from fundraising to budget to hiring and firing instructors, he was, nevertheless, in a position unique to the United States. Some responsibilities, such as interviewing and admitting students, often were in the hands of the college faculty, but more important the president was the public symbol of the institution as well as the person who directed the institution, whether well or badly. The governing board was also relatively unique to the United States, at least in two senses. It offered a portrayal of what the institution represented by its very membership. Furthermore, it held the legal authority for the institution, not the president, faculty, or students. Hence, the 1745 College of New Jersey charter is one of those moments of historical importance worth remembering because widespread representation of social and occupational roles was a central characteristic of the governing board.

The nine colonial colleges, with founding dates, were Harvard College (1636), College of William and Mary (1693), Yale College (1701), College of New Jersey, now Princeton University (1746), College of Philadelphia, now the University of Pennsylvania (1749), King's College, now Columbia University (1754), Rhode Island College, now Brown University (1764), Queens College, now Rutgers University (1766), and Dartmouth College (1769). Age matters, enough to set in motion a seemingly interminable debate about who is older, carried out in all sorts of ways. The College of William and Mary is older than Yale by charter, but Yale began college-level education before the College of William and Mary, as is the case with the University of North Carolina and the University of Georgia, respectively. (Discard, if you will for historical understanding, the common quarrels about who was first, as the meaningful variables are complex and what matters is early, not first, except for marketing concerns.) Also, it is important to remember that by no means are the oldest colleges of the United States the oldest ones on the American continents. The king of Spain founded two universities in 1551, one in Mexico and the other in Peru.[8] The oldest college in America is not Harvard; it is the oldest college in the United States. What also matters is what these institutions intended to achieve in the education of their students, at a time when a very small fraction of the populace even attended, much less graduated from, institutions of higher education; this intent is far more nuanced than easy portrayals of the colonial colleges would suggest.

MORAL AND ECONOMIC PURPOSES OF HIGHER EDUCATION: GOD AND MAMMON IN THE DEVELOPMENT OF U.S. HIGHER EDUCATION

It is, unfortunately, all too common that examinations of the origins of higher education in the United States focus on the theological, particularly Protestant, characteristics of the early colleges, both those in the colonies as well as those in the Early Republic. Such oft-quoted lines as those from a 1643 pamphlet on the need for Harvard's establishment, dreading "when all our Ministers shall lie in the Dust," ignores the fact that the sentence begins with the specific concern about the need to "advance Learning."[9] The Puritans valued learning, and they understood the importance of learning in civil as well as its highly important ecclesiastical terms.

It is a truism of such examinations to present those institutions as religious seminaries, while simultaneously suggesting that only members of the aristocracy attended them. Careful reflection should quickly reveal the inherent flaw in that argument, as by and large religious seminaries in the United States have never drawn much if any of their enrollment from the elite (except, perhaps, for the Episcopalians) but rather from pious students from families of limited means. The nine colonial colleges successfully attracted white male students from well-to-do, or at least comfortable, families as well from the lower class and, at times, the poor. One only need look at the signers of the Declaration of Independence and ask how many in that group (much less how many of the college-educated) were ministers. Of the 56 signers of the Declaration of Independence, only one (John Witherspoon) was a minister, and another was a physician and a minister (Lyman Hall).[10] In fact, many of them had worked in different professions over their lives, shifting from medicine to law for example. Careers, and more specifically professions, did not have the clear demarcations we now know—consider how carefully the American Medical Association guards the boundaries of who is a physician; in contrast it is worth knowing that in the early decades of the 1800s, professional preparation occurred primarily through apprenticeships and reading books, and in a far more informal manner than the classes and examinations of current professions. Many a reader may remember the story of Abraham Lincoln studying to be a lawyer by candlelight, without classmates.[11] Christian churches were important, indeed central, to the colonial colleges, but faith is not the same as education for the ministry. As a point of comparison, Oxford students had to be members of the Church of England until the 1850s; none of the colonial colleges required such specific allegiance. As Lawrence Cremin details, from 1642 to 1689, of those Harvard alumni with identifiable occupations, 180 were ministers and 113 had other occupations, hardly the mark of a well-focused religious seminary.[12] In the 1600s and 1700s, preparation for the ministry in some denominations was a matter of a college education, not a specific professional preparation (other denominations eschewed higher education as preparation for the pulpit). Our contemporary notion of the seminary is grounded in the idea of modern professional preparation, a form of education that did not take root until the late 1800s, reaching into the early 1900s with the 1910 publication of Abraham Flexner's *Report on Conditions of Medical Education in the United States and Canada.* Here is a point worth reflection, in the framework of presentism, addressed in one of the questions at the end of the chapter: what is a profession today and what was a profession in the colonial era and Early Republic? The intersection of church and civil society expectations deserves special attention in regard to the development of U.S. society and more specifically, institutions of higher education and preparing students for their futures.

What the early colleges succeeded in doing was establishing that ecclesiastical and civil accomplishments were good, good for white men and good for the nation, reflecting strains of both Protestant and Enlightenment ideologies. In a brief explication of Max Weber's *The Protestant Ethic and the Spirit of Capitalism*, the acquisition of material goods reflected the hard work that God expected of believers. Neither a comfortable life nor life in heaven belonged to the lazy, and thus it was moral to work hard, and as a result to gain material wealth.[13] While aspirations to the moral life went beyond the capitalist desires of the residents of the colonies and the citizens of the Early Republic, colleges were clever in their efforts to identify themselves as places where young men (and almost always, young white men) could acquire the knowledge necessary for Protestant and economic success. For example, by the late 1700s college leaders had developed commencement as a locus of important local identification, a time and a place where the college could show its links to the community as a social and economic place that mattered. Commencement ceremonies honored graduates and important people, as we do now with diplomas and honorary degrees.[14] In addition, such expectations offered a simple and enduring notion about the United States, that anyone can work hard enough and get ahead, a meritocratic individualistic notion with clear roots in Protestantism that does not attend to broad analyses of what various groups experience in the American Dream. However broad that goal of creating a meritocracy, nevertheless the institutions were small, particularly in their early years, Harvard for example rarely having more than 16 students during the 1600s. Access to higher education was limited in the colonies and the Early Republic not only because of the costs of attending college but also because it was a time when fortunes, or at least a fairly steady life, could be attained without a higher education.

The degree to which the colonial colleges valued meritocracy—specifically, meritocracy for whom—is carefully examined by Bobby Wright in such publications as "The 'Untameable Savage Spirit': American Indians in Colonial Colleges" (this endnote discusses the challenges of naming, such as American Indian and Native American).[15] In his works on the efforts of the colonial colleges to tame the American Indian— the term "tame" is deliberate, the very phrasing of leaders at the colonial colleges (here one might want to say the colonizing colleges given the efforts of their instruc- tors to subjugate young men from several tribes), Wright shows how the colleges of the colonialization period defined what higher education for whose purposes. Presidents at Dartmouth, Harvard, and William and Mary established programs to Christianize young American Indian males, taking them from their families and com- munities to live and learn at their campuses, an effort that proved to be not only a failure but also caused great pain and even death among the young men. Forced into northern European clothing, diet, and habits, the young men typically rebelled, often fleeing their college captors to return home. Horrifyingly, mortality rates were as high as 50 percent. A few graduated from their colleges, but they were caught between two worlds. And, both the programs and the graduates were used to raise money to support the institutions and their causes, funds that did not necessarily end up funding the education of the young Indians but for other purposes. Education for citizenship in the colonizing efforts was at the cost of these young men, figuratively and literally.

In contrast to the Native American experience with higher education, there is evi- dence of some participation by African Americans in the colonial period and the Early Republic, including institution-building. For example, there was an effort to establish a college for African American men in New Haven, Connecticut, in 1831, an effort begun on the very day that Nat Turner began his rebellion in Virginia. That untimely coincidence as well as racist resistance to the proposed institution resulted in ending the effort to establish the college.[16] Although schools for African American children and white girls were not uncommon with dame and ornamental schools developed for the latter to offer both the fine arts and liberal arts subjects, colleges as named were not available to either group as a group. While there were occasional instances of admis- sion in terms of race and ethnicity, there were no women in higher education in the colonial period. They also resisted, albeit in ways different from the young American Indian men at the colonizing colleges, evident in events discussed later in this chapter in the discussion of academies for young white women. Then again, a Yale rule of 1745 did forbid "wearing women's Apparel," suggesting either an institutional formalization of gender identity or, perhaps, student pranks, although a colleague once suggested that wearing women's clothes could have been a way of sneaking women in students' housing.[17] There was, however, some element of diversity among the young white men enrolled in college in the colonial period as well as the Early Republic, because to some degree the institutions not only enrolled white men from the middle and upper middle class (more appropriately at the time, the mercantile and landed classes), but also students from limited means, known as scholarship boys who, typically, were preparing for the ministry. The former group, however, often presented formidable challenges to the institutions and their faculties.

Older historical descriptions of student life during the colonial era and the Early Republic were often prone to describe a stultifying classroom and very little to do outside the classroom because the only common extracurricular activity was the co-curricular, and often required, attendance at church services. Indeed, colonial colleges typically had carefully delineated student schedules from morning prayers to classes to afternoon studying to vespers. The Yale Report offers a description of tutors, instructors without full faculty rank, as closely overseeing the young men even in their rooms, a form of *in loco parentis* now eschewed by student services administrators and staff members.[18] Nevertheless, there are clear indications that not all was pious. For example, one reason for the departure of Harvard's first headmaster, Nathaniel Eaton, was that students had rioted, even in their small numbers, because there was no beer served at meals and, most curiously given the current proclivity for an occasional food fight, because the food itself was poor. In a clear differentiation from more recent student disruptions, even pious did not always mean obedient, as was the case at Yale in the mid-1700s. While the older denominations typically had substantial influence at the colonial colleges, followers of the developing Great Awakening exhibited what was known as enthusiasm, not dissimilar to Protestant revivals today. Yale, with its more religiously conservative approach to higher education, resisted the enthusiasm, the board of trustees even establishing a rule in 1744 that applicants over the age of 21 could only be admitted by "special permission" in order to ensure that followers of the Great Awakening, New Light adherents, had little access to the college. At first the president (known as the rector), Thomas Clap, resisted the New Light movement, but later in his presidency he began to support it. He eventually resisted allowing students to choose their own place of worship during the 1750s, arguing for the church as he understood it, resulting in student rebellions (as well as the departure of tutors disagreeing with his conclusions about religion). As one historian noted, "Harvard and Yale were both founded as colleges of sectaries and both had the problems incident to evolving into colleges of gentlemen."[19] One set of colleges that had no problem insisting on remaining sectarian were the Catholic colleges, beginning with Georgetown College, opening in 1791 with one student; shortly thereafter a Catholic bishop established St. Louis College. These institutions served as places for the higher education of Catholics, and often instructors were members of religious orders who had full belief in the Roman Catholic ways of knowing and expected students to be the same.

Despite those depictions of highly regulated life with likely serious discipline issues, colleges found ways to forgive miscreants, hardly surprising in an era of inadequate tuition revenue and precarious enrollment rates. At Harvard in the 1700s, for example, students often participated in activities in violation of the detailed rules of conduct, such as celebrating holidays with far too much enthusiasm. Although piety was the fundamental expectation of the college leaders and faculty members, often it was only the pious students preparing for the ministry who typically maintained appropriate behavior. The College's solution to the more boisterous was fairly consistent, with a student admission of guilt and request for forgiveness met with a pardon or a brief expulsion followed by readmission. Students' social violations even resulted in the establishment of a grading system at one institution, the University of Pennsylvania, in the early 1800s. The provost, struggling to maintain a sufficient enrollment with many students from wealthy backgrounds who clearly felt a sense of privilege (that too was an issue at Harvard in the 1700s), was alarmed by the formation of student combinations, horizontal student groups that protected their members from investigations by the vertical group of college educators, who were putatively in charge of student behavior, although often overruled by the trustees. (These student combinations were for the most part informal. There was no student expectation for the array of formal extracurricular activities evident nowadays on campuses.) Provost Beasley suggested implementing an academic evaluation (Yale had established the 4.0 scale in 1813); by establishing a seemingly meritocratic system of evaluation for students, he was advocating for competition among the students in order to receive recognition. Here the Enlightenment appears specifically: not by birth but by competition does one achieve status, even legitimizing students' rebellion against "patriarchal authority" at the time. In a fitting description of leadership life, the governing board (largely composed of members of wealthy Philadelphia families) dismissed the academic leader, the provost, before his solution was put into place, concerned that student dismissals with an enrollment of 57 in 1824 would cause further financial woes, but the provost's successor chose to implement the system, which also strengthened the role of the faculty in student dismissal cases, as a step not to further the moral codes of the time but to establish a more democratic way of life for the nation's future leaders, future leaders who came by and large from wealthy families in the area. The meritocratic system rewarded a mostly wealthy group of students.[20] Nor was student enthusiasm limited to the institutions in the North. The University of Virginia began under the direction of Thomas Jefferson in 1819, with his clear expectation that students would be adults. And while some were, many others indulged in excessive drinking, parties, and gun play; their version of Southern honor (and many were the sons of plantation owners, where honor had meaning in race as well as assumed cultural heritages brought from England) meant that they cared little for the rules of the University. A series of student rebellion began in the mid-1820s, in one instance with students whipping a professor, and it did not slow until the 1840s. More frightening, at the University of Alabama, students, sons of slave owners and some as young as 12 years old, kidnapped a young African American slave and kept her in their quarters for about three weeks. Six years after the institution's 1831 inception, "more than half of the students had been expelled and all the original faculty had resigned."[21] Despite the extensive rules at many colleges in the colonial era and the Early Republic, student misbehavior was widespread, and whether their combinations resulted from shared socioeconomic class backgrounds or those backgrounds and a notion of Southern honor, those combinations often proved at least temporarily successful. Meanwhile, the poor and pious students at the colleges were more likely to study, readying themselves for the ministry.

Hence the moral and economic characteristics of higher education would serve the individual, the community, and the nation, whether the immediate institutional control sought to advance Christianity by attempting to control young American Indians or produce graduates with civil and ecclesiastical authority despite the desire among many of these young white men to resist those efforts. As the authors of the 1828 Yale Report argued, their college was a place where young men learned to discipline themselves in order to better serve the nation and God. The Yale Report deserves special attention, given that it is a landmark piece in the definition of U.S. higher education. The faculty authors of the report, in response to demands to make the institution's graduates better prepared for a useful adulthood based on a useful education, sought to defend both the classical curriculum with its focus on Latin and Greek languages and literature, with a goodly dose of moral philosophy, and a very slow but deliberate effort to respond to modern notions of, for example, the natural science. They argued that such an education was instrumental, indeed the best form, of providing students and graduates with the necessary faculties of the mind (i.e., a knowledge of particular bodies of knowledge such as the ancient Roman and Greek authors) and the equally necessary discipline of the mind. These, the authors argued, would be the leaders of the new Republic, thoughtful and reflective on weighty matters in both business and government affairs—a reminder of the enduring notion that higher education in liberal education in both antique and contemporary form as well as higher learning is meant for those capable of higher thought; their role was to ensure the continued development of the nation.

Faculty Lives in the Colonial Era and the Early Republic

In some ways the lives and characteristics of the faculty members of the colonial era and the Early Republic were uniform. The earned doctorate, while to some degree a part of university life in Europe starting in Germany in the mid-1600s, was not available in the United States; Yale awarded the first six doctorates in 1861, so often prior to then the faculty members held master's degrees. This was a time when graduate education was far from the state of affairs in the early 2000s. At some institutions, graduates who remained at the college for a few years received master's degrees on the basis of further study. Often these young white men were waiting for a call to the ministry and not anticipating a lifetime career as a professor.

Faculty members (including the president, who at some institutions was the only teacher of three or four years of a required moral philosophy course) were typically responsible only for students' academic and moral growth rather than focused on advancing their own expertise. The beginnings of the modern academic profession with divisions by areas of study and rank are, however, visible in the colonial era and the Early Republic at Harvard. Because of the institution's comparative wealth even in its early years, Harvard was able to have both tutors and professors; the former were responsible for student behavior and discipline as well as teaching in the general curriculum, the latter taught in specific fields and did not live on campus, although many of them boarded students. Tutors could not marry, professors could. By the 1690s at Harvard, before any other colleges had begun college-level education, tutors were beginning to plan futures not in the ministry (almost three-quarters of those who were Harvard tutors before 1680 became ministers) but as schoolteachers or professors. As the length of service increased for tutors (one of whom served for 55 years), tutors became more involved in college governance, in one case protesting the actions of a president for over-turning student discipline decisions as well as the three-year renewal of tutor appointments given their increased responsibilities. Even at the colonial colleges, faculty members at times challenged norms, although by and large disagreements were enacted by the establishment of additional colleges. It is important to know that the foundation of the northern European university at the University of Paris began with cathedral schools, so named because erudite commentators such as Abelard gave lectures at places near Notre Dame in Paris; those lectures might explicate Christian teachings, but they might also offer careful challenges to the standing notions of Christian society. Furthermore, by the 1700s most of the tutors had their master's degrees before their appointments and had served in other roles at the college prior to their appointments. In the case of the professors, the college began appointing professors to chairs in the 1720s, moving from five-year appointments to lifetime ones. Eventually the tutors also began teaching in specific fields, in the 1750s, with eight-year terminal appointments. Internecine conflicts were present, albeit different from those of the European universities in the Middle Ages, because oddly, the tutors often had appointments to the Corporation, one of two oversight boards for the institution while professors did not have such positions. Finally, after a number of non-physical battles between the two groups over that control, in 1824 the professors succeeded in a reorganization with specific academic departments headed by professors, and student discipline was assigned to a faculty committee with a professor in charge. Over more than a century, the academic profession in the United States began to develop and other colleges began to adopt such characteristics.[22]

The Institutions of the Early Republic

These roles also expanded as different institutional types began to appear, institutions such as the U.S. Military Academy, dame schools and then women's colleges, and practical colleges such as Rensselear Polytechnical Institute came into being. Variations in terms of pedagogy also developed. The European methods focused on disputation, highly formalized arguments about a subject (not unlike formal debate competition today), and recitation (or oral translation) of a text. (While historians of higher education in the 1950s and 1960s often disparaged these methods, it would be wise to admit that many a boring lecture occurs today; not simply the pedagogy but the implementation of the pedagogy has had a lot to do with its ability to engage students.)

The point of a classical college education at that time was not the imparting of scholarly expertise (much less preparation for an academic life) but rather learning what were considered great books, at the center of which was the Bible, perhaps best named as a classical curriculum, one that provided roots for the modern liberal arts curriculum. The liberal arts remain a powerful component of the college curriculum; so too do other curricula, with roots in the Early Republic. The Yale faculty reflected one aspect of the nature of the professoriate at the time in terms of curriculum, and teaching, and it faced pressure to reform the college's curriculum from the state legislature of Connecticut in order to address a more useful education. There were early colleges that had just such a curriculum, such as the U.S. Military Academy (1802),

Norwich University (founded as an academy in 1819), and Rensselaer Polytechnic Institute (1824). They serve as early examples of notions about practical education espoused by such early U.S. leaders on educational thought as Benjamin Franklin and Benjamin Rush. By the early 1800s, with the continued expansion west (and the horrifying efforts to remove or kill those who were native to the land), the country needed engineers, and those institutions were highly important in producing graduates who were instrumental in developing the infrastructure of the states and territories, through the construction of roads, bridges, canals (once a, if not the, primary means of transportation across long distances), and then the railroads. They also focused on leadership; at the U.S. Military Academy, mathematics instructors in the early 1800s used an early teaching technology to develop not only students' mathematical talents but also their ability to handle challenging situations and show the calm so necessary for leadership in those situations. The technology was, simply, the chalkboard. Instructors expected each student to stand at the chalkboard, solve complex problems on the board, and respond to questions and corrections in a collected manner. In contrast to the commonly dulling PowerPoint presentation of today, no different from a dulling lecture of the early 1800s as described with poignant clarity by one West Point student, instructors were determined to ask pointed questions to challenge the students' academic conclusions and their ability to deliver answers with confidence. This form of recitation meant that while the chalkboard was a powerful technology giving instructors the means to display information to a large group of students, they also served at West Point as yet another means to develop the nation's leaders.[23] Not simply curriculum, but also the development of innovative pedagogical practices was a means to creating leaders.

Of particular interest for some higher education institutions in creating leaders was the preparation of engineers given the nation's need for infrastructure, often at the expense of the American Indians. Some institutions began as separate entities (such as West Point, Norwich, and Rensselaer), others added engineering programs—and in a phrase that could well serve as a motto for all colleges and universities, "it was a cheap and simple pattern to follow"—some included the engineering curriculum in their undergraduate degrees, and some developed a "nontraditional degree" program, the bachelor of science. Finally, there were institutions of higher education that separated those programs of study from the young men studying the liberal arts, all located in New England. Yale had the Sheffield Scientific School (gradually merging with Yale after World War I), while Harvard had the Lawrence Scientific School. Prior to the passage of the 1862 Morrill Land Grant Act, engineering education was part of higher education, with as many as 50 institutions offering programs in the field. For many of them, their enrollments rose and fell, but then again, enrollments across the United States for all institutions of higher education followed the same pattern or remained small.[24]

While colleges focused on the development of leaders, notably young white men, another question arose in the Early Republic: how would the nation prepare its citizens? The answer, scholars have argued, was that the mother was the best choice for educating the children of the family in preparation for their lives as members of the democracy. That choice was situated in assumptions about the primary role of a white woman as a caretaker, born to nurture the children, assumptions that also carried the powerful ideas about two spheres of life, the public sphere occupied by men and the private sphere occupied by women (the dualism of those two spheres has been well challenged by some scholars, but it is a useful starting point for this discussion). The man was responsible for business and governmental affairs outside the home, the woman for the work of the home, including raising children appropriately. In contrast, the owners of enslaved African American women forced them to work outside the home, but whether as enslaved people or as free women, they held the primary responsibility for the home too and were far less likely to experience separate spheres.

Dame schools and women's institutions of higher education viewed their role as preparing young women for life in a new society, and Troy Female Seminary (New York) provides a clear example of expanding notions of the meaning of college with specific attention to the higher education of women. An early leader in the formal efforts to educate white women was Emma Willard (founder of Troy Female Seminary in 1821 for teacher education, preceding the establishment of normal schools for training teachers in the 1830s); her arguments for a higher education for women began the decade before as she went to the governor and state legislature to present plans for educating women as teachers. She was careful to protect the women; one scholar suggests she selected the name seminary to avoid offending men and their hold on the name "college," but she also was clearly dedicated to the advancement of women. For example, the norm against women speaking to large audiences was very powerful, but Emma Willard challenged the norm by sitting in a chair on the stage and conducting a conversation with the audience. She sought to expand the role of women beyond the private (or domestic sphere) by educating them as teachers. The seminary's curriculum included science and the modern languages (the former slowly adopted by the Yale faculty members, the latter dismissed by them) as well as more of the classical curriculum. Emma Willard through Troy Female Seminary was highly successful, educating and graduating hundreds of young women who traveled throughout the nation, in many instances establishing schools that lasted for decades. At the same time, these young women as well as Emma Willard and the Troy teachers began to establish another role beyond teachers of citizens; they themselves were leaders in their communities and states.[25] Slowly the gender differences were lessening in the early nineteenth century.

Two issues in considering the nature of higher education in the colonies and the Early Republic are the nature of the institution—college? female seminary?—and who entered those institutions. Distinctions between institutional types are problematic given admission age requirements at Yale while female seminaries admitted students of similar age. Admission requirements appear to be often a common difference, as knowledge of Latin and Greek was required for admission to colonial colleges. Admission requirements slowly expanded, continuing to be academic subjects; arithmetic (becoming mathematics) had been included by the mid-1700s, and by the late 1800s, history, geography, and English were admission expectations, if not requirements.[26] These changes represented very different curricular expectations from the colonial colleges, and hence it is challenging to define the formal organization of higher education in the United States in the early 1800s by relying on an institution's formal name. Colleges' admission requirements by age differed little, but there were curricular differences at some institutions. As Church and Sedlak argued, there was overall little difference between colleges and academies in the first half of the 1800s. The age range of students (most between 14 and 24), formal education providing the knowledge and skills for a successful life, and very low tuition were common for both institutions. Further confusing the distinction between the two institutional types is that many colleges had preparatory departments so that students could still come, pay tuition, and ready themselves for college—a key reminder that public secondary schools were very rare throughout much of the 1800s as well as that colleges seek many ways to create revenue, and more troubling, that contemporary notions of under-prepared students ignore the very deep historical foundation of that challenge. Curiously, they also shared a likely setting, the small institution in a small town (although the meaning and size of urban was very different two centuries ago).[27] Nevertheless, at least in the minds of the authors of the Yale Report, likely reflecting a more widespread set of ideas among educators at other institutions claiming the name college (and soon, university), those were the institutions most responsible for sustaining the meritocracy.

Hence the higher education of women is a salient example of the developing breadth of the curriculum in the Early Republic. The curricular range, from the liberal arts (i.e., the classical curriculum developing into a more modern version of that form of liberal education) to the more practical education, from the study of classics and the inclusion of modern languages and the sciences to the education of young women for teaching, would increasingly become characteristic of U.S. higher education institutions. Although unable to offer a baccalaureate education for women, these women's seminaries, academies, and institutes represented an important range of studies. Even for-profit institutions developed in the colonial era, in the case of what were called venture schools, institutions that not only enrolled women but also in a number of cases, women established them during the Early Republic.[28] Nevertheless, even in the case of utility, women were not allowed to enter those colleges and universities that addressed the need to provide infrastructure for the developing nation; in the case of the considerable breadth of engineering education, these were institutions for white men. The classical curriculum indeed faced direct challenges, such as various types of engineering education, and women's separate institutions of higher education were challenges from a different, gendered perspective.

The goals for higher education articulated in the Yale Report of 1828 became more expansive at other institutions as national interest in higher education, and higher education leaders, began to address two new and remarkably important characteristics: *utility* and *research*.[29] Nevertheless, the commitment to the classical curriculum endured, in part because graduates of Yale and Princeton were often involved in the establishment of colleges in the Midwest (where hundreds of small towns have small colleges). Ensuing chapters address those characteristics as well as continue the discussion of the construction of the meritocracy. To some degree the nature of utility reflected the efforts of such educational leaders as Emma Willard, although it slowly shifted in the 1800s, as advocates of utility saw some broader dimensions. The next chapter, in discussion of the Midwest, South, and West, addresses these topics and introduces some additional arguments about the development of higher education.

DISCUSSION QUESTIONS

1. How might presentism inform or misinform our ideas about post-college careers in the past? For example, what does it mean to say that Abraham Lincoln was a lawyer?

2. In view of Emma Willard and her work, what tensions between the present and the possible future do people in higher education experience when they focus their efforts on change?

NOTES

1 Pierre Bourdieu, "Cultural Reproduction and Social Reproduction," in *Power and Ideology in Education*, ed. Jerome Karabel and A.H. Halsey (New York: Oxford University Press, 1971), 504. This is an instance in which the specific page number is highly important; arguments about moving on up (to coin a phrase from a popular 1970s television show) do not reflect the elites' considerable desire and effort to keep their status. I am, however, also acknowledging the possibilities of upward movement, despite the structural constraints; on structuring opportunity, see for example Joel Spring, *The Sorting Machine: National Educational Policy Since 1945* (Boston: Addison-Wesley Longman, 1976).

2 Elizabeth McHenry, "Dreaded Eloquence: The Origins and Rise of African American Literary Societies and Libraries," *Harvard Library Bulletin* 6 (1995): 32–56.

3 Eldon L. Johnson, "The 'Other Jeffersons' and the State University Idea," *Journal of Higher Education* 58, no. 2 (March–April 1987): 127–150.

4 Jane Fiegen Green, "'An Opinion of Our Own': Education, Politics, and the Struggle for Adulthood at Dartmouth College, 1814–1819," *History of Education Quarterly* 52, no. 2 (May 2012): 173–195.

5 Here is a moment to consider what thinking historically means. Admittedly, history begins when the act is seemingly concluded (thus, acknowledging that acts of the past have meanings for the present and future, so they are only seemingly concluded). It is probably a safe generalization that many historians would say that history begins about 20 years ago—which very nearly constitutes, interestingly, a population generation—but I am comfortable with the idea that history begins about 10 years ago. So, bringing the historical analysis to the early 2000s safely keeps me in a historical frame of mind.

6 Mary Ann Dzuback, "Gender and the Politics of Knowledge," *History of Education Quarterly* 43, no. 2 (Summer 2003): 171–195. I am indebted to Mary Ann for her insights on meanings of difference as centering social constructions of gender (and for me, in other areas such as race and ethnicity).

7 Charles Homer Haskins, *The Rise of Universities* (Ithaca, NY: Cornell University Press, 1923).

8 Harold Benjamin, *Higher Education in the American Republics* (New York: McGraw-Hill, 1965).

9 "New England's First Fruits," in *American Higher Education, A Documentary History*, ed. Richard Hofstadter and Wilson Smith, vol. 1 (Chicago: University of Chicago Press, 1961), 6–7.

10 www.archives.gov/exhibits/charters/declaration_signers_gallery_facts.pdf (retrieved May 23, 2008). On enrollments at colonial colleges, see, for example, Lawrence Cremin's detailed examination of Harvard College graduates; Lawrence Cremin, "College," in *American Education: The Colonial Experience* (Harper & Row, 1970), 196–224.

11 John S. Brubacher and Willis Rudy, *Higher Education in Transition: A History of American Colleges and Universities*, 4th ed. (New York: Routledge, 2017).

12 Lawrence Cremin, "College," in *American Education: The Colonial Experience* (New York: Harper & Row, 1970).

13 Max Weber, *The Protestant Ethic and the Spirit of Capitalism*, trans. Talcott Parsons (New York: Charles Scribner's Sons, 1952).

14   Phyllis Vine, "The Social Function of Eighteenth Higher Education," *History of Education Quarterly* 16, no. 1 (Winter 1976): 409–424.

15   Bobby Wright, "The 'Untameable Savage Spirit': American Indians in Colonial Colleges," *Review of Higher Education* 14, no. 2 (Summer 1991): 429–452. One challenge, of course, in naming, is how to name whom, and by something of a default, I have chosen to follow those who have led the way in naming in recognition. In the case of the term American Indian, the field of ethnic studies includes American Indian studies and a number of scholars highly critical of the repeated efforts of Whites to commit genocide. In a historical sense, the genocide of entire American Indian tribes and the intentional weakening of remaining tribes caused a broad designation, Native American, to serve as a necessary substitute for the loss of individual tribes. A thoughtful discussion of this challenge is in the Introduction to *Postsecondary Education for American Indian and Alaska Natives*, ed. Bryan McKinley Jones Brayboy, Amy J. Fann, Angelina E. Castano, and Jessica A. Solymon, ASHE Higher Education Report 37, no. 5 (San Francisco: Wiley/Jossey-Bass, 2012).

16   Hilary J. Moss, "Education's Inequity: Opposition to Black Higher Education in Antebellum Connecticut," *History of Education Quarterly* 46, no. 1 (March 2006): 16–35.

17   "Yale Laws of 1745," in *American Higher Education, A Documentary History*, vol. 1, ed. Richard Hofstadter and Wilson Smith (Chicago: University of Chicago Press, 1961), 57.

18   There are a variety of versions of the Yale Report of 1828 available online. Do not read excerpts, however tiresome the language of the time might seem; the Report represents not only clear arguments about the meanings of a college education in the Early Republic that resonate today among some educators, but also a remarkable use of rhetoric, the art of convincing readers (or listeners) of an argument.

19   Richard Hofstadter and Walter P. Metzger, *The Development of Academic Freedom in the United States* (New York: Columbia University Press, 1955), p. 165.

20   Kathryn McDaniel Moore, "Freedom and Constraint in Eighteenth Century Harvard," *Journal of Higher Education* 6 (November–December 1976): 649–659; Rodney Hessinger, "'The Most Powerful Instrument of College Discipline': Student Disorder and the Growth of Meritocracy in the Colleges of the Early Republic," *History of Education Quarterly* 39, no. 4 (Autumn, 1999): 237–262.

21   Stephen Tomlinson and Kevin Windham, "Northern Piety and Southern Honor: Alva Woods and the Problem of Discipline at the University of Alabama, 1831–1837," *Perspectives on the History of Higher Education: History of Higher Education Annual 2006* 25: 1–42.

22   John D. Burton, "The Harvard Tutors: The Beginning of an Academic Profession, 1690–1825," *History of Higher Education Annual 1996* 16: 5–20. Burton notes, in an endnote, that the Harvard model may have had its precedent at Emmanuel College, which had tutors expected to leave shortly after completing their advanced degree.

23   Christopher J. Phillips, "An Officer and a Scholar: Nineteenth-Century West Point and the Invention of the Blackboard," *History of Education Quarterly* 55, no. 1 (February 2015): 83–108.

24   Terry S. Reynolds, "The Education of Engineers in America before the Morrill Act of 1862," *History of Education Quarterly* 32, no. 1 (Winter 1992): 459–482. See also, Stanley Guralnick, *Science and the American Antebellum College* (Philadelphia: American Philosophical Society, 1975) and Colin B. Burke, *American Collegiate Populations: A Test of the Traditional View* (New York: New York University Press, 1982).

25   Linda Kerber, "Daughters of Columbia: Educating Women for the Republic 1787–1805," in *The Hofstader Aegis: A Memorial*, ed. Eric McKitrick (New York, 1976), pp. 36–59. See also Linda Kerber, *Women of the*

Republic: Intellect and Ideology in Revolutionary America (Chapel Hill: University of North Carolina Press, 1997); Anne Firor Scott, "The Ever Widening Circle: The Diffusion of Feminist Values from the Troy Female Seminary," *History of Education Quarterly* 19, no. 1 (Spring 1979): 3–25.

26 John S. Brubacher and Willis Rudy, *Higher Education in Transition: A History of American Colleges and Universities*, 4th ed. (New York: Routledge, 2017).

27 Robert Church and Michael Sedlak, "The Antebellum College and Academy," in *Education in the United States: An Interpretive History*, ed. Robert Church (New York: The Free Press, 1976).

28 Kim Tolley, "The Rise of the Academies: Continuity or Change?" *History of Education Quarterly* 41, no. 2 (Summer 2001): 225–239.

29 I am indebted to a single scholar, Laurence Veysey, *The Emergence of the American University* (Chicago: University of Chicago Press, 1965), for his insightful articulation of the importance of utility and research in changing the goals, curriculum, and professors in U.S. higher education from the mid-1800s to the early 1900s. As many colleagues have pointed out, there are many problems with Veysey's analysis (bluntly put, he wrote from the typical white male perspective of the 1960s, and with a perspective grounded in valuing research institutions), but I return to his articulation of the importance of utility and research time and again when seeking to understand how colleges and universities arrived at their station in national life by the early 1900s.

3

A CENTURY OF DESTINY BUILT ON
DEVELOPING TRADITIONS

Higher Education Expands

It is no mere platitude to argue that the nineteenth century was one of destiny for U.S. colleges and universities, although for historical analysis, a century is sufficiently long that a historian might be hard-pressed not to find any destiny in 100 years. What makes the 1800s so key in U.S. higher education, however, is the development of events, institutions, and people that resulted in so many of the myriad definitions and meanings that exist today. The list is long and contains both impressive and depressing characteristics. Some of the characteristics receive more lengthy treatment in other chapters, with only brief comment in this chapter, but overall, the import of the nineteenth century is clear. As Brubacker and Willis argue in a discussion of curricular innovations, "It will be well to get a running start by reminding ourselves that the budget of discontent with the college program in the twentieth century was in part a balance brought forward from the nineteenth."[1] The 1800s also represent several key shifts in the nature of the nation, such as the European-American movement westward from the East and to the East from the Pacific coast that often took Native American lives and ensured the destruction of several tribes in order to expand the nation to the Pacific, the development of a women's movement, the development of an African American movement, the industrialization and urbanization of large parts of the North, and the development of large corporations. Careful examination of the 1800s and the vast expanse of the Midwest, South, and West reveals the sources of many of the innovations in U.S. higher education that we still know today; there were also important changes in the other region, the Northeast.

Across the nation during the 1800s, despite the concerted efforts of many college presidents and faculty members, both public pressure and the work of other college presidents and professors slowly eroded the dominance of God in the work and curriculum of the college in the second half of the nineteenth century. This is not to say that the moral, Protestant (and in a somewhat different way, Catholic, as Catholic colleges came into existence in the 1800s) perspective dissipated. While other religions, such as Judaism, had some representation across the spectrum of higher education, as Paul Ritterband and Harold Wechsler point out in *Jewish Learning in American Universities*, the dominant institutional perspective was Protestant. In contrast to the Bible's centrality at colleges of the 1600s and 1700s, many Protestant colleges and universities increasingly saw their goals as necessarily addressing the daily lives of citizens who wanted to be economically productive, serving the nation in a Christian, or christian, manner, what one historian of higher education termed utility, or utilitarian education. Practical courses of study became much more common. In terms of research, a goal for higher education that by and large followed the institutions' embrace of utilitarian education, colleges and universities increasingly came to see themselves as the logical places for understanding, and providing to the nation, the rational, scientific characteristics of humans and their lives.[2] These goals should sound remarkably idealistic, because they were. There is fervor in the voices and actions of many college presidents and professors in the mid to late 1800s in the United States, a conviction that they were doing right—often arguing that it was God's will to make better the lives of individuals through practical economic activity, activity that slowly became presumably based on rational, scientific examination.

Nevertheless, the ideal of the liberal arts sustained in a remarkably persistent way. As one historian pointed out in 1971, it has long been popular to declare that liberal arts colleges are dead and that large numbers of liberal arts colleges have died and many are on the verge of dying; the reality is far different. Early estimates of college mortality rates were based on college charters and those institutions that resulted and lived after their charters, a very weak measurement. A state legislature granting a charter is a far simpler process than establishing a brick and mortar institution with professors and students. Remembering history reminds a person that even when enrollments were uniformly paltry (in the colonial era but also throughout the 1800s), colleges persisted.[3] The socioeconomic contract between higher education institutions and their communities was increasingly powerful, and as John Thelin has noted, many institutions of higher education learned how to survive with scarce resources.

Just as important as the combination of Christianity and utility was the increasing societal belief that college was worth the time and effort (often couched in the non-academic behaviors of students, discussed further in Chapter 6), a belief oddly captured in the Rudyard Kipling book, *Captains Courageous*; once the spoiled young man is brought safely back to land after months at sea working on a commercial fishing boat, his father offers him two choices, a valet and a yacht or four years of college. The young man chooses college, and this lengthy quote is highly instructive, the father telling his son of his own sense of inferiority:

> "I can't compete with the man who has been taught. I've picked up as I went along, and I guess it sticks out all over me."
>
> "I've never seen it," said the son, indignantly.
>
> "You will though, Harve. You will just as soon as you're through college. Don't I know it? Don't I know the look on men's faces when they think me a—a—'mucker,' as they call it out here? I can break them to little pieces—yes—but I can't get back at 'em to hurt 'em where they live. I don't say they're 'way 'way up, but I feel I'm 'way 'way 'way off, somehow. Now you've got your chance. You've got to soak up all the learning that's around, and you'll live with a crowd that are doing the same thing. They'll be doing it for a few thousand dollars a year at most; but remember you'll be doing it for millions. You learn law enough to look after your own property when I'm out o' the light, and you'll have to be solid with the best men in the market (they are useful later); and above all, you'll have to stow away the plain, common, sit-down-with-your-chin-on-your-elbows-book-learning. Nothing pays like that, Harve, and it's bound to pay more and more each year in our country in business and in politics. You'll see."
>
> "There's no sugar my end of the deal," said Harvey. "Four years at college! Wish I'd chosen the valet and the yacht instead."[4]

Thus, an outside observer greets the end of the 1800s in the United States; Rudyard Kipling (writing in Vermont, in one of those fine historical curiosities, the home of Justin Morrill of the 1862 and 1890 Morrill Land Grant Acts) offers an evaluation of the shifting characteristics of advancement in the nation, the need for a higher education. Just as telling, it is a wealthy man, one who earned his money without having attended college, who advocates the importance of a college education, not just for academic knowledge but also for social opportunities.

That is not to say that the newly wealthy and other newcomers to higher education in the United States came to campus and became a single community. There was a history of residential segregation, segregation based on race, gender, and class. These divisions were even more subtle than a matter of money. These patterns of economic segregation sustained larger enrollments as well as a thin veneer of college community. A number of historians of higher education have noted that not only did institutions such as many of those in the Ivy League systematically limit or exclude Jews, but also German Jews who had come to the United States in the mid-1800s, rather than the large numbers of Jews from central and eastern Europe in the late 1800s and early 1900s, supported limitations on the admission of the new Jews, whose interest in attending college had much to do with first-generation students' aspirations for career and success rather than following the footsteps of established parents.[5]

It should not be much of a surprise to many readers that in like manner, colleges and universities often engaged in similar fashion in regard to the enrollment of white women and African Americans, either excluding them or ensuring that they had minority status. Nevertheless, both groups succeeded in the 1800s in gaining access to higher education. For white women, it was typically enrollment at one of four institutional types: a female seminary (many of which included college-level curricula); a normal school for teacher training, one of the coeducational midwestern colleges; or a college for white women located throughout the nation. For African Americans, it was more likely to be enrollment at a black college—in the South and on occasion in the Midwest, West, and the Northeast.

COLLEGES AND UNIVERSITIES IN THE 1800S: AN INSTRUCTIVE DEVELOPMENT IN THE MIDWEST

Historical understanding of the nation's need for higher education as expressed by citizens and non-citizens is key to understanding colleges and universities; this discussion starts with Beloit College, Wisconsin, because it has an apocryphal story. Other discussion in this chapter includes the admission of white women, the admission of Blacks, the development of black colleges, colleges for white women, the state university from the late 1700s to the 1862 and 1890 Morrill Acts and into the late 1800s and concludes with the rise of the administration. The discussion about the Morrill Land Grant Acts reaches back to mid-state New York, specifically to Cornell University, yet quickly moves west and south. Then again, Ithaca, New York (home of Cornell), was thought of as being in the West during part of the 1800s.

Founded in 1846, two years before statehood for Wisconsin and the foundation of the University of Wisconsin, Beloit College began offering classes in 1847. Its first student walked 50 miles from his home in Mineral Point, Wisconsin to enroll at the college when he heard it was opening. There it is. He heard about the college, got on his feet, and marched in. It is a story of almost biblical proportions, diminished only by the fact that he did not need to part the waters of Lake Michigan to get there (Beloit is in the middle of the state, right on the state line with Illinois, far from Lake Michigan). The president there in the 1980s was so charmed by the story that he organized an annual fundraising walk from Mineral Point to Beloit.

The story says a lot about higher education in the United States in the nineteenth century. To start, quoting from the 2011 version of Beloit's website:

> The College's early curriculum was cast mainly in the Yale mold. Aratus Kent, chairman of the Beloit College board of trustees, and the first faculty members, Jackson J. Bushnell and Joseph Emerson, built a solid casing with Yale mortar before another Yale graduate, Aaron Lucius Chapin, accepted Beloit's first presidency in December 1849. He served until 1886, and during his presidency the College became widely known for its scholastic excellence.[6]

So indeed, the College also reflects the powerful influence of Yale often noted by historians of higher education in the development of midwestern colleges and universities. (Princeton, too, was influential.) The influence of scholastic influence stretched through Beloit to other institutions; as Laurence Veysey notes, T.C. Chamberlain, an early Beloit president, had a remarkable influence on the development of research at the University of Wisconsin. Hence, it is not simply the colonial colleges that helped to shape the younger institutions or the larger institutions to shape the smaller ones; the obverse can also obtain. Yet this part of the historical narrative is more illuminating than simply the common alma maters of college founders in the Midwest or the influence of one college upon another. Enrollments continued to be small; the president of the University of Arkansas boasted an enrollment of 1879–1880, which he proudly declared was the fourth largest enrollment in the United States, when in fact two-thirds of the 450 students were in the preparatory program.[7] Many institutions survived simply because they had preparatory departments, important for their tuition revenue and necessary because of the dearth of secondary schools in much of the nation for an extraordinarily long time. It did not matter whether Beloit's first student had attended, much less graduated from, secondary school or had the benefit of a tutor. The secondary school was a rarity in the 1800s; many communities simply did not have the student population for secondary schools, and by and large it was not until the late 1800s and the developing urbanization of the nation that populations were large enough to justify secondary schools; the primary exceptions were the preparatory schools of the Northeast.[8] Beloit, like so many colleges and universities of the time, accommodated students of all sorts of educational levels up to and including the baccalaureate.

What would cause a small group of men to establish a college in the small town of Beloit—and for that matter, many small groups of men in many small towns across the Midwest? After all, it seems as if one cannot walk across a midwestern state today without tripping over a small private college or university. More often than not there were two major reasons for establishing these colleges. Towns (and cities) were very interested in promoting themselves, showing themselves and their neighbors across the territories and states that they were civilized, what David Potts refers to as boosterism, promoting the town or city while creating citizens and leaders in and for the local community.[9] There was a powerful drive to ensure the future of the Republic, and education was at the core of the drive. Colleges and universities would educate the leaders, an argument found in all sorts of documents about those institutions and one that obviously persists today, albeit often for different reasons and outcomes such as individual economic prosperity but not excluding the need to preserve the nation.

In addition, a variety of Protestant denominations wanted to establish their presence. Some of those denominations wanted an educated clergy, such as the Presbyterians and the Congregationalists (both of which had roots in the old colleges of the Northeast). The Methodists, for example, quickly established colleges in the Midwest and the West, starting with Iowa Wesleyan in 1842 and followed by colleges in California, Missouri, and Nebraska). Denominations could sustain themselves through higher education and while some (Baptist in particular) were slower to come to the decision to found a college, or several, there was a widespread movement among both white and black congregations during the 1800s to start colleges.[10] Nevertheless, the will to establish an institution of higher learning is not the same as the annual need for money that has always characterized higher education. And there was (and is) a fundamental problem, one that had an easy yet uncomfortable solution, opening the doors of the denominational institution to students from other denominations. While today many colleges and universities display a distanced uncomfortable relationship with their specific denominations (offering any number of terms to identify themselves, such as denominationally affiliated, or denomination-sponsored, or the broader faith-based), the roots of that distance are old and deep. In the sparsely

BN 5

populated regions of the country, colleges needed students, and the practical pressures of enrollment revenue, coupled with a need for tolerance in a nation with no nationally sanctioned religion—after all, our coins did not include the message In God We Trust until the Civil War (perhaps sanctifying the North's efforts to win the war) and paper money did not have that motto until the mid-1950s, in the midst of another war, the Cold War)—resulted in a focus on the denomination only through the institution's president and, sometimes, the faculty. As early as the mid-1700s, charters for some institutions explicitly prohibited discrimination against denominations other than the founding one, reflecting the context of denominational tolerance of the new nation.[11] The symbol of Christianity, a chapel with the tolling bell to bring students to classes and faculty members and students to chapel services, remains a constant on so many of those colleges campuses, but ironically the bell tolled for denominationalism and in celebration of pan-Christianity born of institutional pragmatism and religious tolerance. Hence like so many other denominations, the Congregationalists who founded Beloit College might well require the president if not the professors to declare themselves members of the denomination, but the students faced no such requirement.

Think, then, the following: local civil and denominational boosters and pragmatism of enrollment including student age and denomination. These conditions have powerful roots in the colonial era but find important characteristics in the colleges of the 1800s. Boosterism also was instrumental in the development of what we know today as the West (roughly, west of the Mississippi River, although much of this chapter's discussion includes consideration of states such as Iowa and Minnesota as part of the Midwest); one difference in the expansion was that it came from two directions, from the east as well as from the western seaboard. In addition, the institutions' founders also followed the path of college establishment beginning in the colonies and moving westward, the education, or removal, or eradication of American Indian tribes as well as ongoing conflict with the Spaniards and then the Mexicans. Development of higher education to the west of the Mississippi by and large occurred after the Civil War, and it often began with denominational colleges. As a curious aspect of the combination of local boosterism and denominational pride, some state universities began as denominational institutions and became state institutions, such as the University of Tennessee (begun as a Presbyterian college, Blount, in 1794) and even as partial state institutions, as in the case of the Mormons founding the University of Utah in 1850.

Despite the support of denominations and a common tolerance of other denominations for enrollment reasons, there were, however, instances of substantial clashes between denominations over control of colleges, as occurred at Transylvania

University in Lexington, Kentucky. Until the mid-1810s, the Presbyterians controlled the institution, but they allowed it to languish; Jeffersonian liberals exerted pressure on the state legislature, which in turn pressured the board of trustees to appoint Horace Holley as president. Holley, a Unitarian (a very liberal denomination), transformed the institution from offering a one-year course of study to one with studies in arts, law, and medicine, with students from 14 of the 24 states. The Presbyterians, in contrast to other area denominations, opposed Holley and campaigned to criticize him, not on the basis of his nonsectarian approach characteristic of Unitarians but rather because of the minority status of his denomination in Kentucky. At the same time, the economy was suffering, and Transylvania raised tuition while critics were emphasizing what they saw as its elite status; eventually even the governor joined the criticism. Holley resigned in 1827, then becoming what might easily be concluded as again an unsuccessful president, this time at the University of Alabama where the student behavior discussed in the previous chapter did nothing to advance the institution's academic work, and meanwhile Transylvania went into decline.[12] When tolerance was not part of the relationships among denominations, the consequences could be deleterious, a reminder that the fissures in the socioeconomic contract, given not only denominational but also tuition problem, were indeed serious issues.

Two other characteristics define some midwestern colleges, exemplifying how they led the nation rather than simply following older institutions. One institution has received much attention for its commitment to educate both Whites and African Americans, the first such institution to do so. Founded in 1833, Oberlin College upon its inception accepted white women and men and in 1835 began to admit African Americans. That decision was as pragmatic as it was idealistic, given that in 1834 the College was facing financial challenges, and students from Lane Seminary in Cincinnati, Ohio, having left that institution for its suppression of public speech about anti-slavery, indicated that they wanted to enroll at Oberlin, thus helping to alleviate Oberlin's financial problems. There had been other attempts to establish colleges for the education of African Americans, as in the case of the effort in Connecticut in 1831. In contrast, Oberlin had both white and African American students. Oberlin was successful and enduring, and the effort shaped U.S. higher education. No longer was a college necessarily a bastion of white men, only rarely admitting individual African American men and never admitting women.[13] The extension of higher education beyond some mixing of males of different socioeconomic classes had begun, men and women both white and African American having the opportunity to pursue higher education. Baccalaureate education for white women and African Americans began in the Midwest.

The Oberlin story has, however, another highly important component, the meaning of access beyond mere matriculation, a reminder that the past is not even past. As Cally Waite documents in her article on African American experience at Oberlin in the late 1800s, the College reflected the pernicious effects of the end of Reconstruction (the important but brief government efforts to reshape race relations in the South after the Civil War), the rise of Jim Crow laws in the South, which disenfranched Southern African Americans in myriad ways, and segregationist expectations in the North. In what must sound all too familiar in contemporary terms, white students were uncomfortable eating with black students in the dining hall, and white female students did not want to live with female African American students in the dormitories. Equally familiar, Oberlin presidents and faculty members were typically either equivocal or supported the white students.[14] Nor were only African Americans the ones who faced nuanced interpretations of who belonged. Among historians of women in education, the story of Lucy Stone is almost iconic. An Oberlin student, she was not allowed to speak at her 1847 commencement because the faculty vote of refusal reflected a powerful norm of the time: women were not allowed to give public speeches. Women were admitted, but their lives were far more circumscribed than the lives of men, particularly white men; often white and African American women were required to do domestic work as part of their enrollment, while expectations of utility for men focused on either more physically demanding labor or, more likely, the completion of programs of study with direct application to immediately practical careers. These experiences are instructive to historical understanding as well as to how history haunts us; even today it is obvious that colleges and universities welcome different groups in different ways, centering on age-old notions of privilege based on ascribed characteristics such as race and ethnicity, gender (and gender identification), and in far less acknowledged terms, socioeconomic class. Ironically, Stone became a noted public lecturer after graduation, speaking to issues of abolition and women's rights; equally ironic, she was the first female college graduate from Massachusetts. Go west, young woman.

The discussion about who came first in U.S. higher education includes black colleges. While it is not uncommon to point to efforts in northeastern states, the Midwest offers a more complete example of the effort to offer a higher education for African Americans. Indeed, Lincoln University received its charter in 1854 in Pennsylvania and as such is likely the first (Cheyney University, also in Pennsylvania, also lays claim to being the first), but Wilberforce (Ohio) began in 1863 as the first black college established by a black religious denomination. Here again, the difference seems to be slim, although the development of a college by African Americans expressly intended to serve African Americans (in contrast to both the enrollment of Oberlin black and white students as well as the experiences of Blacks at the institution) is of considerable import. One of the great and damaging, even brutal, assumptions about many peoples of color on the part of Whites is that they do not have the intellectual capacity for higher learning (or all too often, even rudimentary learning such as memorization of the alphabet). Hence the drive to secure learning, and equally if not more important, to secure formal institutions of education whether schools or colleges, provides insight into the drive for equality through the evidence of intelligence. Such a drive buttresses arguments of equality because, as often shared in the African American community in the past and present, no one can take that learning away. Focusing on Wilberforce given the work of the American Methodist Episcopal Church (AME), a church that was the product of early efforts to establish the right to worship in the Christian world, the AME purchased the institution's buildings and grounds from the Methodist Episcopal Church, a predominantly white denomination, having previously resisted efforts of that church to educate African Americans at the institution, fearing the use of those students to advance the colonization movement (a popular mid-1800s movement to send free African Americans to Africa). The key figure in these developments, Daniel Payne, argued for the purchase despite the fact that other members of the denomination decried the necessity of a higher education for their group; Payne saw the purchase as a means to advance racial uplift, connecting the church, higher education, and racial uplift. As early as 1844 in regard to higher education, the AME had committed to advancing the knowledge of the congregations, deacons, and ministers, and Payne later reflected, "These resolutions, presented . . . were the first strong, entering wedges to rive the mass of general ignorance and force the ministry of our Church to a higher plane of intellectual culture."[15] In 1863, the AME purchased Union Seminary (Columbus, Ohio, founded in 1847 and likely the first school for Blacks founded by Blacks), merging it with Wilberforce, becoming the Theological Department, then incorporated in the early 1890s as Payne Theological Seminary. In 1887 the state of Ohio began to provide funds for normal and industrial department, effectively combining liberal education, theological education, and utilitarian education.

In contrast to the early establishment of black colleges in the Northeast and the Midwest, white women's colleges had their earliest roots in the South (1831, LaGrange Female Institute, now LaGrange College and coeducational; Wesleyan Female College, 1836, now Wesleyan College and still a women's college) and then the Midwest (Rockford Female Seminary, Illinois, 1847, now coeducational Rockford University; Milwaukee Female Normal Institute and High School, Wisconsin, 1848, which became Milwaukee-Downer College and merged with then Lawrence College, Appleton, Wisconsin in 1964). Curiously, histories of women's colleges at times overlook the Catholics; nuns were instrumental as professors in the development of Catholic women's colleges, and the first Catholic college for women was the Academy of Saint Mary-of-the-Woods (Indiana), founded in 1840. The first women's college in the Northeast was Elmira College, NY, 1855, now coeducational, although as mentioned earlier, that part of New York was considered to be part of the West. Much of the discussion about who is first for men's colleges is similar to the discussion about which of these women's colleges was actually the first college-level institution for women, particularly in terms of curriculum, a constant in histories of higher education. While some historians have pointed at Vassar College, opened in 1865, as the beginning of women's colleges in the United States, others have examined events in the South and in the Midwest, and Roger Geiger has estimated that more than 45 women's colleges were degree-granting by the 1850s.[16] In fact, it may well be that the first college for white women is long deceased, Mary Sharpe College, in Winchester, Tennessee. Founded in 1855, it claimed to be the first college for women that offered both Latin and Greek, and it was a successful institution prior to the Civil War; afterward, its fortunes slowly declined given competition from other Tennessee colleges and a faltering economy in the 1890s, and eventually it closed in 1896.[17]

THE PURPOSE OF COLLEGE IN THE 1800S

The important difference between the South and the Midwest in the 1800s was that many midwestern women's colleges offered both the liberal arts and utilitarian education while Southern white women's colleges by and large had a fundamental purpose, as in the words of one book's title, the education of the Southern Belle. At Wesleyan College (Macon, Georgia), young white women and their instructors focused on their becoming appropriate matches for the sons of plantation owners; while the curriculum included aspects of the classical approach (so that they could engage in civilized conversation as the wives of plantation owners), it also included the ornamental arts and social relationships that included in some cases the ownership of enslaved Africans.[18]

Social relationships also mattered in the Midwest, although institutions often enough emphasized life in the public and private spheres rather than only the private sphere, much as Emma Willard had done at Troy Female Seminary. As one scholar noted about the foundation of white women's colleges in the Midwest, the patterns seem to follow family responses to births in the 1800s. She states in her discussion of Rockford and Beloit Colleges,

> Family members poured their dreams and materials resources on the son, who represented their future reputation and fortunes . . . A daughter, whether single or married, could not inure the continuance of the family name or add much to the family's wealth, for women were barred from professions and lucrative occupations. A daughter usually received less education than her brother, very little if the family suffered severe reverses.[19]

The same men who founded Beloit College also established Rockford Female Seminary and included in its charter the right to confer degrees, clearly indicating that the institution would have collegiate standing. Nevertheless, Anna Peck Sill, the head of the Seminary (the trustees maintained oversight but not direct administration of the fledgling institution, even naming the head of Beloit College as president of Rockford while Sill was named principal) made it clear that her ideas about a woman's education were quite different from the all-male Christian board of trustees who saw women as being in the private sphere. Sill saw the opportunities of public sphere missionary work and teaching, and eventually she would encourage her students to enter medicine and law. There were patterns of differences evident at Beloit and Rockford as well as across the nation; men made the decisions about appointments, men's salaries were considerably higher, male students could live off-campus with little of the supervision present at 1828 Yale but boarding houses were potential sites of sin for female students who, according to the male leaders, needed such supervision that they could not talk to men without a chaperone. The Beloit curriculum emphasized classical studies while the Rockford curriculum had some of those courses as well as those in areas such as English literature, history, rhetoric, and science, courses considered as more suitable to women; men debated in literary societies but the trustees thought women too delicate for such arguing. Not only did women take courses suitable to the private or domestic sphere (foreign languages, the fine arts, in order to be more desirable as potential wives), but also they performed domestic chores in their dormitories. As Rockford women gained more confidence, they challenged the Beloit trustees, even threatening at one point to appoint a male president of Rockford. Sill persisted, seeking college status, but it was not until the 1890s that the Beloit trustees named Rockford as a college.

Higher education for African American women had similarities and differences with white women's colleges. There are two black colleges for women, Bennett and Spelman. The former began as a coeducational school in 1873, instituting college-level courses shortly thereafter and becoming a women's college in 1926. Spelman began with two white women, Sophia Packard and her longtime companion, Harriet Giles, who founded Atlanta Baptist Female Seminary in 1881 with classes in the basement of an Atlanta church (a recurring theme in the establishment of a number of black colleges). The Seminary found a permanent home in 1883, initially funded by the white American Baptist Home Missionary Society and securing full funding in 1884 from John D. Rockefeller, renamed Spelman Seminary in honor of Rockefeller's wife and renamed Spelman College in 1926. Unlike white women in higher education, who either came from families of wealth and often had a liberal arts education, or white women from families of lesser means who sought a more career-oriented education but almost always stopped work outside the home after marriage, African American women before and after enslavement faced powerful norms to work outside and in the home. The Spelman curriculum reflected just such a combination, yet also reflected an ongoing commitment to seeming to emphasize industrial (i.e., utilitarian) education while actually focusing on a liberal arts education. White donors to black colleges preferred an education that encouraged such moral virtues of the nineteenth century as "thrift, sobriety, self-discipline, and a rejection of secular pleasures," virtues matching the Northern industrialist goal of a African American workforce educated for manual forms of work.[20] Yet while enrollments at Spelman seemed tilted toward industrial and teaching programs, graduates were more likely to be from academic programs. Hence Spelman, like many other black colleges, was able to present a face of industrial training while offering students the opportunity to pursue a liberal arts education. What is especially important about the higher education of African American women is that the central principle of their colleges was that they had primary responsibility for racial uplift, the drive to establish African Americans on equal footing with white people. This drive meant that African American women were responsible for both public and private spheres, for work outside the home and in the home, hence the importance of industrial training and teacher preparation for those students even as they chose the liberal arts.

At Spelman and at a number of white women's colleges, white women found ways to bond that established relational permanence. In the case of Spelman, the two white Massachusetts women who founded the institution, Sophia Packard and Harriet Giles, were lifelong partners, and two common terms by the late 1800s were Boston marriages and Wellesley marriages, referring to long-term relationships between two women, often living together for decades. Some of their letters were quite romantic, while in other cases, such as Ella Flagg Young, the superintendent of Chicago public schools in the early 1900s, her lifelong partnership is marked only by formal recognition of her partner in print and photographs as well as the graves of her partner and her, side by side.[21]

At times, women academics took on challenges to their abilities in direct fashion, although as in the case of the development of higher education for women, the process could take many years, if not decades. In what is perhaps one of the more infamous events of the late 1800s, a Harvard medical professor argued that women were not suited to higher education because in the act of such intense study, the blood flowing to their brains would lessen the flow to their ovaries, and they would not be able to reproduce. He first offered that argument at an 1872 women's club meeting in New England, and there is a suitable irony in that Lucy Stone (of Oberlin) was in attendance. Although there was apparently little reaction to his comments at the meeting, in the next year he published a monograph in which he furthered his arguments that women needed a different, less demanding higher education than the one offered for men based on his review of the health of seven women college graduates:

> Clarke pronounced female college education a flagrant violation of the laws of nature, one that he predicted would lead to a racial apocalypse. The female college graduate would be renowned for invalidism rather than erudition, sterility rather than achievement, a degenerate femininity rather than true womanliness—if, that is, she lived through the experience at all.[22]

The resultant response was both popular and among women college graduates heated and lasted for years, as the first edition of his monograph sold out quickly and over the next 15 years or so, there were another 16 editions. Written at a time when women's higher education in the Northeast was still relatively young (recall that Vassar began in 1866) and notions of evolution were still developing, his arguments had traction, even among reformers seeking the development of higher education for women because they placed their arguments in the context of the differences between men and women (more accurately, between white men and white women). Women reformers attempted to refute his claims or argue that women were different but still benefitted from a higher education, but Clarke's arguments retained their attraction until a newly formed group of college women graduates began its efforts to refute his claims. The group of those women met in Boston in 1881 (one of its organizers was Marion Talbott, who would become the dean of women at the University of Chicago as discussed later in this chapter) and the next year organized as the Association of Collegiate Alumnae (now the American Association of University Women); using their membership of nearly 300 women college graduates, in 1884 the Association instituted a statistical approach to rejecting his arguments. The 1895 publication of the survey results clearly indicated that the members did not suffer from the health problems described by Clarke. The introduction to the publication exemplified the long efforts of women reformers, both accepting and contesting the commonly held views of women, echoing the work of such women as Emma Willard; the results made clear that women could maintain their health, including their reproductive health, after a college education.

Although Clarke's claims were popular, women entered higher education more and more in the late 1800s. In addition to women's colleges, coeducation was an increasingly acceptable form of higher education in the Midwest and West, started by Oberlin and in many ways furthered by the efforts at seminaries. Reflecting the conditions of local boosterism and denominational pride, one scholar estimates that as many as 29 coeducational colleges, with the preponderance of the institutions' enrollments dominated by students in three-year courses, operated during the 1850s. Those institutions also enjoyed the support of local families who found that sending their sons and daughters to one institution was a financially judicious decision.[23] That last condition was also evident in the spread of junior colleges, discussed in Chapter 4 on Progressivism.

HIGHER EDUCATION INSTITUTIONAL EXPANSION

What were called junior colleges until the 1950s and 1960s, when they increasingly and almost always began to be called community colleges, supposedly began in 1901 when the principal of Joliet High School and the president of the University of Chicago worked together to form a post-secondary institution to prepare students not yet ready to enter institutions such as the University of Chicago (the next chapter offers a more detailed discussion of two-year colleges and refutes that popular claim). The dearth of secondary schools resulted in a variety of ways of preparing students for college study. Curiously, one of those ways was institutionally specific as well as specific to the Midwest, the certification of secondary schools (typically based on visits by university faculty members) within a state so that their graduates could attend that state's university. Those efforts were extensive in such states as Wisconsin and Michigan, yet so extensive that they eventually exhausted faculty members and those institutions moved to more familiar forms of selecting students, the evaluation of secondary school transcripts and the use of standardized testing, a matter discussed more thoroughly in Chapter 7 on research universities.[24]

While neither Wisconsin nor Michigan's efforts led to a permanent method of evaluating and admitting prospective students, their contributions to land grant and research universities is unmistakable. In the case of Wisconsin, its land grant status became a central part of its identity. The idea of using federal land to provide opportunity to create or sustain educational institutions dates back to the 1700s, particularly to the 1787 Northwest Ordinance. (Land grants were also popular in the colonizing era; in 1618 the Virginia Company of London designated 10,000 acres in the Virginia colony for a college for the children of American Indians, a substantial irony in that the natives were obviously the first occupants of that land.) In that 1787 legislation designating the formation of states and establishing rights in the Northwest Territories to white settlement at the cost of American Indian tribes, there was a specific statement that a part of the Ohio Territory would be set aside for a public university, and as a result, Ohio University opened in 1804, graduating its first two students in 1815.

States established almost 20 institutions of higher education because of land grants authorized by the Ordinance. That same act also prohibited slavery in the states developed from the Northwest Territory, ensuring a *de jure* divide between the North and the South that would eventually have serious consequences for the nation, including for higher education and the passage of the 1890 Morrill Land Grant Act. (In 1828, 24 years after its founding, Ohio University conferred an A.B. degree on John Newton Templeton, its first black graduate and one of the first black men to graduate from a college in the United States.) Although states established universities beginning in the late 1700s, it is clear that federal land grant support was key in the beginnings and development of state universities.

It seems that all too often, the story of the 1862 Morrill Land Grant Act and its emphasis on what it termed agricultural and mechanical arts begins with 1862, while in fact it is a much longer story in terms of origins and also necessarily includes the 1890 Morrill Land Grant Act. In terms of origins of practical higher education, West Point, the American Literary, Philosophical, and Military Academy (later Norwich University), and the Rensselaer School (later Rensselaer Polytechnic Institute) serve as important reminders that by the 1820s, practical higher education, perhaps better named as utilitarian education (i.e., in broader terms than simply courses of study, serving a utility for the student, the institution, or the broader society) was underway among institutions of higher education, even in the Northeast in areas such as engineering. Land grant institutions did not appear out of the heads of legislators in 1862 and 1890; rather the nature of land grant goals, much like the use of land grants themselves, has a much deeper history.

For example, in Virginia, the troubled consequences of draining the soil of its nutrients in the 1700s and early 1800s by the production of tobacco (a production by enslaved Africans) created financial problems. Plantation owners, in particular, recognized the need for scientific agriculture, which required the higher education of farmers for success, and several years of lobbying through journals and state associations led to the development of agricultural education at the Virginia Military Institute, a development that ended shortly thereafter with the advent of the Civil War. Nevertheless, it is instructive that in a region long considered a home of non-utilitarian education (the sons and daughters of plantation owners did not need utility but rather sought the veneer of civilization through the classical curriculum, a veneer that was decidedly race-thin), agricultural education took hold, albeit briefly, at a leading Southern institution. The federal movement toward the 1862 act resulted from decades of land grant programs, the goal of advancing science, and graduating students prepared to advance the economic wealth of the nation through utilitarian higher education.[25]

The curriculum was not solely one of utilitarian focus, as the liberal arts were often a prominent feature of early state universities. For example, the University of Oregon (1873) had a classical curriculum. Not surprisingly, given external criticisms resulting in the institutional response to defend Yale College in 1828, Oregon faced sufficient pressure that it quickly developed scientific and utilitarian programs. In fact, the 1862 Morrill Land Grant Act dictated that the institutions would offer agricultural and mechanical education "without excluding scientific and classical studies" as well as military tactics (tactics appropriate for 1862 Northern legislation at the beginning of the Civil War). Nevertheless, the expectation that these institutions were indeed for instruction in agricultural and mechanical areas was powerful, to the extent that one vocal movement for farmers, the Grange, gained control of New England land grant colleges in the last quarter of the nineteenth century and worked for institutions reflecting "the values of working farmers," although eventually losing that control to advocates for state institutions with broader academic programs and higher expectations for prospective students' qualifications by the early 1900s. Another grass-roots movement, the Populists in the Midwest, focused on land grant universities, seeking to influence the social sciences (although they remained skeptical of the privileged social science professors), create greater access for rural students whose preparatory schooling might not be at the same level as that in more popular areas and whose economic backgrounds could preclude college because of cost. While not necessarily successful, their effort is a reminder of the faith in higher education in this nation.[26]

National racial political pressures resulted in the 1890 Morrill Land Grant Act (with careful but quick searches on the Internet, readers can find the full documents for both Land Grant Acts; comparing and contrasting the two acts provides illustrations of how the federal government carefully sustained efforts to keep the races apart and Whites in a superior position of power). Reconstruction had ended, Southern legislators were increasingly developing Jim Crow laws, and judicial decisions affirming "separate but equal" conditions were underway (resulting in the infamous 1896 *Plessy v. Ferguson* decision by the U.S. Supreme Court, a decision never overturned). Consequently the 1890 act allowed separate institutions by race if neither discriminated on the basis of race in admissions (thus, allowing institutional administrators to proclaim a *de jure* position of equality while fully effecting a *de facto* one of segregation in the case of white colleges and universities as far north as Delaware) and, in what ought to be unforgettable wording, states could propose and establish separate institutions with "a just and equitable division of the fund." The 1890 institutions did not receive either just or equitable funding; through the motivation and perseverance of administrators, faculty members, students, and supporters, there are 15 such institutions today.[27]

The land grant universities also offer both an important story in the uneven growth of higher education in the second half of the 1800s as well as a reminder of the dangers of presentism. In the case of the latter, today most land grant universities are widely known in the United States, although those that resulted from the 1890 act are likely better known among African Americans than Whites. Those that are predominantly white are now large, often with extensions across the state, and many have very popular college football and men's and women's basketball teams. Their beginnings were decidedly otherwise. Despite the apparent largesse of the federal government by granting federal land to finance the institutions, few states moved quickly to secure those funds, and even when they did, they did not necessarily use them well. Furthermore, many of these institutions were small, some so small that they had to close for a few years. Some 1862 land grant institutions were small in part because there were so few, if any, secondary schools in their states (when Arizona began its land grant institution, there were no secondary schools in the territory). Even in the cases where there were standing institutions of higher education that became the state's land grant institution, the university was not necessarily much of a college; the University of Wisconsin called itself "a high school for the village of Madison." While Cornell University opened as an 1862 land grant institution, with the motto (coined by the founder, Ezra Cornell), "I would found an institution where any person can find instruction in any study," early enrollments did not sustain. The first class in 1868 had just over 400 male students, with women admitted beginning in 1870, although soon the entire enrollment was just over 300 students.[28]

These institutions suffered both from enrollment problems and their inability to produce research leading to improved agriculture or in the mechanical arts, for the simple reason that such practical research necessarily resulted from discoveries in basic research such as biology and chemistry. As noted previously, good ice cream comes from improved milk that comes from better cattle, and only a field such as genetics could establish the base for that process. Furthermore, in terms of enrollment, students often eschewed the practical areas for liberal education and professional preparation in areas such as law.

Despite the generosity of the land grants offered by the federal government, the states were not necessarily enthusiastic about implementing the act, often avoiding providing any additional funding for the institutions, choosing instead to cut faculty salaries, inviting local or private funding, or on occasion in the Northeast assigning land grant status to existing private institutions. Success in terms of enrollment and high-powered academic programs would come later, an arrangement that ensured some financial balance because the large undergraduate numbers would help to fund the far smaller but more expensive research efforts. The development of extension programs serving citizens of the state and a commitment to preparing teachers for the state would develop in later years. The foremost example of service to the state occurred in Wisconsin, as discussed in the following chapter on Progressivism.

Expansion of state flagship universities occurred before and after the Civil War in the West. In 1868 California established the University of California (at Berkeley); North Dakota established its state university in 1883 and not long after, the University of Idaho began in 1889, and the University of Montana in 1893. Hawai'i established its state university in 1907, and 10 years later Alaska followed suit.[29]

Establishing state flagship universities, such as the land grant institutions, reflected the development of modern professional education as well as the education of the developing middle class. While professional education had often consisted of apprenticeship to someone in the field, including reading works in that field, a convergence of new universities to meet the perceived needs of the people, the development of the elective system, and the ongoing reliance on the individual for success (a measure of the Enlightenment) resulted in higher institutions—old and new, private and public—developing programs that are recognizable today. For example, the dean of Harvard Law School in the last quarter of the nineteenth century successfully argued for a study of law that was seemingly scientific and not the result of reading law books and interning with a lawyer. So too business programs developed, starting with the University of Pennsylvania's Wharton School of Finance and Economy (1881, the first at a private institution) and the University of California at Berkeley's College of Commerce (1898, the first at a public institution), and by the early 1900s the Amos Tuck School of Administration and Finance at Dartmouth College was awarding master's degrees. The Wharton School claims it developed the first business textbooks, an important shift from the Bible as the central text of the classical curriculum, Mammon taking the center from God. As business endeavors grew from companies to corporations, and as middle-class sensibilities developed—in the words of one historian, the middle-class desire for respectability in the late 1800s was almost palpable—university leaders recognized the opportunity for growth in size and reputation and responded accordingly. University leaders (administrators and faculty members) advanced many fields, including business as well as other practical areas such as public health and nursing, in effect teaching practitioners new practices that were scientific approaches to the problems that practitioners were facing. The institutions of higher education grappled with their multiple efforts—liberal arts, utilitarian education, and research—often solving the problem, at least at larger universities, with bureaucratic arrangements, allowing advocates of each of the three approaches a reasonably comfortable home in higher education.[30] The drive of the individual, coupled with a university education, seemed to offer a new future of individual and societal advancement, couched in a respectability of the middle class as a cultural separation from the lower classes. Success mattered, and higher education adopted a utilitarian model of success with a foundation in the liberal arts.

Land grant universities were not the only institutions to combine the liberal arts with utilitarian studies. Three women's institutions in Oxford, Ohio, provide important information about the liberal arts and utilitarian studies as well as socioeconomic class and gender. The Rockford College story exemplifies the slow institutional movement, led by a woman president, toward men's acceptance of higher education for women; the tensions in Miami, Ohio, further the story of that acceptance as well as the curricular issues involved.

GENDER AND SOCIOECONOMIC CLASS

The three women's institutions of higher education in Miami prior to the Civil War were Oxford Female Institute (1849), Western Female Seminary (1855), and Oxford Female College (1856). (The men's college in Miami, Miami University, was the result of a land grant bequest in 1793, eventually resulting in its 1809 opening.) Margaret Nash notes,

> Relatively wealthy students, who were more likely to attend Oxford Female Institute and Oxford Female College, received ornamental education in addition to academics; they learned music and embroidery along with Latin. Less affluent students, who attended Western Female Seminary, participated in an arrangement in which they performed all of the household labor in addition to their academic work, thereby demonstrating that learning Virgil did not make them unfit for the kitchen.[31]

While household labor (a requirement at Mt. Holyoke Female Seminary—founded in 1837, becoming Mt. Holyoke College in 1893—as well as at schools that its alumnae and boosters were instrumental in establishing such as Western Female Seminary) is not the same utilitarian study as mechanical and agricultural education, it was useful for those women who were not so likely to marry into families with sufficient wealth to hire servants. Despite the common requirement of domestic labor, rumors flew about exhausted young women who died from their physical exertions as a result of being overworked; the facts were otherwise, with no such records extant. Here, then, is reminder of how neither gender nor socioeconomic class operate separately. Well-to-do women received an education appropriate to their anticipated station in life, while less well-off women received a different, more practical education, even though their strength was called into question.

Just as Anna Peck Sill at Rockford spent years moving the institution toward degree-granting recognition, so too did these three institutions move slowly toward the same recognition. All three offered college-level instruction, although only Western Female Seminary eventually offered a bachelor's degree, in 1893, becoming a women's college in 1894. It merged in 1973 with Miami University (which became coed in 1903 after the Ohio state legislature mandated that all public schools be coeducational).

These socioeconomic class and gender characteristics extended into students' extra-curricular activities. Chapter 6 on students examines these issues in greater depth; for the moment, a discussion of student literary societies at four-year institutions in Illinois and a broader range of student activities at Wisconsin normal schools (established beginning in the 1830s in Massachusetts for the express purpose of training teachers, especially women teachers) illustrate the origins of organized co-curricular and extra-curricular activities in the nineteenth-century college. They also illustrate the role of socioeconomic class in higher education.

Literary and debate societies were a foremost activity for many college students, the Dartmouth society during the Dartmouth case evidencing the importance of those groups. Midwestern colleges and universities also had literary and debate societies, and a study of the University of Illinois, Illinois State Normal University (now Illinois State University), and Illinois College not only provides continued evidence of student interest in extracurricular academic activities, but also gender roles within socio-economic contexts. Literary and debate societies afforded students the opportunity to write literary works beyond the requirements of the classroom and also to speak to and debate issues of the day, in both cases ensuring that students were participating in the affairs of the day. Of the three Illinois institutions, the University of Illinois societies were the least important, likely because of faculty resistance to extracurricular activities until the rise of athletics; in contrast, the all-male Illinois College modeled its societies on those at eastern colleges, the societies even clearly favoring the wealthy students in admission to the groups. Illinois State Normal University societies were, however, much different, as they were popular and coeducational. As a normal university, the institution saw itself as providing practical higher education to the sons and daughters of farmers, and both male and female students were active in the societies. The range of activities is familiar even today, although typically compartmentalized into different groups now with administrators and professors in charge or advising—a library with a check-out system, readings, theatre productions, student publications, presentations on a variety of topics, and of course, oratory and debate. Furthermore, these were popular student activities, evidencing a desire among the sons and daughters of farmers to be fully participatory in the affairs of the day. Most important in regard to this history, in contrast to the more exclusive University of Illinois and Illinois College, the societies were coeducational.[32] Herein lies an important characteristic, the openness among the lower-class students attending colleges and universities to accept coeducational participation in the classroom and in activities outside the classroom.

A clear indication of that participation at such institutions also occurred at Wisconsin normal schools in the late 1800s and early 1900s. As Christine Ogren shows, women students at those institutions were very much participants in the academic and extracurricular activities; those institutions by and large enrolled students from the middle and lower class.[33] In contrast, more prestigious institutions such as Stanford University, the University of Chicago, and the University of Wisconsin found ways to contain the effects of women on campus. Both Stanford and Chicago capped the proportion of academic awards for women because they had begun to outperform the men in what were seen as alarming numbers. At Wisconsin, fear about women feminizing the liberal arts because so many pursued programs in those areas was such that the University began coeducation with a separate college for women, the Female College. Socioeconomic class differences in terms of institutional types evidenced differing expectations for men (as in the case of lower-income students at the colonial and Early Republic colleges studying for the ministry, in contrast to the education of gentlemen) as well as women.

Yet women students at the University of Wisconsin increasingly resisted their compartmentalization, resistance that began with their admission in the 1860s to a Normal Department and accelerated in the 1870s with President Bascom, who was supportive of coeducation, as they developed arguments for their full involvement in their education. Facing both the societal expectations about their lives as adult, married women (while teachers remained single, the most typical expectation was that they would eventually marry, necessarily leaving teaching, a departure often required by law) and their aspirations for a career, they maintained a balance between constraint and opportunity as best they could. Nevertheless, their participation in such common activities as literary and debating societies was gender-specific, and awards for oration and debate went to the men. In the mid-1870s, the University mandated separate class meetings (this was a form of student government, with officers elected) for men and women enrolled at the institution; when the class of 1877 entered, after years of University faculty requests as well as student requests to allow each class to organize coeducationally, President Bascom directed that the meeting become unified. In following years, the issues of coeducation took a different turn, focusing less on academic issues and more on social ones, including participation in sorority activities.[34]

Broad issues of socioeconomic class were evident at other midwestern institutions as well. Jana Nidiffer and Jeffrey Bouman offer a compelling discussion of the conditions of poor students in the late 1800s and the early 1900s at the University of Michigan.[35] As the idea of a middle class, of being middle class, developed in the 1800s, so too did the idea of who was below the middle class. President Angell in an 1879 address declared that access for the poor (likely the lower class with subsistence wages and not those without jobs) to higher education was essential to the nation as a democratic republic, apparently hoping to gain more state funds to keep tuition low. Despite his stated commitment, tuition fees rose during his presidency (he served in that role until 1909); while tuition was relatively cheap, President Angell's successor generated more revenue by encouraging out-of-state students, whose fees were higher. (Michigan did not have dormitories, a common arrangement at many universities, and even at those that did, including colleges, it was not unusual for the community to have boarding houses for students; hence, those costs were not part of Michigan's charges.) Nor was this a time of financial aid at the University, except for two loan programs, although students were able to find off-campus jobs, a number that declined in this period. In addition, the rise of the middle class resulted in students with better secondary preparation and more family income, offering them rather than the poor a place at the University. As costs increased, Michigan also increasingly focused on research, a means to increase its prestige; furthermore, the rise of Progressivism brought to the forefront the idea of studying the poor in order to improve their lives. In brief, enrolling poor students met the ideals of the institution's mission, but studying them resulted in more prestige, and the University chose the latter.

THE RISE OF WEALTH, THE RISE OF ADMINISTRATION

The growth of two additional characteristics mark the late 1800s in U.S. higher education, and both are easily recognizable today. Some institutions of higher education began the long path toward institutional wealth and the development of administrative organization to meet the demands of a larger enrollment, more faculty members, and more facilities.

Colleges and universities have long paid careful attention to their wealth, especially in terms of their endowments. While private higher education has a longer history of focusing on those monies, public higher education has also increasingly developed similar fundraising efforts. The origin of the endowment is clearly evident in the late 1800s and early 1900s, when the national economy experienced rapid growth, a growth substantially based in the successes of large corporations. While large gifts typically marked philanthropic efforts to support higher education in the late 1800s (at the time Stanford likely received $20,000,000 from Leland and Jane Stanford according to some estimates), one president was determined that his institution's wealth would be the result of steady annual contributions to a general operating fund, and the distribution of money from that fund would be at the discretion of the university's administration, particularly its president. Charles W. Eliot, president of Harvard, recognized that the race for institutional success nationally and internationally was dependent on who had more money. He argued for business efficiency yet also an annual deficit, thereby offering a convincing portrait of a well-run university that nevertheless had to struggle financially to meet its goals each year. Rather than imploring donors to assist in filling large or small budgetary gaps, Eliot emphasized a permanent fund based on unrestricted gifts that would ensure institutional growth, and he succeeded. Other institutions had annual funds (the first annual alumni fund began in 1891 at Yale), whose purpose was to provide immediate financial support. Eliot's vision eventually took hold, no doubt in part because it took the lead on endowment size with $141,000,000 in 1920, and it has not looked back.[36]

In many ways, college and university administration began and developed into a currently recognizable form in the Midwest in the late 1800s and early 1900s. As Veysey remarked in his 1965 history of higher education, "The second stage of administrative growth began during the early nineties; it has never stopped."[37] One important reason for this growth was development of increasing enrollments; as institutions of higher education became larger, they became more complex, and no longer could a president and a few faculty members handle all of the tasks that the larger organization needed to complete. Efficiency in administration became increasingly important, often characteristic of principles of efficiency in labor and management espoused by Frederick Winslow Taylor. Unfortunately, and as John Thelin lamented many years ago, we have few histories of administration (other than presidents). What few we have, however, are instructive.

One highly important development in administration was in the area of student services. Unfortunately, all too often both practitioners and scholars in higher education claim that student services resulted from faculty members increasingly focusing on research and becoming less interested in student development. In fact, coeducational institutions were coming to the conclusion that someone had to work with women students. Examining the early deans of women and deans of men highlights the historical accuracy of the arguments in this book about the reasons for the development of student services.

As women increasingly enrolled at colleges and universities, presidents and some faculty members grew increasingly concerned about what to do with this new student population. They needed someone to work with women students in a variety of areas, such as appropriate housing and, more important, behavior. To a great extent, these presidents and faculty members were concerned about the influence of the female presence, both in terms of their impact on the classroom and on male students outside the classroom. Outside the classroom, presidents at several midwestern institutions decided that appointing a woman administrator was the solution. Here then, even at those universities with a developing focus on research, it was not research, but gender, that was the context for the development of student services.

These early midwestern deans of women faced a myriad of challenges. Young women needed guidance and support, in a broad range of activities both academic and social. Deans of women saw their roles as crucial to the development of young women students and also recognized the need to develop themselves, and over the course of several decades beginning with Marion Talbott's appointment at the University of Chicago in 1892, they organized as a developing profession with a 1903 meeting in Chicago, called by Marion Talbott, that eventually resulted in the formation of the National Association of Deans of Women. The deans of women at the first meeting came from almost exclusively midwestern and western institutions—the Universities of Colorado, Illinois, Indiana, Iowa, Kansas, Michigan, and Wisconsin, as well as Indiana, Northwestern, and Ohio State Universities, and Ripon, Carleton, Oberlin, Beloit, and Illinois Colleges. The sole dean of women from an eastern college, Barnard College, is an interesting participant because of the eventual development by the deans of women of graduate study of student services at Teachers College, Columbia University; at the time, Barnard was affiliated with Columbia. The topics for that first meeting covered mostly extracurricular issues ranging from etiquette to leadership, reflecting roles of college women in the late 1800s, facing powerful societal norms while finding ways to become not just full citizens but leaders, in effect increasing the permeability of the border between the private and public spheres begun at such institutions as Troy Female Seminary. The appointment of deans of men was the result of a very different set of assumptions, the first occurring much later than the appointment of deans of women, with Thomas Arkle at the University of Illinois. Robert Schwartz describes their meetings, which began in 1919, as "the opportunity to converse, to enjoy local hospitalities and activities, and to regale each other with tales from their campuses."[38]

At another level of administration, presidents of the newly large universities (a handful had enrollments of more than 5,000 students by the early 1900s) also found themselves in need of someone to handle tasks that previously were the purview of presidents. Beginning with the creation of a position of vice president at Cornell University in 1868, over the next four decades either presidents or boards of trustees developed similar positions at six other developing research universities from coast to coast. Their roles varied, as Jana Nidiffer and Timothy Cain discuss, with three types: "vice presidential modes-jack-of-all-trades, presidential confidant, and official administrator-that generally trace the development of the office from the merely next-in-line to the position as recognized today."[39] The pattern of administrative growth, whether in regard to student services or central administration, was indeed well underway by the late 1800s.

This discussion of administration could have easily been placed in the next chapter, in the examination of Progressivism and its impact on higher education, but the chapter provides examinations of other, equally salient, historical characteristics of higher education. As David Tyack successfully argued, in the late 1800s and early 1900s in U.S. education, two forms of Progressive education developed, pedagogical Progressivism and administrative Progressivism (more recently, education scholars have argued for more nuanced forms of Progressive education). The former is most recognizable in terms of John Dewey, the educational philosopher who argued for student-focused (not student-centered as is too glibly uttered by scholars and politicians alike) education that was useful for citizenship and knowledge in a democratic society, while the latter focused on efficient and effective ways of organizing the schools, the teachers, and the curriculum. Curiously, both pedagogical and administrative Progressives wanted social and moral reform, although the individualized attention of the pedagogical Progressives was clearly different from the collective approach of administrative Progressives. As a scholar noted in the 1960s, much of the development of student services resulted from a focus on student development intrinsic to pedagogical Progressivism, and arguably the field of student services increasingly developed as a combination of the two.[40] In other areas of administration the precepts of Frederick Winslow Taylor and administrative efficiency increasingly took hold. As the twentieth century wore on, the two Progressive groups differed more and more in the schools, yet in higher education each still reflect important aspects of the impact of Progressivism, aspects that receive substantial attention in the next chapter, how a century of destiny, with serious questions about whose destiny and for what purposes, leads in interesting ways to a substantial political, economic, and social reform movement of the late 1800s and early 1900s.

DISCUSSION QUESTIONS

1. Is there presentism evident in the contemporary and recurring criticisms of schools for not adequately preparing students for post-secondary study? How would you prepare evidence for one of two arguments, to either accept and improve the

opportunities for multiple pathways into higher education or to improve elementary, middle, and secondary schools so that their graduates are ready for college?

2. The 1800s mark the advent of utilitarian goals in educating college and university students. What balance was there for an institution in offering both the liberal arts and utilitarian education?

NOTES

1 John S. Brubacher and Willis Rudy, *Higher Education in Transition: A History of American Colleges and Universities*, 4th ed. (New York: Routledge, 2017), p. 267.

2 On the subtle but sustained influence of Christianity on the supposedly secular university, albeit in muted ways, see George M. Marsden, *The Soul of the American University: From Protestant Establishment To Established Nonbelief* (New York: Oxford University Press, 1994) and Julie A. Reuben, *The Making of the Modern University: Intellectual Transformation and The Marginalization of Morality* (Chicago: University of Chicago Press, 1996).

3 James Axtell, "The Death of the Liberal Arts College," *History of Education Quarterly* 11 (Winter 1971): 339–352.

4 Rudyard Kipling, *Captain's Courageous* (New York: Bantam Books, 1896/1946), 170.

5 Harold S. Wechsler, "An Academic Gresham's Law: Group Repulsion as a Theme in American Higher Education," *Teachers College Record* 82, no. 4 (Summer 1981): 567–588. On the exclusion of central and eastern European Jews, see Harold S. Wechsler, *The Qualified Student: A History of Selective College Admission in America* (New York: Wiley Press, 1977); Marcia Synnot, *The Half-Opened Door: Discrimination and Admissions at Harvard, Yale, and Princeton, 1900–1970* (Westport, CT: Greenwood Press, 1980); David O. Levine, *The American College and the Culture of Aspiration, 1915–1940* (Ithaca, NY: Cornell University Press, 1986).

6 www.beloit.edu/about/history (retrieved March 26, 2011).

7 Eldon L. Johnson, "Misconceptions About the Early Land-Grant Colleges," *Journal of Higher Education* 52, no. 4 (July–August 1981): 333–351.

8 William J. Reese, *The Origins of the American High School* (New Haven, CT: Yale University Press, 1995); David Tyack, *The One Best System: A History of American Urban Education* (Cambridge, MA: Harvard University Press, 1974).

9 David B. Potts, "'College Enthusiasm!' As Public Response, 1800–1860," *Harvard Educational Review* 47, no. 1 (February 1977): 28–42.

10 Lester F. Goodchild, Richard W. Jonsen, Patty Limerick, and David A. Longanecker, eds., *Higher Education in the American West: Regional History and State Contexts, 1818–2010* (New York: Palgrave Macmillan, 2014).

11 Jurgen Herbst, "The Eighteenth-Century Origins of the Split Between Private and Public Higher Education in the United States," *History of Education Quarterly* 15 (Autumn 1975): 273–280.

12 Richard Hofstadter and Walter P. Metzger, *The Development of Academic Freedom in the United States* (New York: Columbia University Press, 1955), 247–251.

13 Russell W. Irvine, *The African American Quest for Institutions of Higher Education Before the Civil War: The Forgotten Histories of the Ashmun Institute, Liberia College, and Avery College* (Lewiston, NY: Edwin Mellen Press, 2010).

14 Cally L. Waite, "The Segregation of Black Students at Oberlin College after Reconstruction," *History of Education Quarterly* 41, no. 3 (Autumn, 2001): 344–364.

15 As quoted in Shannon A. Butler-Mokoro, "Racial Uplift and Self-Determination: The African Methodist Episcopal Church and Its Pursuit of Higher Education" (Ph.D. dissertation, Georgia State University, 2010).

16 Roger L. Geiger, "'The Superior Instruction of Women' 1836–1890," in *The American College in the Nineteenth Century*, ed. Roger L. Geiger (Nashville, TN: Vanderbilt University Press, 2000), 183–195.

17 Linda Rose Buchanan, "Not Harvard, Not Holyoke, Not Howard: A Study of the Life and Death of Three Small Colleges" (Ph.D. dissertation, Georgia State University, 1997).

18 Christie Anne Farnham, *The Education of the Southern Belle: Higher Education and Student Socialization in the Antebellum South* (New York: New York University Press 1994).

19 Lucy Townsend, "The Gender Effect: The Early Curricula of Beloit College and Rockford Female Seminary," *History of Higher Education Annual* 10 (1990): 69–70.

20 Johnetta Cross Brazzell, "Bricks Without Straw: Missionary Sponsored Black Higher Education in the Post-Emancipation Era," *Journal of Higher Education* 63 (January/February 1992): 26–49.

21 Jackie M. Blount, "Individuality, Freedom, and Community: Ella Flagg Young's Quest for Teacher Empowerment," *History of Education Quarterly* 58, no. 2 (May 2018): 175–198.

22 Sue Zschoche, "Dr. Clarke Revisited: Science, True Womanhood, and Female Collegiate Education," *History of Education Quarterly* 29, no. 4 (Winter 1989): 545–569. Of particular note here is that this was a time when the rise of evolutionary thought was often coupled with social characteristics and consequences, seemingly buttressing Clarke's arguments.

23 Doris Malkmus, "Small Towns, Small Sects, and Coeducation in Midwestern Colleges, 1853–1861," *History of Higher Education Annual* 22 (2002): 33–65.

24 Harold S. Wechsler, *The Qualified Student: A History of Selective College Admission in America* (New York: Wiley, 1977); Marc A. VanOverbeke, *The Standardization of American Schooling: Linking Secondary and Higher Education, 1870–1910* (New York: Palgrave Macmillan, 2008).

25 Michael Wallace, "Agricultural Education at the Virginia Military Institute During The 1850s: The Development of a Practical Education" (Ed.D. dissertation, University of Alabama, 2018); Nathan M. Sorber, "Introduction," *Perspectives on the History of Higher Education* 30 (2013): 3–12; https://nifa.usda.gov/sites/default/files/asset/document/First%20and%20Second%20Morrill%20Act.pdf.

26 Nathan M. Sorber, "The Rise and Fall of the Grange's Yankee Land-Grant Colleges, 1873–1901," in *Science as Service: Establishing and Reformulating Land-Grant Universities, 1865–1930*, ed. Alan I Marcus (Tuscaloosa: University of Alabama Press, 2015), 61–92; Scott M. Gelber, *The University and the People: Envisioning American Higher Education in an Era of Populist Protest* (Madison: University of Wisconsin Press, 2011).

27 Nathan M. Sorber and Roger L. Geiger, "The Welding of Opposite Views: Land-Grant Historiography at 150 Years," in *Higher Education: Handbook of Theory and Research*, ed. Michael B. Paulsen (New York: Springer, 2014), 385–422; https://nifa.usda.gov/sites/default/files/asset/document/First%20and%20Second%20Morrill%20Act.pdf; Ralph D. Christy and Lionel Williamson, eds., *A Century of Service: Land-Grant Colleges and Universities, 1890–1990* (Brunswick, NJ: Transaction Publishers, 2012).

28 Eldon L. Johnson, "Misconceptions About the Early Land-Grant Colleges," *Journal of Higher Education* 52, no. 4 (July–August 1981): 333–351.

29 Lester F. Goodchild, Richard W. Jonsen, Patty Limerick, and David A. Longanecker, eds., *Higher Education in the American West: Regional History and State Contexts, 1818–2010* (New York: Palgrave Macmillan, 2014).

30 Burton J. Bledstein, *The Culture of Professionalism: The Middle Class and the Development of Higher Education in America* (New York: W.W. Norton & Company, 1978); Richard Hofstadter, *The Age of Reform: From Bryan to F.D.R.* (New York: Vintage Books, 1955); Laurence Veysey, *The Emergence of the American University* (Chicago: University of Chicago Press, 1965).

31 Margaret A. Nash, "'A Salutary Rivalry': The Growth of Higher Education for Women in Oxford, Ohio, 1855–1867," *History of Higher Education Annual* 16 (1996): 21.

32 Becky Bradway-Hesse, "Bright Access: Midwestern Literary Societies, with a Particular Look at a University for the 'Farmer and the Poor,'" *Rhetoric Review* 17, no. 3 (Autumn 1998): 50–73.

33 Christine A. Ogren, "Where Coeds Were Coeducated: Normal Schools in Wisconsin, 1870–1920," *History of Education Quarterly* 35, no. 2 (Spring 1995): 1–26.

34 Amy Hague, "'What If the Power Does Lie Within Me?' Women Students at the University of Wisconsin, 1875–1900," *History of Higher Education Annual* 4 (1984): 78–100.

35 Jana Nidiffer and Jeffrey P. Bouman, "'The University of the Poor': The University of Michigan's Transition from Admitting Impoverished Students to Studying Poverty, 1870–1910," *American Educational Research Journal* 41, no. 1 (Spring 2004): 35–67.

36 Bruce A. Kimball and Benjamin Ashby Johnson, "The Beginning of 'Free Money' Ideology in American Universities: Charles W. Eliot at Harvard, 1869–1909," *History of Education Quarterly* 52, no. 2 (May 2012): 222–250.

37 Laurence Veysey, *The Emergence of the American University* (Chicago: University of Chicago Press, 1965), 306.

38 Jana Nidiffer, *Pioneering Deans of Women: More Than Wise and Pious Matrons* (New York: Teachers College Press, 2000); Robert A. Schwartz, "Reconceptualizing the Leadership Roles of Women in Higher Education: A Brief History on the Importance of Deans of Women," *Journal of Higher Education* 68, no. 5 (September–October 1997): 502–522.

39 Jana Nidiffer and Timothy Reese Cain, "Elder Brothers of the University: Early Vice Presidents in Late Nineteenth-Century Universities," *History of Education Quarterly* 44, no. 1 (Winter 2004): 487–523.

40 Eleanor M. Schetlin, "Myths of the Student Personnel Point of View," *Journal of Higher Education* 40, no. 1 (January 1969): 58–63.

4

THE PROGRESSIVE ERA AND ITS ENDURING IMPACT ON HIGHER EDUCATION

Efficient, Rational Solutions to Moral and Social Problems

Many historians of higher education, regardless of the topic of their inquiry, have indicated that the late 1800s and early 1900s form a key period in a number of changes in U.S. higher education. There is little reason, if any, to argue against those conclusions. The 1800s set several factors in motion, such as the increasingly substantial enrollment of white women and African Americans and the development of institutions enrolling those students as well as shifts in the curriculum, which have had a lasting influence on colleges and universities. It was also when research universities began to develop, as discussed in Chapter 7. The central part of this chapter's investigation, however, is a revision of other examinations of higher education in the period from the late 1800s through the mid-1900s through consideration of the role of higher education in presenting efficient and rational solutions to national problems to create a better future. In a word, Progressivism. (Although many contemporary scholars seem to prefer the lower case in reference to Progressivism, the upper case marks the movement as real, powerful, and enduring as well as distinct from generalized notions of progress and progressive behavior—terms used often enough in the early 2000s and, hence, all too prone to presentism.) And there are curious but not incidental links to the previous chapter in that Progressivism has its roots in the Midwest; in addition, as will be shown in this chapter, even during wartime Progressivism had an impact on higher education, thereby anticipating in part the chapter on war.

While historians of education have investigated a variety of events and institutions related to Progressivism and the school as well as higher education in the Progressive era, there is no work on the lasting effects of Progressivism in higher education other than discussion of the Wisconsin Idea and pedagogical experiments at some institutions of higher education. This chapter offers conceptions of the relationship of higher education to state and national interests that began in the late 1800s and early 1900s and left a heritage of those conceptions to the present, presenting the argument that leaders in higher education increasingly turned to varying forms of Progressivism to address problems in higher education as well as societal problems that higher education could presumably solve, furthering the reach of the socioeconomic contract. Hence, this chapter begins the break with a simple chronology because some of the discussion reaches into the 1960s, and the break continues with the next three chapters. After an overview of Progressivism, this chapter offers five investigations of how fundamental characteristics of Progressivism have long affected, and continue to affect, higher education. In the first case, I highlight the work of women academics, both in terms of the scholarship that they pursued, particularly in the 1920s and 1930s, as well as a broader context of what one historian has called, in centering gender in the study of the history of higher education, the politics of knowledge. Second, the work of Abraham Flexner in the substantial reform of medical education in the early 1900s in the United States highlights rational approaches to solving societal problems. In the third example, the discussion of the development of junior colleges exemplifies the strong drive to establish a middle class and create educated workers, particularly for important local and state employment. In the fourth case, employing a contemporary of Flexner who shared some similar principles as well as disparate ones, the economist Thorstein Veblen, offers the argument that the slow development of faculty unionization in the early 1900s exemplified the anti-corporate sentiments of Progressivism. (The rapid development of unionized faculty members at other than research universities in the 1960s and 1970s is one of several examples of the important differences in organizational goals in U.S. higher education.) In the final example, the use of apparently scientific approaches to solve social problems, served as guiding principles in the development of the 1944 G.I. Bill; that more lengthy discussion is based on primary and secondary sources and, thus, both illustrates how key elements of Progressivism have endured for colleges and universities and provides readers new to historical inquiry with another understanding of how a historian employs primary and secondary sources to form historical arguments. The drive to establish a rational and planned future through such government actions as the G.I. Bill (the 1944 Serviceman's Readjustment Act), in the midst of the horror of global warfare, had roots in Progressivism. Comments by a variety of participants in the development of the G.I Bill indeed reflect "the cultivation of a *public philosophy*," what one historian identifies as "the principal ingredient of a political realignment" that occurred as a result of Progressivism.[1]

PROGRESSIVISM

Historians, including historians of education, have identified many problems in attempts to define Progressivism. As Lynn Gordon remarks, "Historians disagree about the nature and meaning of progressivism." She goes on to note the focus on scientific solutions to natural and social problems as a key component of Progressivism on college and university campuses, a focus with important consequences for women in college seeking places in higher education and in the society at large.[2] In one sense, then, it might appear as if Progressivism is simply a historical convenience, a means of marking, albeit indefinitely, a critical time in this nation's history with substantial meaning, yet admittedly rife with ambiguity. Nevertheless, Progressivism is a real historical force, perhaps with its roots in the Enlightenment. Enlightenment philosophers argued that humans were capable of reason, a capacity long ignored in the presumptions about an aristocracy and rule by kings and queens based on the Christian God's precepts. Hence, with the use of reason, humans could achieve reform, progress, and happiness, in other words, life, liberty, and the pursuit of happiness (a rather long content endnote follows).[3] Despite the ambiguities surrounding Progressivism, there is, indeed, a defensible definition of the movement based on rational approaches to societal issues.

By the end of the 1800s the Progressive movement was underway, offering a blend of reform and restraint by emphasizing the importance of providing social and economic opportunity while often assigning societal roles on the basis of gender, race and ethnicity, and class. The rise of testing in the early 1900s was one such means of assigning societal roles—an effort largely based on attempts in the Armed Services during World War I (examined in the next chapter) to determine the seemingly appropriate fit of individuals to various tasks and responsibilities. One strand of Progressivism (it was not, much like other political movements, uniform in its principles except in very broad form) advocated efficiency, and testing appeared to be socially efficient. That claim too easily overlooked differences in background, such as level of schooling, quality of schooling, and a person's first language, which could affect test results, or in other words, testing could be willfully used to marginalize or exclude groups.[4] That strand of Progressivism intersected with the powerful efficiency movement, symbolized by the work of then-prominent Frederick Winslow Taylor. It is instructive that Taylor's first instruction in efficiency occurred in a mathematics classroom at Phillips Exeter Academy (a New England prep school), where the instructor used a specific instructional technique to ensure that he tested all students for their comprehension in each class meeting.[5] Members of the elite educational institutions devised means for efficiency that would serve not only pedagogical goals but also economic, political, and social ones.

In broad form, Progressivism represented three fundamental concerns: limiting "the power of business, a commitment to 'pure democracy,' and the dedication to new rights as a bulwark against the uncertainties and injustices of the marketplace."[6] It was also a distinctly middle-class movement. Remember Richard Hofstadter's assessment of Progressives as so middle class as to be "palpably, almost pathetically respectable"; that assessment foreshadows Burton Bledstein's argument that the middle class reformers of the middle and late nineteenth century were almost obsessed with proper social position and behavior.[7] Achieving that respectability came in great part from education, a primary concern for the Progressives and a vehicle "through which the people could gain an understanding of civic obligation." In Progressive terms, education served as the fountainhead for the preservation of democracy.[8]

The goals of Progressivism, brought about by the challenges of a new era characterized by the phenomenal growth of the large corporation and resultant opposition and the remarkable influx of immigrants, needed means for implementation. Progressives did not have to look very far in their new world; the new social sciences beckoned. The growth of the social sciences in the late 1800s, especially economics, political science, psychology, and sociology, provided ample opportunity for reformers to claim a new means for improving society, a means replete with rationality.[9] The way to control excesses—whether those of large corporations, of ill-educated classes, or of immoral enemies—was through rational assessment of the problem and efficient solution.

Thus, as a definition, Progressivism is the predominantly middle-class impulse that represents the need for political, social, economic, and even moral reform through administrative, often governmental, structures. Education was one of those structures.

No single university better exemplifies the fervor, the moral code, the importance of offering a useful curriculum, and the power of scientific examination in social and political arenas than the University of Wisconsin and the Wisconsin Idea. Although the Wisconsin Idea had few statewide imitators, its focus on the use of academic expertise to solve social problems, a key element of Progressivism, eventually permeated higher education; University of Wisconsin professors offered "a new role for trained intelligence in government" in the development of laws as well as in administration of government agencies.[10] There were early and direct efforts to link Progressivism and higher education at the University of Wisconsin. Although University presidents advocated for the Wisconsin Idea before the development of the Progressive political movement, the university in the service of the state as a rational, social instrument, was in fact lauded by perhaps the most visible of all Progressives, Wisconsin's U.S. Senator Bob LaFollette.[11] President Charles Van Hise's inaugural address at the University of Wisconsin in 1903 is, according to Lawrence Cremin, "the classic Progressivist statement of the role of higher education in a democracy. Its theme from beginning to end is service to the state."[12] There must be, of course, a note of caution about such an assessment; as Frederick Rudolph observes, service to the state is the only consistent theme in U.S. higher education from the colonial colleges to the 1950s.[13] What distinguishes the Wisconsin Idea is the degree of cooperation between the university and the state, the extension education program (first in agriculture, later in engineering), and perhaps most important for the Progressive movement, the social sciences. Some of the University of Wisconsin social science professors were tireless advocates of the University's capacity to initiate social change, based on rational approaches to social, political, economic, and moral problems (a phrase I at times shorten to societal problems in the remainder of the chapter), and remarkably, at one point nearly all of the social science professors at Wisconsin were also working with state agencies.[14]

Service to the state, however, had its obstacles because at times faculty members in the social sciences challenged the norms of the business community (despite a common conception of the conflicts between the social scientists and external constituencies, it was business people more than politicians who proved to be the antagonists in academic freedom situations). One early case of academic freedom occurred at the University of Wisconsin. Economist Richard T. Ely opposed the laissez-faire claims of businessmen (again, the gender use is intended), favoring government controls to provide a defense for the public at large. A committee of Wisconsin's governing board reviewed his work, and although it was a committee of "conservative lawyers and businessmen" (who were also well represented on the board), the committee conclusion was in fact a clear defense of his right to conduct research and teach, offering a lengthy statement on the necessity of such freedom; two sentences are poignant, and perhaps sardonic, in refuting the idea that universities ought to dismiss or criticize professors with contrary views: "Such a course would be equivalent to saying that no professor should teach anything which is not accepted by everybody as true. This would cut our curriculum down to very small proportions."[15] In the matter of social science research and instruction, the Progressive movement in higher education had one stalwart defender.

There were some institutional experiments of Progressivism in the 1920s and 1930s, most notably at Sarah Lawrence, Bennington, Black Mountain, Bard, and Rollins Colleges as well as the General College of the University of Minnesota, although in contrast to the University of Wisconsin, these were by and large pedagogical experiments. While one historian of education argues that the General College experiments found life in post-World War II community colleges (linked in this chapter to Progressivism), these institutional approaches differed from the Wisconsin Idea. Most notably, the institutional experiments of the 1920s and 1930s addressed the importance of the liberal arts as a means for student growth rather than the application of scientific expertise to social and economic problems.[16] And, the experiments occurred only at a handful of institutions; the broad Progressive movement seemingly ended at Wisconsin's borders.

White women's colleges, however, furthered the practice of Progressivism in solution of social problems. The first generation of women faculty members began in the 1870s.[17] Geraldine Clifford edited a book, *Lone Voyagers*, which speaks to the experience of seven white and African American women who were among the first women on different campuses in the late 1800s and early 1900s, women who succeeded despite isolation.[18] And then there was the second generation, as increasing numbers of women entered colleges and universities, as students and as faculty members (most often in the case of the latter, at women's colleges). Women entering academe faced multiple challenges at the same time that they were creating opportunities. In a very important sense, their primary institutional means of creating a scholarly identity occurred at women's colleges, specifically the white women's colleges. All-male and coeducational colleges for many years had no interest in appointing women as full-time faculty members, although a number of universities were most assuredly interested in having women in their doctoral programs, a curious turn on the meaning of Jefferson's idea about seeking talent. Their tuition revenue was welcomed, their employment was not. Furthermore, women were far more likely to enter the humanities or the social sciences, although as Margaret Rossiter has thoroughly documented, many women entered the natural and physical sciences, for example creating and securing space in laboratories and working with eminent male scientists. At times, not surprisingly, those women scientists were instrumental in advancing the frontiers of knowledge, without, again not surprisingly, receiving much if any recognition.[19]

Another area where women were instrumental in advancing knowledge was in the social sciences. Here Progressivism and gender intersect. As Mary Ann Dzuback and Patricia Palmieri have shown, women social scientists as well as their institutions' deans and presidents focused on the social sciences, and in particular on social science research with direct implications for practice. For example, in the case of Bryn Mawr College, its president, M. Cary Thomas, as well as a department chair and several faculty members, developed a research culture that supported both faculty members and graduate students interested in the applications of social science research examples. The department chair, Susan Myra Kingsbury, helped students to identify research problems and methods, analyze their data, and publish their dissertations. Topics covered a wide area in the social sciences, with careful attention to social conditions and the effects of policies and social norms; in one case, Bryn Mawr researchers found in a Philadelphia study that over half of the families in working-class neighborhoods did not rely solely on the father's income, although the mothers still had responsibility for household demands. In a different form in great part because Bryn Mawr faculty included a number of men because President Thomas wanted to ensure recognition for the College's research, while all of Wellesley's faculty members and the president were women and they, more than Bryn Mawr's faculty, represented gendered approaches to the social sciences. (Wellesley College is the sole women's college to have only women presidents throughout its history and to hire only women faculty members in its early years.)[20] Wellesley faculty members tended toward direct social activism, in working for and advocating such Progressive solutions as settlement houses, developed to educate immigrants in American ways—both in basic improvements such as healthy eating as well as acculturation into the dominant culture—based on the research done by Wellesley faculty members and students. Perceiving the need to address social problems (including support for the suffrage movement) and being a patriotic American was compatible, remarkably evident in one Wellesley professor's case, Katherine Bates, who authored "America the Beautiful."[21] At both institutions, the women faculty members and students pursuing social science research, using the quantitative approaches that were the norm of the day, were intent on scientific planning that would provide the means for governmental or private agency efforts to effect social, even moral, reform.

The idea of the social sciences as rational instruments of societal and moral judgment informing decision-making—in government, in business, in individual life—marks the enduring effect of Progressivism in higher education. Such an idea does not represent a radical departure from college intent over the centuries, but adds an essential element, the results of empirical research, to the moral virtues practiced and professed in previous centuries, whether those virtues were expressed in the destructive efforts to acculturate members of American Indian tribes in the colonizing colleges era or in the words of the Yale faculty in 1828. The reform of professional education symbolizes that combination of moral virtues and empirical perspectives.

MEDICAL EDUCATION

The decisive reform of medical education in the United States in the late 1800s and early 1900s, highlighted by the critically important 1910 work by Abraham Flexner, *Medical Education in the United States and Canada*, illustrates how social science study could lead and often has led to reform. In this case, the reform was more enduring and with deeper impact than many other attempts at reform.

By the late 1800s, physicians represented what would now be seen as an unusual range of practices—not in the modern sense of specialties but rather in terms of how they perceived the fundamental principles of curing human ailments. Nor were they typically educated in medical schools as is the case today; instead apprenticeships or brief educations in medical schools (many of which were for-profit institutions with very small enrollments) were the primary forms of preparing physicians. One consequence of such an education meant that, in one historian's words, "Democratic ideology received its sharpest expression in lay medicine." Beginning with the colonial period, members of Native American tribes and white women were often doctors; in the latter case, in some communities, white women were often the only doctors. By the late 1800s, however, efforts to reform medical education and practice, led by physicians in creating, for example, state licensure of physicians, were well underway. Concerned about the poor conditions of medical practice, Henry Pritchett of the Carnegie Foundation for the Advancement of Teaching commissioned Abraham Flexner to conduct a review of medical education and practice. He was an educator, not a physician, who had majored in classics at the Johns Hopkins University (in two years) and completed graduate courses at Harvard and the University of Berlin; he was also an advocate of a liberal arts education to develop the whole person. Flexner conducted the review with enthusiasm, preparing an extensive report after visits to all of the medical schools across the United States, and he provided a scathing statement for reform of medical education and practice.[22]

Drawing attention to poor and often common practices, such as the absence of laboratories, or perhaps worse, autopsy laboratories with rotting corpses, Flexner argued for a new form of medical education and practice, one reflective of the reform efforts already extant yet also sharply divergent from such practices as providing medical education through for-profit institutions. He drew on the John Hopkins University model of a teaching hospital with formal relationships to the university, providing medical education that was at once clinical and academic with students in the hospital and studying the natural sciences. The report proved to be a catalyst, and within a few short years, by and large medical education and practice, including control of access, education, and certification of physicians themselves, began to resemble what is now modern medicine. The issue of access, however, was highly problematic for white women and African Americans (although curiously, Flexner at times argued for equality of the sexes and races and equal treatment). In 1900, approximately 10 percent of all medical school students were women, and there were seven medical schools in the thoroughly segregated United States (North as well as South, East as well as West) that provided access for African Americans. With a few short years of the Flexner report and the surge of reform, white women faced near exclusion with outright quotas of 5 percent at some medical schools, and there were only two medical schools for African Americans.[23]

The exclusion continued for decades, and the efforts of medical educators and physicians to effect the exclusion were not surprising, but remarkable and disingenuous. As Charlotte Borst shows, the entrance requirements for medical school in the 1920s and 1930s relied on different means of evaluation—whether they were interviews or standardized tests or both—to ensure that "the right man" would be selected. Gender and race played a role, with questions on the medical school entrance examination regarding, for example, the Civil War battle of Chancellorsville far more likely to reflect the knowledge base of middle- and upper-class white men than white women or African Americans. For white women, even given multiple commission reports on nursing that mirrored the Flexner report in the 1920s and beyond, for those controlling the field of medicine, the Civil War meant that nursing was their appropriate choice. For African Americans, for whom the Emancipation Proclamation was likely the deep meaning of the Civil War, exclusion was a matter of fact. Furthermore, the selection of the right man reflected concerns about ethnicity, with clear references to Eastern or Central European men, as well as Jews, as not having the right character (typically prior to World War II, both Jews and people from eastern and central Europe were considered to be non-white).[24] And as medical schools slowly but surely increased the requirements for admission, with more focus on a baccalaureate degree and background in both the sciences and the liberal arts, efforts on the part of African American educators to introduce black literature, history, and social sciences at black colleges meant that those students would either not have the specific knowledge of the white canons or would have to work twice as hard to have the knowledge base required by both the college and medical schools.[25] The challenge was even more considerable, as the Southern Association of Schools (the regional accrediting association) consistently gave black colleges a B rating, second to the A rating of white male and coeducational institutions and insufficient for admission to medical schools. While medical schools slowly opened their doors to white women and African Americans starting in the 1960s, exclusion persisted in both subtle and institutional patterns; female physicians often entered lower-paying specialties such as obstetrics-gynecology, pediatrics, and family practice, and the third medical school on a black college campus, Morehouse School of Medicine, did not open until 1975, preceded by Charles Drew Medical University in Los Angeles, opened in 1966 (this institution differed from the others in that it did not have a specific affiliation with a college or university).

This was not simply a price of exclusion from a higher-class status as a physician. Health care remained a segregated system, and not only did African Americans have less access to health care, but also it was not uncommon for an African American after a serious injury or illness to die, either refused care at an all-white hospital or unable to gain access to health care in the African American community.

In contrast to the results of the Flexner report, in the early part of the 1900s the nursing profession attempted reform with little success. The 1923 Goldmark Report (arguably the primary report among others on nursing reform) did not have the broad support that the Flexner report enjoyed, and the nursing profession was unable to develop the coherent strategy of reform that was evident in the call to reform the education of physicians. "However, despite this inability, the fundamental issue that challenged nurses was how to elevate a practice field dominated by women in a culture where the role of women was one of subservience." Black nurses faced particularly strong challenges because the racist policies of Southern white hospitals would not allow them to practice at those institutions; nevertheless, they held high regard in the African American community, but in both cases of gender and race, the ability of white male medical professionals to control medicine remained paramount.[26]

Here, then, is an unsettling and fundamental tension resulting from a Progressive approach to higher education, a tension that historical understanding illustrates. Clearly health education and health care improved as a result of the reforms promoted by Abraham Flexner, but the reforms were deliberately exclusionary, implemented to ensure a form of professional education that defined gender as well as race and ethnicity as exclusionary characteristics.

THE JUNIOR COLLEGE

Another organizational problem in higher education in the early 1900s was the increasing enrollment of four-year institutions because of the perceived need for a higher education in order to succeed in life. Universities and communities sought solutions, and the two-year college, the junior college, was one attractive possibility. On the surface, it appears that the increasingly selective four-year institutions, particularly universities, needed an efficient means for sorting students, offering access but with varied opportunities.

By and large the literature on the origins of the two-year college is thoroughly inaccurate. Over the decades, beginning as early as the 1920s, scholars and observers attached great importance to university presidents and a national movement of advocates for the junior college, but in a remarkable dissertation by Robert Pedersen, the historical record becomes clear.[27]

The earliest junior college was not Joliet Junior College (Illinois) in 1901 as a result of negotiations between William Rainey Harper of the University of Chicago and the principal of Joliet High School (who, interestingly, is rarely named in these discussions). As early as the 1880s, Joliet High School was offering college-level courses, and by the end of the 1890s the school's courses were recognized by the University of Michigan, indicating not the efficiency of administrative Progressivism but rather the blurred lines among educational institutions in the 1800s. The first appearance of the term "junior college" in school records was in 1913, and not until 1916 did the school board distinguish between the high school and the junior college. It is far better to understand this part of the origin of the two-year college as murky, different secondary schools offering some college-level instruction that in some cases slowly developed into a junior college. While national leaders in education advocated for different means of efficiently organizing higher education, standardizing the types of institutions, they offered a variety of solutions (the 6-4-4 organization, six years of elementary school, four years of secondary school—i.e., grades 7, 8, 9, 10—and four years of post-high school education was a very popular one), the junior college was only one proffered solution among several. More important, those leaders were simply not as influential as the more common claims suggest.

In terms of the actual decisions to establish public junior colleges, one characteristic ought to be familiar, local boosterism. Especially in small cities of the early 1900s, local civic leaders saw the potential to grow into large cities (as had happened at Chicago, for example), and one of the many means to do so was to have a college; hence, junior colleges were a viable solution. In addition, often regardless of location, parental preference played a role in establishing these institutions because parents did not want their children far away from home, perhaps exposed to the Godless state university or simply as a means to keep the family intact; reinforcing that aspect was the common student desire to attend a college close to home, a much cheaper and convenient arrangement. In all cases, the junior college presented the opportunity for a higher education.

Nor were these open-access, egalitarian institutions, despite the sweeping claims of retrospectives and histories that have been popular since the 1950s. They often had admission requirements that were just as rigorous as those for four-year institutions, and they were typically segregated. Even more fascinating is that the presentism seems to have taken a powerful hold on the authors of the retrospectives, arguing from the knowledge that many two-year colleges charged little or no tuition. Pedersen examined the actual tuition charges of public junior colleges and flagship state universities, using Arizona, Iowa, Oklahoma, and Texas as examples, and found that in each case public junior colleges charged more for tuition and fees than the universities. Free or low tuition was the exception, not the rule.

Furthermore, student life would presumably be quieter on public junior college campuses because students from lower-income backgrounds would need to work in order to finance their education. Pedersen's investigation resulted in a much different portrait: "There is more than ample evidence that the student culture of the typical pre-1940 junior college was no less self-absorbed and self-indulgent than the student cultures at Stanford, Ann Arbor, Berkeley, and Minneapolis."[28] Much like at the normal schools, although their students typically came from lower-income backgrounds, student life included athletics, debating societies, student newspapers, and social gatherings. While appearing to be the result of efficiency in organizing higher education and the influence of national leaders, one Progressive principle, these institutions were actually much more reflective of a more fundamental characteristic of Progressivism, the rising middle class and the desire for respectability.

FACULTY UNIONS

There were, of course, parts of higher education that clearly reflected the efficiency of administrative Progressivism. Eight years after completing his manuscript and looking for a publisher willing to publish his book, Thorstein Veblen succeeded, and Huebling published *Higher Learning in American: A Memorandum on the Conduct of Universities by Business Men* in 1918. Veblen excoriated colleges and universities for their unrelenting movement toward corporate practices in higher education, or as Laurence Vesyey observed a half-century later, the second stage of administrative growth began in the early 1900s, and it has never ceased. Such practices found their way into details of the college and university, such as the rise of the credit hour.[29] Veblen took a less sanguine view of the movement, and in a telling passage on page 202 (of early editions), he states that the best thing to happen to colleges and universities would be the removal of presidents and boards of trustees. That suggestion never took form in reality.

What both Veblen and Veysey illustrate, however, is that the rise of business practices on campus across the nation in the late 1800s and early 1900s was prevalent, and the long-held position that faculty members were employees was as popular as ever. One possible response to such a position was the identification of the professor as a professional, situated at an institution that needed to provide the professor with such protections as to ensure freedom of inquiry and freedom in the classroom. Such a response was deeply embedded in two German principles about professors, *Wissenschaft* and *Lehrfreiheit* (both discussed in greater detail in Chapter 7 on research universities). The former was a principle of scientific investigation, and the latter was the freedom of German professors to discuss topics of their choosing in the classroom, although such freedom had much to do with the fact that they were civil employees of various German states and, thus, the principle of *Lehrfreiheit* offered protection against professorial dismissal by irate political leaders as well as distinction as professors rather than ordinary civil servants. In an act of banding together, a small group of white male scholars called for a new organization of professors, which became the American Association of University Professors (AAUP) in 1915.[30] The AAUP wanted to focus on the professional role of professors including faculty governance of colleges and universities but found itself more often addressing issues of academic freedom, initially on an ad hoc basis (as contrasted with the AAUP's own history on its web page), encouraged to do so by an early AAUP leader, Arthur O. Lovejoy.[31] The AAUP maintained a level of exclusion at its onset, inviting only distinguished scholars to become members, and not until 1939 did the Association accept members from two-year colleges. By 1940 the AAUP had also developed in its final form (earlier iterations occurred in 1915 and 1925) its statement on academic freedom, one that incorporated processes regarding tenure and dismissal.[32] To date, the 1940 Statement on Principles of Academic Freedom and Tenure remains the primary document addressing academic freedom; the American Federation of Teachers and the National Education Association also have such statements but the AAUP is often the organization highlighting the issue of academic freedom.

Another act of organizing also began in the early 1900s, faculty unionization. The AAUP was adamant for decades that it was not a union, despite on occasion being identified as such; the American Federation of Teachers (AFT), in contrast, embraced the possibilities of defending professors against corporate control effected by higher education administrators.[33] The AFT was also an advocate for academic freedom, but its focus both nationally and in local activity tended to be on such matters as negotiating with the administration on such matters as faculty hiring and dismissal, faculty salaries, and faculty authority in regard to curriculum and teaching responsibilities.[34] Nevertheless, AFT locals on campuses were rare well into the 1960s, in part because of faculty indifference or opposition to unionization (often on the basis of the professional arguments about faculty life) and in part because of the need for state or federal enabling legislation that would authorize formal bargaining units with the power to negotiate on behalf of faculties with administrations.[35] Successes tended to be local and not necessarily consistent, as Timothy Cain shows in his examination of unionization efforts at Howard University from 1918 to 1950. Howard's local was the first in the nation, affiliated with the AFT, lasting briefly until 1920, with the faculty organizing a second local in 1936, which closed in 1943. In that same year faculty and staff members in the Howard University School of Medicine organized a local affiliated with the Congress of Industrial Organizations (organized by labor leaders in the mid-1930s as a competitor to the American Federation of Labor); it lasted until 1950, by and large a victim of the increasing anti-Communist fervor of the post-World War II era.[36] Although not a continuously successful organization, the Howard locals are prime evidence of faculty resistance to corporate control.

Here then, is the Progressive characteristic of controlling corporations, or at least constraining the power of corporation in regard to their employees. It would not be until the early 1960s that faculty unionization began in its full form, only occurring when an administrative structure was in place—state or federal enabling legislation and the concomitant appointment of state or federal labor relations boards with the responsibility of determining a faculty union's right to bargain—to effect reform.

THE EXIGENCIES OF WAR

One of Progressivism's fundamental characteristics was political engagement, and college and university advocates recognized the potential for their role in the polity. While important Progressive politicians such as President Theodore Roosevelt and Senator Bob LaFollette were no longer part of the national picture by the mid-1920s (the former passed away in 1919, the latter in 1925) the efforts of the movement continued. The New Deal represents, in a variety of ways, the goals that Progressives espoused. For example, assistance to parents without adequate resources, Aid to Families with Dependent Children (AFDC), passed as part of the New Deal, and was the result of earlier Progressive proposals to assist those very families.[37] Progressivism indeed focused on creating a better life for the poor and for the uneducated, although that focus derived from white middle-class perspectives on the meaning of a better life and complicated by assumptions of who belonged where, as in the case of medical education and the practice of medicine. By the 1940s, although Progressive leaders continued to be visible, such as Henry Wallace, vice president under Franklin Roosevelt, nevertheless the direct impact of Progressivism appeared more in specific forms of legislation and more broadly and importantly, in the policies of the federal government.[38]

The need to educate veterans once World War II ended had three over-riding and extremely important goals, girded with the assurance that the United States was the world's repository of democracy and justice. One goal was to ensure that never again would the nation be so complacent about the power of evil in the world, especially in totalitarian governments. This goal was more often implicit than explicit, but most certainly it was an important one when it was acknowledged. In terms of higher education, the report of the President's Commission on Higher Education, *Higher Education for American Democracy*, clearly and eloquently voiced that goal.[39] Another goal was to make life sane for service men and women who had experienced terror and horror and survived. Finally, the polity recognized that service men and women deserved a reward for their sacrifices. Only a well-organized effort could accomplish such goals. By the end of the war the nation was not only immediately celebratory but also anticipatory of a brighter future. One of the key programs, the 1944 Serviceman's Readjustment Act, popularly known as the G.I. Bill, emphasized such readiness.

During World War II the American Council on Education (ACE) worked with federal government agencies and officials in its efforts to create a focus on higher education and its capacity to work on behalf of the nation. These efforts reflected the use of an administrative structure—in this case, committees staffed by political and higher education representatives—to solve moral and social problems in the interests of the middle class. President George Zook of the American Council on Education reported in a 1939 editor's note of the *Educational Record* that the Council had begun preparation to implement services that would aid the federal government in the effort to combat Germany, two years before the United States officially entered World War II. As a result of the Council's decisions, Zook was able to secure funding from the General Education Board to hire Francis Brown, a New York University professor who had already coordinated two conferences of educational leaders (one in Washington, DC and one in New York City) to discuss preparation for the possible war.[40]

Brown's dedication to the development and passage of the G.I. Bill is a key example of higher education's work with the federal government. His work represents the first legislative implementation of higher education as a means to national defense in the policy terms later articulated in *Higher Education for American Democracy*, and to a lesser degree, to civil rights. Brown's work is also a powerful example of the underlying assumptions about effective, rational solutions to the moral and social problems of the time.

The impact of the GI Bill is as much mythological as it is empirical. While empirical studies tend to show that for the most part those who attended college on the GI Bill after World War II were either those whose higher education was interrupted by the war or those who were likely to have attended college if it were not for the war, nevertheless the stories of veterans who decided that this was a unique opportunity abound. Veterans most certainly went to college in unprecedented numbers, popularized by the press and by Hollywood, as Daniel Clark has ably shown in his work. And, many of the veterans—in particular the white male veterans—had attended college prior to becoming a member of the Armed Services or would have been likely to attend college.[41] Raccoon coats and college banners were no longer the only icons of college life—although it is an error to think that those were the only aspects of college life, given the number of poor students who attended college well into the late 1800s, if not later. Even the spouses and new families of veterans went to college; the G.I. Bill provided support to married veterans, and often their families lived with them in

Quonset huts placed on campuses across the nation. Now new phrases about college became common: "The thought of college never even entered my mind," or "I was the first one in my family to go to college." The meaning of college access changed. Even many of those veterans who left college to join the armed services or deferred college for military service were not traditional college students; they returned home having experienced the brutality of war and were certainly not the young men and women who wore raccoon coats and waved college banners at sporting events.

While the New Deal often seemed to offer proof that direct federal intervention in state and local affairs would result in benefits for individual citizens and for the nation as a whole, it was World War II that offered not only compelling proof, but more important, compelling patriotic proof that direct federal intervention—in a variety of settings, including education—was an effective and efficient way of addressing social and moral problems. The early years of planning for a successful 1944 G.I. Bill through the education of U.S. soldiers and sailors provides a clear illustration of the ongoing importance of Progressivism.

The G.I. Bill had a powerful political history. Veterans of World War I, bitterly disappointed by the federal government's refusal to pay them their promised stipend, gathered in Washington, DC, in 1932 in an encampment known as the Bonus March Camping Ground. Unable to convince the angry veterans to move, eventually President Herbert Hoover ordered U.S. Army troops to disperse the veterans and destroy the camp. Pictures of the attack, led by General Douglas MacArthur, capture the terrible irony of the event, as soldiers gas and attack ex-soldiers. President Franklin Roosevelt, the American Legion, and armed services commanders wanted no such protest much less those counter-measures, and they all also wanted to recognize the veterans for their sacrifices. Furthermore, placing the veterans in education suggested there would be some relief for the tremendous shift from a wartime to a peacetime economy. Efforts to establish a well-adjusted veteran in a peacetime democracy and economy began early. Several scholars have documented the political context for the G.I. Bill.[42]

Yet in addition, the G.I. Bill has an important organizational history within the federal government, especially the executive branch, one not yet investigated, a history that reflects the rational, planned society that was so attractive to Progressives at the turn of the century. Part of the organizational history addresses policy development, and there has been some investigation of that characteristic, but the larger organizational history has not been addressed in terms of Progressivism.[43] While the armed services had long engaged in technical education and training for officers and enlisted men and women, during World War II another form of education, one substantially based in the traditional liberal arts, developed. The armed services coordinated the educational developments with several educational organizations, the most influential being the American Council on Education (ACE). The development was based on assessment, experiment, implementation, organization, and planning, a highly rationalized approach to the social problem of educating members of the armed services. In addition, the use of existing educational activities and facilities provided much needed efficient use of resources. Hence rational planning based on social science expertise joined with efficiency to inform the federal government's interest in educating soldiers and sailors. Initially the Navy and the Army ran their own programs—conducting with ACE assessment, experiment, implementation, and organization—although rational use of resources eventually dictated a joint program.[44]

Long-term planning occurred through two committees, the Post-War Manpower Re-Adjustment Conference and the Armed Forces Committee on Post-War Educational Opportunities for Service Personnel (these were the days before the sound-bite titles and acronyms that now force acronyms from words). Each would eventually issue a report leading to the G.I. Bill.[45] Both the conferences and federal committees benefited from contributions by educators, most of all those from the American Council on Education. In the following, there is a brief summary of the process of developing the G.I. Bill and then a more extended discussion of the administrative, executive branch development of the education of soldiers and sailors, a development that was part of the foundation for the G.I. Bill.

In July 1942 the Conference on Post-War Readjustment of Civilian and Military Personnel met (the name was later changed to the Post-War Manpower Re-Adjustment Conference). Its chair was Floyd W. Reeves, a University of Chicago professor and ACE staff member, and its membership included Francis Brown. Reeves developed the agenda for the first meeting, an agenda focused on the problems of a post-war economy and the need to educate both civilians and veterans after the war's end. The agenda also included the proposal that the government provide direct financial assistance. Keith Olson reports that the agenda "provided the conceptual framework of the group's final report, and aroused no opposition at the meeting."[46] The conference members studied both past efforts to provide veteran education, the limited federal and state efforts following World War I, and 1941 Canadian legislation that offered veterans stipends and fees depending on their length of service. The final report, issued in June 1943, offered more than 90 recommendations, and while many were general, some specified veteran benefits for education. Shortly after the Post-War

Manpower Conference submitted its report, another committee, the Armed Forces Committee on Post-war Educational Opportunities for Service Personnel also issued a report focused on veteran education, a report very similar to the one by the Post-War Manpower Conference. Floyd Reeves, an advocate of planning, worked very closely with that committee.[47]

In October 1943 the American Council on Education also proposed a plan for veteran education, one developed by its Committee on Relationships of Higher Education to the Federal Government—whose membership included Rufus C. Harris, president of Tulane University and a member of the Armed Forces Committee on Post-War Educational Opportunities for Service Personnel. The ACE report, as had occurred with the Osborn report, resulted both from committee deliberations and a survey of member colleges and universities. All three reports were very similar and served as the basis for the G.I. Bill.[48] The ACE monitored the passage of the G.I. Bill carefully, as Francis Brown attended all of the hearings on the bill, and at one hearing Brown even corrected Senator Claude Pepper on the issue of subsistence grants for veterans.[49]

Thus, the American Council on Education, in continuous cooperation with a variety of federal agencies and Congressional committees, was instrumental in the development of the plan for the 1944 Serviceman's Readjustment Act. Planning also occurred in specific organizational approaches in standardization of courses, student achievement, and the evaluation of the educational experience for service personnel as well as veterans, providing in a very real way a social science experiment in preparation for the G.I. Bill (i.e., evidence that veterans wanted an education and were capable of achieving one). In cooperation with the armed services, the ACE helped to develop a process that experimented with ways of providing education to service personnel and veterans that reflected national democratic goals, used federal resources yet preserved local, institutional characteristics, and rested on rational means. The roots of such national activity appear in the late 1800s and early 1900s, specifically in Progressivism. The general education efforts are reminders that Progressives consider schooling an intrinsic part of the democratic process, and that educated citizens are necessary components of a healthy democracy. The use of experts in such matters as test development, in the use of a social science to solve a social problem, is also clearly a mark of Progressivism.[50] Just as important, however, are far more subtle manifestations of Progressivism, means to accomplishing Progressive goals. A telling example exists in the development of procedures for assessing U.S. Armed Forces Institute (USAFI) courses for academic credit. Progressives worried about the relationship between a national, central government and the local agencies, arguing that both had to have robust lives in order for democracy to grow. The American Council on Education implemented a program whereby centralized information about the USAFI courses was available for all colleges and universities, so that those institutions could make local judgments about appropriate credit, with expert advice from the ACE.[51] This was the Wisconsin Idea writ large, to give expert advice so that local entities (individuals or institutions) could make informed, rational, effective decisions to solve social problems.

Who, then, would use rationality to serve the state? Not only the politicians and citizenry in need of expertise, but also the experts themselves in order to advance their institutions as well as society. As Hawkins argues in *Banding Together*, the first half of the twentieth century represented a period when representatives of higher education increasingly recognized the national opportunities for cooperation, especially but not exclusively among like institutions. Given the lack of a national system of higher education characteristic of many other countries, such coordination could indeed prove more fruitful than hundreds of colleges and universities pursuing related but individual goals. The ACE membership was broad by the 1940s, and the Council's work represented administrative Progressivism, what David Tyack and Elizabeth Hansot identify as the search for efficient ways to run educational institutions.[52] In terms of rational planning and expertise in education, the American Council on Education was at the center of the cultivation of a public philosophy, and its staff members and committee members provided the very sort of academic links to the government that were evident in the Wisconsin Idea.

In the nearly three centuries from the 13 colonies to the mid-1900s, colleges and universities increasingly identified themselves as central to the nation's political and economic growth, although the public-at-large did not fully embrace that identification. College and university enrollment was typically no more than 5 percent of the college-aged population (an age range just as broad then as it is now) well into the 1900s. Nevertheless, by the early 1900s colleges and universities had begun to seize upon a new means of being central to the nation, through Progressive service to the nation, serving as the core of rational planning to solve moral and social problems.

PROGRESSIVE PRINCIPLES AND HIGHER EDUCATION

While it would not be a wise use of historical inquiry to insist that Progressivism lurks behind every desk on campuses nationwide, it is appropriate to understand two key issues and to raise a third that is implicit in this chapter. First, the very sort of reform evident in arguments by Enlightenment philosophers and at the core of the reasons for establishing the great experiment, the United States, echoes into the reform movement of the late 1800s. Sometimes history has constants, and human behavior and values as individuals or institutions obtain over time; the arguments of the Enlightenment and the broad goals of Progressives sustain over centuries. Second, the tensions of control and social resistance are evident in different ways across the examples. Neither white women nor African Americans were completely excluded from modern medical education. Advancements in professorial contributions to government problems occurred at the University of Wisconsin but were widespread among white women's colleges advancing practical solutions based on social science research. Administrative control over colleges and universities was substantial, but professors sought social control of the institution and had some limited successes. Organizing and passing a bill to provide higher education for veterans resulted in a shift, as much mythical as real but no less important, in understanding who could and ought to benefit from a higher education. Finally, an important shift occurred in how citizens and leaders viewed the mechanisms of the government, especially the federal government, during the Progressive Era. As Ellen Lagemann argues in her work on the Carnegie Corporation, up until the late 1800s, government was viewed not so much as a direct instrument but as a broad implementation of policy. Slowly during the late 1800s and the early 1900s, people increasingly viewed government as a direct mechanism, with a civil service, for the implementation of the details of policy; it is possible to extend her arguments to include the processes of controlling entry into the medical profession, examining social conditions using social science research, implementing the G.I. Bill, and enabling faculty unionization.[53] The idea of government mechanisms of such detail plays out in formidable ways in the late 1900s, whether in the matters of football or research universities. War too had a response in rational approaches, although such issues as patriotism challenged notions of rationality.

DISCUSSION QUESTIONS

1. How is it in regard to the reform of medical education that both "the issue of access . . . was highly problematic for white women and African Americans [while] (curiously, Flexner at times argued for equality of the sexes and races and equal treatment)?" More broadly, can reform be well intentioned if it clearly excludes or marginalizes certain groups, or do the mores and values of the time constrain the perspectives of reformers?

2. What does it mean in Progressive approaches, in a society founded in Enlightenment principles, when a supposedly rational approach to solving problems only partially addresses power relations?

NOTES

1   Sidney M. Milkis, "Introduction: Progressivism, Then and Now," in *Progressivism and the New Democracy*, ed. Sidney M. Milkis and Jerome Mileur (Amherst: University of Massachusetts, 1999), 6.

2   Lynn D. Gordon, *Gender and Higher Education in the Progressive Era* (New Haven, CT: Yale University Press, 1990), 3 on meaning, 3–5 on consequences.

3   John Locke's arguments about government and education reflect a form of rationality based on the rule (and also logic) of men rather than God. Douglas Sloan offers a great deal of insight into the key roles that the Scottish utilitarians played in the institutional development of higher education in the United States as well as some major philosophical themes about humans and social problems. Sustaining moral concerns, but with rational solutions, appears to be precedent to the acts and thoughts of Progressives. See John Locke, *Two Treatises of Government* (New York: Cambridge University Press, 1689/1963) and Douglas Sloan, *The Scottish Enlightenment and the American College Ideal* (New York: Teachers College Press, 1971). See also Clarence J. Karier, "Liberalism and the Quest for Orderly Change," *History of Education Quarterly* 12 (Spring 1972): 57–80, on the shift from classical to modern liberalism in the late 1800s and early 1900s. Karier argues that both John Stuart Mill and John Dewey were concerned with "individual freedom, dignity, and well-being" (58), but Mill advered state power while Dewey advocated the "positive use of state power" (59). Thus, a new cooperative and efficient order (one that Jane Addams and John Dewey saw as moral, even Christian) among business, government, educational institutions, and social institutions became a public goal (61–62).

4   Lynn D. Gordon, *Gender and Higher Education in the Progressive Era* (New Haven, CT: Yale University Press, 1990) and Joel Spring, "Education and Progressivism," *History of Education Quarterly* 10, no. 2 (Spring 1970): 53–71. On testing, see Joel H. Spring, "Psychologists and the War: The Meaning of Intelligence in the Alpha and Beta Tests," *History of Education Quarterly* 12, no. 2 (Spring 1972): 3–15; John L. Rury, "Race, Region, and Education: An Analysis of Black and White Scores on the 1917 Army Alpha Intelligence Test," *Journal of Negro Education* 57, no. 1 (Winter 1988): 51–65; David F. Noble, *America by Design: Science, Technology, and the Rise of Corporate Capitalism* (New York: Oxford University Press, 1977), 19, 50–65. While these four scholars differ in their interpretations of why these events occurred, all focus on the development and importance of testing.

5   Robert Kangel, *The One Best Way: Frederick Winslow Taylor and the Enigma of Efficiency* (New York: Viking Penguin, 1997), 215.

6   Sidney M. Milkis, "Introduction: Progressivism, Then and Now," in *Progressivism and the New Democracy*, ed. Sidney M. Milkis and Jerome Mileur (Amherst: University of Massachusetts, 1999), 9. There were, not surprisingly, different strands of Progressivism, with varying interpretations of appropriate ways to address the concerns. One strand favored federal regulation of corporations, the other the prevention of monopolies and state regulations. Both strands, however, recognized the importance of schools. See 18–19.

7   See Richard Hofstadter, *The Age of Reform: From Bryan to F.D.R.* (New York, Alfred A. Knopf, 1955), 131 and Burton J. Bledstein, *The Culture of Professionalism: The Middle Class and the Development of Higher*

Education in America (New York: W.W. Norton & Co., 1976), especially on the professional norms that defined what were problems for whom, 330.

8   Sidney M. Milkis, "Introduction: Progressivism, Then and Now," in *Progressivism and the New Democracy*, ed. Sidney M. Milkis and Jerome Mileur (Amherst: University of Massachusetts, 1999), 19 on civic obligation, 20–21 on critical role of educational institutions. See also Lawrence A. Cremin, *The Transformation of the School: Progressivism in American Education, 1876–1957* (New York: Alfred A. Knopf, 1961), 168 on the essential connection between politics and education in Progressivism.

9   For disparate views that nevertheless conclude that the social sciences offered opportunities for rational approaches for reform, whether self-serving or in the interests of other constituencies, see Mary O. Furner, *Advocacy and Objectivity: A Crisis in the Professionalization of American Social Science, 1865–1905* (Lexington: University Press of Kentucky, 1975); Edward T. Silva and Sheila Slaughter, *Serving Power: The Making of the Academic Social Science Expert* (Westport, CT: Greenwood Press, 1984); and Dorothy Ross, *The Origins of American Social Science* (New York: Cambridge University Press, 1991).

10 Samuel Haber, *Efficiency and Uplift: Scientific Management in the Progressive Era* (Chicago: University of Chicago Press, 1964), 106.

11 Lawrence A. Cremin, *The Transformation of the School: Progressivism in American Education, 1876–1957* (New York: Alfred A. Knopf, 1961), 87.

12 Lawrence A. Cremin, *The Transformation of the School: Progressivism in American Education, 1876–1957* (New York: Alfred A. Knopf, 1961), 161.

13 Frederick Rudolph, *The American College and University: A History* (New York: Alfred A. Knopf, 1962), 496.

14 Lawrence Cremin, *The Transformation of the School: Progressivism in American Education, 1876–1957* (New York: Alfred A. Knopf, 1961), 162–163. On engineering, see Noble, *America By Design*, 133. See also J. David Hoeveler, "The University and the Social Gospel: The Intellectual Origins of the 'Wisconsin Idea,'" *Wisconsin Magazine of History* 59 (Summer 1976): 282–298.

15 Richard Hofstadter and Walter P. Metzger, *The Development of Academic Freedom in the United States* (New York: Columbia University Press, 1955), 427.

16 Lawrence Cremin, *The Transformation of the School: Progressivism in American Education, 1876–1957* (New York: Alfred A. Knopf, 1961), 167–168. See 308–318 on the institutional experiments.

17 Christie Anne Farnham, *The Education of the Southern Belle: Higher Education and Student Socialization in the Antebellum South* (New York: New York University Press 1994); Geraldine Jonçich Clifford, *Lone Voyagers: Academic Women in Coeducational Institutions, 1870–1930* (New York: The Feminist Press at CUNY, 1989).

18 Geraldine Jonçich Clifford, ed., *Lone Voyagers: Academic Women in Coeducational Institutions, 1870–1937* (New York: The Feminist Press at CUNY, 1993).

19 Margaret W. Rossiter, *Women Scientists in America: Struggles and Strategies to 1940* (Baltimore: Johns Hopkins University Press, 1982).

20 Mary Ann Dzuback, "Women and Social Research at Bryn Mawr College, 1915–1940," *History of Education Quarterly* 33, no. 1 (Winter 1993): 579–608; Patricia Ann Palmieri, *In Adamless Eden: The Community of Women Faculty at Wellesley* (Yale University Press, 1995); Ellen Fitzpatrick, *Endless Crusade: Women Social Scientists and Progressive Reform* (New York: Oxford University Press, 1990).

21 Patricia Ann Palmieri, *In Adamless Eden: The Community of Women Faculty at Wellesley* (New Haven, CT: Yale University Press, 1995).

22   Paul Starr, *The Social Transformation of American Medicine* (New York: Basic Books, 1982), 47–125.

23   Paul Starr, *The Social Transformation of American Medicine* (New York: Basic Books, 1982), 118–119, 124.

24   Charlotte G. Borst, "Choosing the Student Body: Masculinity, Culture, and the Crisis of Medical School Admissions, 1920–1950," *History of Education Quarterly* 42, no. 3 (Summer 2002): 181–214; Nancy Cheal, "Medicine and Nursing: Professions Bound by Gender, Prescribed by Society" (Georgia State University Ph.D. dissertation, 1999).

25   Philo A. Hutcheson, "The University, Professionalization, and Race in the United States," in *Beyond the Lecture Hall: Universities and Community Engagement from the Middle Ages to the Present Day*, ed. Peter Cunningham, Susan Oosthuizan, and Peter Taylor (Cambridge, UK: University of Cambridge, Faculty of Education and Institute of Continuing Education, 2009), 103–115.

26   Nancy Cheal, "Medicine and Nursing: Professions Bound by Gender, Prescribed by Society" (Ph.D. dissertation, Georgia State University, 1999).

27   Robert Patrick Pedersen, "The Origins and Development of the Early Public Junior College, 1900–1940" (Ph.D. dissertation, Columbia University, 1999). Bob and I first met when I began doctoral studies in 1978, and after my first year he left to take an administrative position. Harold Wechsler reintroduced us as Bob was preparing to defend his dissertation, and we remained friends until he passed away. Despite my repeated urging that he publish his dissertation, he always declined, insisting that he had no interest in all of the additional work of writing a book, particularly since he was not at a college or university, very much his choice.

28   Robert Patrick Pedersen, "The Origins and Development of the Early Public Junior College, 1900–1940" (Ph.D. dissertation, Columbia University, 1999), 54.

29   Jessica M. Shedd, "The History of the Student Credit Hour," in *How the Student Credit Hour Shapes Higher Education: The Tie That Binds*, New Directions for Higher Education, ed. Jane V. Wellman and Thomas Ehrlich, Issue 122 (Wiley Periodicals: 2003): 5–12.

30   Walter P. Metzger, *Academic Freedom in the Age of the University* (New York: Columbia University Press, 1969).

31   Walter P. Metzger, "The First Investigation," *AAUP Bulletin* 48 (June 1961): 206–210.

32   Philo A. Hutcheson, *A Professionalized Professoriate: Unionization, Bureaucratization, and the AAUP* (Nashville, TN: Vanderbilt University Press, 2000).

33   Philo A. Hutcheson, *A Professionalized Professoriate: Unionization, Bureaucratization, and the AAUP* (Nashville, TN: Vanderbilt University Press, 2000).

34   Timothy Reese Cain, *Establishing Academic Freedom: Politics, Principles, and the Development of Core Values* (New York: Palgrave Macmillan, 2012).

35   Philo A. Hutcheson, *A Professionalized Professoriate: Unionization, Bureaucratization, and the AAUP* (Nashville, TN: Vanderbilt University Press, 2000).

36   Timothy Reese Cain, "Faculty Unionization at Hoard University, 1918–1950," *Perspectives on the History of Higher Education* 29 (2012): 113–150.

37   Sidney M. Milkis, "Introduction: Progressivism, Then and Now," in *Progressivism and the New Democracy*, ed. Sidney M. Milkis and Jerome Mileur (Amherst: University of Massachusetts, 1999), 9. For an in-depth discussion of the continuing characteristics of Progressivism during the New Deal, see Alonzo L. Hamby, "Progressivism: A Century of Change and Rebirth," in *Progressivism and the New Democracy*, ed. Sidney M. Milkis and Jerome Mileur (Amherst: University of Massachusetts, 1999), 40–68.

38   Alonzo L. Hamby, "Progressivism: A Century of Change and Rebirth," in *Progressivism and the New Democracy*, ed. Sidney M. Milkis and Jerome Mileur (Amherst: University of Massachusetts, 1999), 40–68.

39   Philo A. Hutcheson, "The 1947 President's Commission on Higher Education and the National Rhetoric on Higher Education Policy," *History of Higher Education Annual 2002* 22 (2003): 91–107.

40   Samuel P. Capen, "The Effect of World War 1914–18 on American Colleges and Universities," *Educational Record* 21 (January 1940): 47. On Zook and international issues, see George F. Zook, "The President's Annual Report," *Educational Record* 21 (July 1940), 327–328 on the nation's first responsibility as result of hostilities in Europe to bolster efforts for international intellectual cooperation. See also John W. Rieken, "George Frederick Zook: Educational Leader in a Crucial Decade" (Ph.D. dissertation, Georgia State University, 2005).

41   Robert C. Serow, "Policy as Symbol: Title II of the 1944 G.I. Bill," *Review of Higher Education* 27, no. 4 (Summer 2004): 481–499; Daniel A. Clark, "'The Two Joes Meet. Joe College, Joe Veteran': The G.I. Bill, College Education, and Postwar American Culture," *History of Education Quarterly* 38, no. 3 (Summer 1998): 165–189. See also Helen Lefokowitz Horowitz, *Campus Life: Undergraduate Cultures from the End of the Eighteenth Century to the Present* (Chicago: University of Chicago Press, 1988), 185–187.

42   Glenn Altschuler and Stuart Blumin, *The G.I. Bill: The New Deal for Veterans* (New York: Oxford University Press, 2009); Keith W. Olson, *The G.I. Bill, the Veterans, and the Colleges* (Lexington: University Press of Kentucky, 1974); and Theodore R. Mosch, *The G.I. Bill: A Breakthrough in Educational and Social Policy in the United States* (Hicksville, NY: Exposition Press, 1975). The protesting veterans wanted their promised bonus, and as Mosch points out, "Education was substituted for the bonus" in the G.I. Bill, 11. See Milton Greenberg, *The GI Bill: The Law That Changed America* (New York: Lickle Publishing, 1997), especially 25–29 for pictures of the Bonus March attack. See also J.M. Stephen Peeps, "A B. A. for the G. I. . . . Why?" *History of Education Quarterly*, 24, no. 1 (Winter 1984): 513–525. Peeps focuses on the bill's political history, argues that educators served primarily as "consultants," 521. There are additional, highly important issues attendant upon the development and implementation of the G.I. Bill, including issues of access and civil rights as well as the role of general education. I have addressed the first set of issues in an earlier paper (see Philo A. Hutcheson, "Exploring the Roots of Federal Language on Discrimination: The 1947 President's Commission on Higher Education," Association for the Study of Higher Education, November 2001, Richmond, Virginia, November 2001), available upon request.

43   Keith W. Olson, *The G.I. Bill, the Veterans, and the Colleges* (Lexington: University Press of Kentucky, 1974), 13–14; Theodore R. Mosch, *The G.I. Bill: A Breakthrough in Educational and Social Policy in the United States* (Hicksville, NY: Exposition Press, 1975), 34; Hugh Hawkins, *Banding Together: The Rise of National Associations in American Higher Education, 1887–1950* (Baltimore: Johns Hopkins University Press, 1992), 165–167.

44   Ralph A. Sentman, "The Program of Voluntary Education in the Armed Services," in *Higher Education under War Conditions*, ed. John Dale Russell (Chicago: University of Chicago Press, 1943), 9.

45   Ralph A. Sentman, "The Program of Voluntary Education in the Armed Services," in *Higher Education under War Conditions*, ed. John Dale Russell (Chicago: University of Chicago Press, 1943), 9.

46   Keith W. Olson, *The G.I. Bill, the Veterans, and the Colleges* (Lexington: University Press of Kentucky, 1974), 6–7 on conference membership and agenda, 7 on acceptance of agenda. The conference was actually a sub-committee of the National Resources Planning Board, 5–6; Floyd W. Reeves, "Education for Social and Economic Planning," *Educational Record* 22 (October 1941), 479–490.

47   Keith W. Olson, *The G.I. Bill, the Veterans, and the Colleges* (Lexington: University Press of Kentucky, 1974), 7–11.

48   Keith W. Olson, *The G.I. Bill, the Veterans, and the Colleges* (Lexington: University Press of Kentucky, 1974), 13–14, 15, 18.

49   Hugh Hawkins, *Banding Together: The Rise of National Associations in American Higher Education, 1887–1950* (Baltimore: Johns Hopkins University Press, 1992), 166.

50   Joel H. Spring, "Psychologists and the War: The Meaning of Intelligence in the Alpha and Beta Tests," *History of Education Quarterly* 12, no. 2 (Spring 1972: 3–15. For an in-depth discussion of the ACE role in test development and the enthusiasm of the President's Commission on Higher Education for using tests to assess college applicants, see Michael Ackerman, "Mental Testing and the Expansion of Educational Opportunity," *History of Education Quarterly* 35 (Autumn 1995): 279–300.

51   George F. Zook, "The President's Annual Report," *Educational Record* 25 (July 1944): 206–208.

52   David B. Tyack, *The One Best System: A History of American Urban Education* (Cambridge, MA: Harvard University Press, 1974) and David B. Tyack and Elisabeth Hansot, *Managers of Virtue: Public School Leadership in America, 1820–1980* (New York: Basic Books, 1982). Tyack and Hansot argue for two forms of Progressivism, administrative and pedagogical (the latter reflecting the institutional experiments with general education and pedagogy at those few institutions in the 1920s noted earlier).

53   Ellen Condliffe Lagemann, *The Politics of Knowledge: The Carnegie Corporation, Philanthropy, and Public Policy* (Chicago: University of Chicago Press, 1989), 4.

5

WAR

Meanings of Patriotism in Higher Education

War has had a variety of important effects on U.S. higher education, and indeed the wars in the colonizing era had effects on the colonial colleges. Such campus and higher education matters as changes in enrollments in regard to men and women, faculty attrition due to contributions to winning the war, institutional and faculty commitment to national interests, and definitions of citizenship are common themes in times of war. This chapter addresses, in some detail or another and some manner or another, the American Revolution, the Civil War, World War I and World War II, the Cold War (part of the section on the war on terrorism), the Vietnam War, and the war on terrorism, with an important final discussion of the sustained war against Native Americans, which was in fact the first war of the colonies and continued well past the American Revolution and the Civil War.

One important effect of World War II up until the Vietnam War,[1] might be summarized in a single phrase: The men left. While to some degree the phrase is simplistic, it is also highly representative of how institutions of higher education in this nation reacted to war. These institutions found out that white women could pay tuition, succeed in the classroom, take leadership positions on campus, and after college (either as graduates or having left before completing their degrees) pursue careers.

War too had a powerful effect on African Americans. The most poignant example may well be World War II and African Americans' participation in multiple efforts to win the war, from working in factories that manufactured weapons and machines to serving in the armed services; whether they fought the war on the home front or in theatres overseas, many came to realize that the battle for the Double V was the real battle—Victory at home for equality and Victory overseas to defeat totalitarian forces. Both of those battles were fraught with challenges.

For many people on campuses across the nation, one theme seems clear: often framed in terms of enthusiastic if not strident patriotism, college and university leaders, faculty members, staff members (once the administration began its growth in the early 1900s), and students heeded the national call to win the war. Dissent was rarely tolerated, and dissenters typically faced marginalization, rebuke, or dismissal.

THE AMERICAN REVOLUTION

One distinct difference between many other nations and their higher education institutions and the United States is that in the United States, there is no federal ministry of education that controls most if not all colleges and universities in the nation.[2] As a result, nor is there one (nor are there two or more) colleges or universities that are the exemplars of what the nation as a political entity wants to accomplish in terms of higher education. Nevertheless, in the early years of the Republic, national leaders argued for such an institution. Expectations about education for the nation varied by such characteristics as gender.

As noted in the Introduction, the American Revolution occurred as the Enlightenment was having a powerful effect, especially among leaders in the colonies. Formal schooling was a highly appropriate mechanism for ensuring that the values of the Enlightenment as expressed in the Early Republic were part and parcel of each white citizen's understanding of his or her role in the new nation. White women articulated their participation in new ways, as Barbara Solomon voiced:

> This war, like all wars, heightened the importance of women; some overcame their lack of confidence during the long struggle. Moreover, those identified with the patriots discovered that their political ideology about the rights of man had meaning for the female sex.[3]

Works such as Linda Kerber's "Daughters of Columbia: Educating Women for the Republic" are instructive for understanding what higher education needed to achieve.[4] Since the nation was not to rely, in philosophical argument, on an aristocracy that transferred power and control from generation to generation, education became the means for creating a citizenry that knew how to govern itself. Most proposals paid scant attention to the higher education of citizens, focusing instead on the need for basic literacy and numeracy. And as Kerber argues, mothers of the Republic were well situated to educate children who would be ready for the self-governing demands of a democratic republic.

The former colonial colleges claimed the role of educating the elite, the leaders of the governing councils, a claim made obvious in the Yale Report of 1828. Nevertheless, national leaders fretted about the lure of the venerable universities of Europe and their ability to draw the most talented students. Fearing the possibility that those students would return with notions of aristocracy, some national leaders called for a national university. While the idea would never come to fruition, even George Washington (who was neither college educated nor even schooled at the lower grades) deeded land to the United States for a national university campus.[5] Hence the need for both citizens and leaders educated in the ways of the new republic was an early and important goal for higher education.

Then too another critical issue for higher education arose, academic freedom. Although more than a century would pass before the process of codifying the meaning of academic freedom would begin, nevertheless, concerns about the loyalty of professors and their rights to freedom of speech began with the American Revolution. One important aspect of professorial loyalty prior to the Revolution was in regard to denominational interpretations of the Bible, and a New Light minister's attack on the Harvard faculty because "bad books were being read at Harvard" resulted in a careful refutation by the professor of divinity, Edward Wigglesworth. In another instance at King's College (now Columbia University) in 1775, Alexander Hamilton, then a student, was able to forestall a mob long enough for the Loyalist president (most students, faculty members, and presidents supported the Revolution) to escape tar and feathering.[6] While the latter is not a matter of academic freedom but rather an issue of civil liberty, the two incidents serve as a reminder that external or internal criticism on college or university campuses easily elevates to outright attacks.

THE CIVIL WAR

The Morrill Act of 1862 had a role in the Civil War, as its required military training resulted in what we now know as the Reserve Officer Training Corps (ROTC); its graduates fought for both the Union and the Confederacy. Campus military training was popular throughout the nation even among institutions that were not Morrill

Land Grant institutions, including at several Southern colleges and universities such as the Citadel, the University of Alabama, and the University of Tennessee. Participation in this training was a patriotic duty of the white male student.

Citizenship required different forms of citizenship, however, when the nation split apart and then reunified. The Civil War devastated much of the South and re-arranged education in the public schools. In order for the states of the Confederacy to return to the Union, one requirement was that each state have free and public education for all citizens, a condition hardly followed in the North. As a consequence, one fully implemented following the end of Reconstruction in 1877 and the return of white domination in the South, Southern states created separate public school systems for white and black citizens. In similar form, the passage of the 1862 Morrill Land Grant Act, while putatively for all citizens, reflected the racism in the nation in the need for the passage of the 1890 Morrill Land Grant Act. The Morrill Acts also represent increased forms of student access, as noted in the chapter on the 1800s, a reminder that in nearly any careful scholarly investigation, simple answers may not obtain since the two Acts represent both discrimination and increased access.

On campus during the war, women were engaged in discussions about the conflict; in the case of one Ohio college for white women, there were frequent "scraps" between Northern and Southern students; as was the case with the American Revolution, white women articulated their engagement with the political setting.[7] In the South after the Civil War, large numbers of white women found themselves suddenly responsible for the care of their families, including the financial affairs of the family. For those women from wealthy backgrounds, educated to be the wife of a plantation owner, their education rested more in the liberal arts in classical terms, with additional emphasis on the fine arts. As Christie Ann Farnham observed, their education was intended to show how they could complement their husbands. Nevertheless, Southern white women often rose to the challenge, managing farms, running small businesses, or becoming schoolteachers.[8] Both Southern and Northern white women taught in schools in the South that served both black and white students or black students only. They were often teachers out of economic necessity or called to teach (often in the context of evangelical backgrounds), and they brought education to the young even in the face, at times, of deeply racist responses in their communities.[9]

The Civil War also brought emancipation from enslavement with the 1863 Emancipation Proclamation and then the passage of the 13th Amendment to the Constitution in 1865, and hundreds of thousands of newly emancipated African

Americans faced the challenge of securing financial stability and ensuring their citizenship. Education became a central goal in what many scholars identify as racial uplift, a concerted effort across the African American community to establish equality with white people in social, economic, and political terms. Given the rampant racism across the nation, even seemingly well-intentioned efforts by Whites to assist African Americans often had results that continued the marginalization and oppression of African Americans. The matter of what sort of college would best serve African Americans had advocates of differing opinions, although it appears that the now-popular distinctions between the advocates (usually portrayed as Booker T. Washington in support of practical education and W.E.B. Du Bois in support of the liberal arts and the training of a Talented Tenth) may be more a construction of social scientists, especially historians, than a principled division; disagreement between those two may well have been more personal than recognized, and Black colleges readily incorporated both practical and liberal education while valuing the latter, as did White colleges.[10] In any regard, it is not wise, however, to under-estimate the efforts of African Americans and the minority of Whites who were supportive of equality, and the growth of Black colleges across the South, both private and public, speaks clearly to the intent and will of African Americans to secure what could never be taken away, an education. The private institutions often began as the result of efforts by missionary societies (during the nineteenth century and earlier, these groups were instrumental in the development of Western forms of formal education, both in the United States and elsewhere in the world), and the public ones as a result of African American presence and lobbying in state legislatures. In both cases, the colleges had to begin with their students, who were either literate at a basic level or just learning to read and write. As James Anderson has richly documented, the stories of Black education in the South after the Civil War and through the Jim Crow era manifest a strength of will and commitment that is enviable. Resisting efforts to develop a curriculum heavily focused on practical or industrial education, steadily across the decades these institutions developed into four-year colleges, even as critics (ignoring the need for preparatory academies at white institutions of higher education) called for cutting the number of Black colleges in order to create a more selective group of institutions.[11]

The white colleges and universities in the South had to respond to what essentially constituted their near extinction during the Civil War. Not only did the white male students and professors leave (the white women attended only women's colleges), but also the Union forces often destroyed many of the buildings on campuses, either burning them to the ground or using them for housing or hospitals and effectively ruining the interiors. Consequently, rebuilding these institutions entailed both curricular and architectural decisions, and in both cases, the general tendency was toward an affirmation of traditions, both of the South and Western Europe. The curriculum at many all-white colleges and universities before the Civil War focused on the classical curriculum, what might well be considered a forerunner of the modern liberal arts with their division on disciplines such as physics, sociology, English, and theatre; the classical curriculum evidenced little such division given the centrality of the Bible and ancient Greek and Latin texts but nevertheless was of less immediate practical use than majors in such areas as engineering or, in the later decades of the 1800s, business. The curriculum after the Civil War drew upon the classical curriculum but began to include such subjects as modern languages, evidencing what one historian identifies as liberal Christian education, as well as practical subjects such as engineering. New architecture much resembled the old architecture, with Georgian and Federalist buildings, red brick and white-columned, arising on many campuses. One historian identifies three important consequences of the Civil War on colleges and universities not only in the South, but also in the North. Michael David Cohen explores the effect of the war in terms of the war mobilization efforts throughout the nation (one might well attend to the Civil War memorials scattered across campuses), an effort reflective of a budding commitment of the federal government to higher education as well as the commitment of the institutions' constituencies to provide assistance to the federal government. This assistance extended to the provision of assistance to formerly enslaved Africans, primarily through the efforts of the Freedman's Bureau. So too was the assistance to veterans a new governmental approach, often done at the state level by offering educational benefits to them, including in the Deep South, an early version of the 1944 G.I. Bill.[12] Second, as noted earlier, the state university (also identified as the comprehensive university) was developing, and efforts to create higher education access after the Civil War accelerated as states strove to provide more higher education to more people. Finally, and a curious tension with the increasing federal role, institutions of higher education enrolled more local students.[13]

Hence the meaning of citizen shifted for white women, highlighting their need to be economic providers. For African Americans, decided steps toward citizenship occurred, although the advent of the Jim Crow era when Reconstruction ended in 1877 meant the pace slowed greatly; nevertheless, their institutions of higher education continued to make gains even in the face of virulent racism. Finally, the federal government had taken important steps in its involvement with colleges and universities.

WORLD WAR I

Perhaps because World War I was the first war in which the United States engaged an enemy on European soil (as opposed to such actions as invading the Spanish colonies of Cuba and the Philippines in 1898), signaling in another form the newfound might of the nation, patriotism on campuses was palpable. For example, the Student Army Training Corps (SATC) was a highly visible presence on campus, as young men went into military training offered at colleges and universities in preparation for the battles in Europe.

At some institutions, such as Columbia University, faculty members and the president, Nicholas Murray Butler, viewed the role of the university as the creator of the nation's leaders. As such, the formation of those leaders had two dimensions—beyond the clear assumption that they would be men. In terms of educating those leaders, Professor John Erskine organized a seminar of Western civilization, a seminar designed to present the unifying and superior dimensions of Western civilization for the men of Columbia. Just as important, the university needed the right men, men of character; character, however, was defined by class as well as race and ethnicity. African Americans were not threatening to break open the doors of the institution, but the Jews were, and institutions such as Columbia developed sophisticated and at times explicit mechanisms to ensure that white Protestant males were the men of character best suited to a higher education preparing them for national leadership.[14]

Butler not only led the effort to properly educate the proper man, but also he was adamant about the need for the institution to be fully and unequivocally committed to winning the war. As a result, he saw the need to dismiss faculty members who remained uncertain or in opposition to the war, including the prominent historian Charles Beard, author of *An Economic Interpretation of the Constitution*, a radical interpretation of the U.S. Constitution that did not elevate the Founding Fathers but rather found them wanting in their creation of a document that safeguarded their financial interests. Beard did not, however, receive much assistance from the newly formed American Association of University Professors (AAUP), organized as a result of a call to professionalize the professoriate, and immediately faced expectations about supporting the nation in its efforts to win the war. The AAUP had found itself unexpectedly and quickly responding to threats against the developing notion of academic freedom, yet at the same time its members were called upon to provide justifications for the war and promote the nation's superiority in moral and political terms over Germany. The irony of such promotion lay not only in the AAUP and its efforts on behalf of academic freedom but also in the fact that many of the nation's more prominent social scientists had earned their doctorates in Germany. Even the AAUP itself was engaged in the promotion and propaganda that so often has characterized the verbal and written national responses to war.[15]

World War I brought about the popularization of a specific form of assessing students, one that persists today with no end in sight. As the armed services increasingly recognized, in an increasingly sophisticated and specialized industrial world, the need to assign people (especially white men) to different roles in order to achieve the goal of efficiently winning the war, they drew upon the nascent efforts in standardized testing to identify levels of intelligence.[16] Ignoring such characteristics as level and extent of schooling and quality of schooling, proponents of standardized testing effectively began a march toward numeracy in the evaluation of students' potential for success that privileged any group that had more access to more education, within the context of defining education in terms as specific as Western civilization courses. A careful analysis of the 1917 Army Alpha Intelligence Test by John Rury highlights this issue; the U.S. Army tested about 1,750,000 men and determined that native Whites were more intelligent than immigrant Whites and Blacks (and Northern Blacks tested better than Southern Blacks). According to the test results and in deeply disturbing language of the time, "89 percent of the black men qualified as 'morons.'" Rury's quantitative analysis illustrates the strong relationships between level and extent of schooling and standardized test results, but the test (based on Stanford professor Lewis Terman's model and administered by a team led by Harvard professor Robert Yerkes) was foundational in using standardized testing to stereotype groups. Indeed, as Christopher Loss notes, World War I marks the implementation of the idea of a personnel movement, specifically an ideal person (whose characteristics did not change) based on white, male, upper-class and middle-class notions of a person, a movement.[17]

Finally, in view of the heavy preponderance of male student enrollments in higher education until the late 1800s, World War I was the first time that the men left (although in this case, only the classroom and extracurricular activities). In the fall of 1918, in "simultaneous assemblies at 516 colleges and universities throughout the country, 140,000 male students were inducted into the U.S. Army and assumed the novel status of student-soldiers, in a program known as the Students' Army Training Corps (SATC)."[18] This program effectively changed colleges into military training sites, signaling their commitment to the effort to win the war, and fortuitously, providing many of them with much-needed income because their tuition revenue seriously declined as young men volunteered to go to war. The ROTC units (not named as such until 1916) were replaced by the SATC. Although faculty members across the nation initially welcomed the program, as SATC regulations (such as the requirement that students march to class) and the loss of academic courses (which increasingly focused on military matters) became more important, they lost their enthusiasm. One course, however, elicited faculty interest, on the issues of war, a course that cast the German as evil and the U.S. citizen as good. In regard to military training at civilian institutions, despite concerns about the SATC effect on campuses, after the war colleges and universities increasingly re-adopted ROTC units. The measure of citizenship for men included commitment to military education.

White women often supported the war effort too, although in different ways. The most common approach was in the form of supportive activities such as preparing warm clothing for shipment to men serving at the front, as discussed in a biography of two teachers who were at the University of Maine during World War I.[19] The identity of patriotism, developed in the American Revolution, now stretched into modern warfare and international efforts to defeat an enemy.

MODERN WAR, MODERN HIGHER EDUCATION: WORLD WAR II

It is hard to grasp the dimensions of World War II. Two facts are informative; first, every single continent, including Antarctica (albeit to a very small degree) experienced some form of military engagement. Second, there is no firm number of how many people lost their lives because of the war, but estimates go as high as 60 million.

The origins of rational, effective use of such national resources as "scientific personnel and equipment" to win a war were as early as World War I, if not earlier in the Civil War. World War I set the pattern for military–business cooperation and planning in World War II. In regard to the Civil War, the period between Civil War and World War I was the key period for the development of military–business cooperation and planning; the historical role of higher education, evidenced in the passage of the 1862 Morrill Land Grant Act with its explicit conditions of vocational education and military training (the latter of which assured passage by the United States Congress) remains largely unexplored in these complex relations.[20] Yet the rise of science in World War II, culminating in devastation created by the atomic bomb, is far more notable than in the Civil War or World War I. The capacity of universities to produce basic and applied scientific discoveries, the understanding that an increasingly broad range of students could benefit from higher education, and the beginning identification of higher education as a critical, if not the central institution for the advancement of national interests, all make World War II a particularly important time for colleges and universities.

Science, and more particularly departments in the natural and physical sciences, benefitted greatly from World War II, in great part because of their willingness to work with external organizations (both industrial and federal) to define their work and receive external funding, a willingness underway in the 1930s prior to the war. Rebecca Lowen provides an especially instructive examination of the Department of Physics at Stanford University, where the department faculty split along the lines of practical science (of immediate use to industry or the government) and basic science (i.e., theoretical investigations and laboratory work not necessarily leading to practical application). Those faculty members advocating the practical application eventually took the day, while receiving generous external funding from industry (they were well aware that there were possibilities for government funding as well).[21] By the time of World War II, at a university without an engineering program until the early 2000s, one that has long declared its commitment to the life of the mind, the University of Chicago was the center of the development of the most powerful practical application of science, the atom bomb.[22] All of this led to a report to President Roosevelt by Vannevar Bush called *Science, the Endless Frontier*, a report resulting, after political struggles, to the establishment of the National Science Foundation in 1950.[23]

In addition to the planning for the education of veterans as discussed in the previous chapter, the armed services and the American Council on Education (ACE) developed educational programs for armed services personnel, programs that illustrated the broad range of individuals who could benefit from further education. As early as 1940, prior to the nation's entry into World War II, Francis Brown, an ACE staff member, was working directly with the Army and the Navy to develop educational programs for officers and enlisted personnel.[24] In October 1940 the ACE Subcommittee on Military Affairs met and recommended that the armed forces establish a committee on education, and in November of that year the Subcommittee met again to formulate a plan and also met with representatives of the Army and Navy to discuss educational programs for armed forces personnel. In February 1941 the Joint Army and Navy Committee on Welfare and Recreation was appointed, and that committee established a subcommittee on education with Francis Brown as executive secretary.[25]

This discussion focuses on the educational programs of the Department of the Navy; the War Department, with responsibility for the Army, followed a similar pattern although the programs themselves differed. The Navy began assessment of the educational needs of its personnel in 1941, beginning with a base in the Caribbean where officers and sailors had no contact with females, excellent recreational facilities, and considerable off-duty time. Concern about the men wondering about present dangers and future uncertainties, "(their 'thinking time' period)...the danger period," led to a report resulting in two high school teachers being sent to the base. By 1943 about 15 percent of the men were taking courses, with technically trained men preferring liberal arts courses and liberally educated men preferring mathematics, science, and technical subjects. Following the experiment, the Navy established Educational Service Centers throughout the Caribbean, North America, and in Iceland and Ireland. In Alaska, instruction occurred essentially as a result of members of construction battalions organizing informal courses ranging from cabinet-making to art appreciation, a program jokingly called the University of Kodiak.[26] Education, then, was both an external need, as the Navy determined that its personnel needed certain forms of education, and an internal need established by the personnel themselves.

The Navy also implemented an off-duty program so that officers and enlisted men and women could continue their interrupted educations, or learn skills essential to their Navy jobs, or address "a concern for the eventual return to civilian life and a desire to understand better the problems of that life in a rapidly changing world." The off-duty program included a component for those men and women in hospitals suffering from "cases of nervous disorders, such as those caused by severe shock," since they were "capable of educational rehabilitation."[27] Thus the Navy very clearly recognized that education was a means of re-adjusting the sailor to civilian life, even for those suffering from debilitating emotional states. An assessment of the Navy's off-duty program in 1944 confirmed that objectives of the program included officers' and sailors' preparation for return to education after the war, including the specific responsibility of officers in charge of the program to counsel students concerning their educational and vocational choices.[28]

In January 1942, the armed services established the United States Armed Forces Institute (USAFI), a program offering hundreds of courses at the secondary school and college levels. The program had five objectives, three of which focused on training needs for the armed forces, one on the preparation of personnel for citizenship, and one "to enable those whose education had been interrupted to return to civilian educational activity." Unlike the Navy's program, USAFI courses were initially only correspondence courses. In addition, the armed services offered self-teaching, and the Navy's off-duty courses. The Armed Forces Institute developed "measures of general educational development" to assist students who wanted educational institutions to be able to evaluate their work in the armed services educational programs, indicating government and institutional preparation for veterans' entry into colleges and universities. The program also foreshadowed the unprecedented level of access that the G.I. Bill offered, as African American service personnel enrolled in USAFI courses too. The issue of access for African American veterans very nearly halted the passage of the 1944 Serviceman's Readjustment Act, as the American Legion had to fly a Georgia representative to Washington, DC to ensure approval of the bill, in response to opposition by the racist chair of the conference committee for the bill, Representative John Rankin of Mississippi.[29]

The USAFI leadership favored using tests to measure student achievement, in part because of the various ways in which students could learn (even including "miscellaneous" as well as "informal and individual" approaches), and the ACE was able to supply the necessary expertise.[30] In terms of instruction on college and university campuses, both the Department of the Navy and the War Department instituted programs, the Navy College Training Program (eventually known as the V-12 Program) and the Army Specialized Training Program (ASTP), respectively. An evaluation in 1944 suggested that the most important positive conclusions were that colleges and universities were far more flexible than most people assumed—including a willingness to "meet the needs of new types of students"—and benefited from federal aid.[31] Both the federal government as well as colleges and universities were learning during World War II the apparent benefits of government–higher education cooperation, especially in educating a broader range of students.

The implementation of the G.I. Bill, the Serviceman's Readjustment Act of 1944, began a substantial shift in perceptions of who belonged on college and university campuses, especially in terms of class issues (one aspect of its passage, in organizational terms, was discussed in detail in Chapter 4 on Progressivism), reflecting the USAFI experience. Colleges and universities had limited scholarships and loans for needy students, but the sheer size of the G.I. Bill was a fundamental shift in student financial support.[32] The federal government had previously signaled its willingness to use higher education to achieve national purposes, through the 1862 and 1890 Morrill Acts and also through New Deal programs such as the National Youth Administration, which provided loans and campus jobs to college and university students in an effort to keep them in college and away from unemployment lines. The jobless rate was nearly 25 percent in 1933 (a rate likely under-measured given the struggles of poor people, especially rural poor people, throughout the nation); many college and university students faced financial stress, and jobs and loans benefitted them, and often institutions of higher education. Although administrators at some private colleges balked at the idea of the federal government dictating institutional programs as well as the problem of supporting students at the same financial rate regardless of public or private institution tuition, the program was moderately successful. It may be also seen as the first instance of federal aid for students, as opposed to the financial support for institutions evident in the Morrill Acts.[33]

Whether in popular magazines or in terms of classroom experiences, veterans who had little time for cheering on the football team or joining a fraternity (given that the vast majority of the G.I. Bill beneficiaries were men, particularly white men) showed that they were determined to succeed in the classroom and did so. Such potential for success had social as well as academic characteristics, with even popular magazines and advertisements increasingly turning to portrayals of the veteran on campus, succeeding and smiling.[34] Although popular accounts of the G.I. Bill, and some historians of higher education, are prone to point to the G.I. Bill as a major impetus in the democratization of U.S. higher education, a step toward mass higher education, it was mostly a democratization by class for white men; for example, about 75 percent of the veterans attending Harvard had been previously admitted to that institution. The democratization was also as much symbol as reality, inasmuch as the majority of veterans who took advantage of the educational benefits of the bill would have gone to college nonetheless; one estimate suggests that only about 20 percent of the veterans using those benefits enrolled as a result of the bill. African American veterans faced a very different set of issues because so many white institutions of higher education either resolutely remained segregated or admitted African Americans in small numbers while many black institutions of higher education faced substantial financial constraints and could not afford enrollment increases given their limited facilities and little chance of further funding to increase their enrollment capacities. One aspect of the veterans that had an impact on the administrative side of higher education, regardless of whether the veteran had been to college or was likely to have enrolled, was the widespread concern about his (in a far more limited sense, her) readjustment after experiencing the brutalities of war. Colleges and universities began to develop student personnel staffs, to some degree extending the vision of the 1937 statement, *The Student Personnel Point of View*, authored by a committee of the American Council on Education.[35]

The G.I. Bill captured the public imagination, and of course Hollywood responded. In *An Apartment for Peggy*, an old white male philosophy professor, a member of a campus classical music group, ready to commit suicide as logical response to a rewarding life, rents his attic to a G.I. Bill couple, and despite the challenges, the husband succeeds in college. The ending is, of course, a Hollywood happy one, without suicide.[36] The veterans' success provided a powerful symbol for the possibilities of mass higher education, and the G.I. Bill represented a landmark in the movement toward federal funding of college and university students. It was, however, a targeted program for veterans rather than providing general support for any student qualified to enter college. Nevertheless, the massive surge of white male students showed that college could be for a far broader range of students than originally assumed, if, of course, they had adequate funding.

As suggested in the inclusion of African Americans in the USAFI programs and the G.I. Bill, matters of citizenship in the United States experienced renewed importance during World War II. This time, however, elements of inclusion appeared, in contrast to the general tendency of exclusion during previous wars. While the historical context of civil rights in the 1940s is obvious in view of a growing body of scholarship,[37] that context provided little environmental pressure on colleges, universities, and education associations; what follows is a discussion of the remarkable levels of visibility of the issue in the 1940s, a visibility dimmed in the Eisenhower years (see the following long endnote).[38]

There was some discussion within higher education about African Americans and their role in higher education's efforts to further the effort to win the war. For example, at a 1941 conference organized by the American Council on Education, with eight sectional meetings divided by types of institutions and constituencies, the shortest and most succinct report was titled "Rights of Minorities." That report stated in full:

> The Negroes pointed out that they had to "fight for the right to fight," that they are discriminated against by draft boards, that they frankly do not know where they stand in America today. They are loyal and want to share responsibilities as well as rights. The feeling in the group was that minorities should be protected, especially when we are fighting for democracy.[39]

In general, those voices were unheard or dismissed in higher education during the 1940s, as there were few efforts to desegregate colleges and universities, other than those of the Legal Defense Fund of the NAACP. That those voices were public is, however, now clear.

Furthermore, African American leaders were able to convince President Truman of the importance of equal opportunity, and he repeatedly made clear that this particular topic held urgency. Although initially evidencing little concern about racism, he changed his mind during a meeting with Black leaders who told him of lynchings and brutality in the South and "the flood of viciously anti-Semitic, anti-Catholic, anit-labor, and anti-foreign-born literature." One of Truman's fondest memories was his service in an artillery battery during World War I, and the descriptions of racist attacks on African American veterans returning home left him aghast. Walter White, president of the NAACP at the time, recounts Truman's reaction at the September 19, 1946 meeting: "When I had finished, the President exclaimed in his flat, Midwestern accent, 'My God. I had no idea it was as terrible as that. We've got to do something!'" While he balanced principles and politics in a number of matters, Truman acted upon the issue of civil rights despite its lack of salience in the polity and the public.[40] He appointed the Committee on Civil Rights immediately following the meeting, and it issued a frank report in 1947, *To Secure These Rights*, preceding the 1948 report of the President's Commission on Higher Education (which in fact referenced the report on civil rights). *To Secure These Rights* offered a highly critical view of race relations in the United States. It was remarkably inclusive, specifically naming and addressing discrimination faced by such groups as (in the language of the time) Negroes, Mexicans, Hispanos, American Indians, Chinese, Japanese, Filipinos, Koreans, Eskimos, Indians, Polynesians, Micronesians, and Puerto Ricans; the Committee was most concerned, however, about African Americans. It designated four essential rights: "the right to safety and security of the person," "the right to citizenship and its privileges," "the right to freedom of conscience and expression," and "the right to equality of opportunity," which included educational opportunity.[41] Although much of the report addressed problems of law enforcement, voting, housing, and health care, the Committee took a brief but harsh look at higher education. The document highlighted Northern higher education and the exclusion of Jews. It also discussed liberal arts colleges' tendency to argue for a "representative and diversified student body" as means to exclude on the basis of race or religion. It even identified the explicit mechanisms by which colleges and universities used application questions on race and religion to exclude and noted that in Northern institutions Jews and Blacks never had much representation. Nor were professional schools exempt from criticism, with medical schools in New York City identified as discriminatory—with a later argument that Blacks as a result had more health problems than Whites.[42] White institutions of higher education, however, were not often interested in these issues. As James Anderson has shown in his discussion of

African American professors and white colleges and universities in the 1940s, Northern white institutions of higher learning were unwilling to provide places, much less create supportive institutional mechanisms, in order to integrate their faculties.[43] There were instances of institutional desegregation, for example linked to wartime shifts in populations; at Spring Hill College in Mobile, Alabama, desegregation occurred in the early 1950s in part because of some Catholic educators committed to equality and in part because the industrial effort to win the war brought white Northerners and African Americans closer in the community and the factories.[44] One step toward greater desegregation at Northern colleges and universities resulted from a program initiated by a Smith College alumna concerned about the small number of African Americans at the Seven Sister colleges. The National Scholarship Service and Fund for Negro Students began in 1947 and providing its search for talented Black students until 1974, its origins evidencing the goal of the Double V.[45] For the most part, however, both Northern and Southern colleges and universities either remained fully segregated or only nominally desegregated, a few people of color across the students and, rarely, the faculty (the first African American scholar appointed to a tenure-track position at any white university was Allison Davis, in 1942 at the University of Chicago).

In concert with the Committee on Civil Rights, the 1947 President's Commission on Higher Education offered a clarion call for equality, in rich language and persistent presentation of data. Arguing that the world would not succeed without the achievement of equality of all and respect for each other, the Commission members authored a report that subtly shifted the conversations about the meanings and uses of higher education as the central actor in creating a better democracy:

> If we cannot reconcile conflicts of opinion and interest among the diverse groups that make up our own Nation, we are not likely to succeed in compromising the differences that divide nations. If we cannot make scientific and technological progress contribute to the greater well-being of all our own citizens, we shall scarcely be able to exercise leadership in reducing inequality and injustice among the other peoples of the world. If we cannot achieve a fuller realization of democracy in the United States, we are not likely to secure its adoption willingly outside the United States.[46]

While this call would eventually fall prey to the demands for higher education to educate for the sake of economic gain, for decades the idea of the college and university as a place for the achievement of democracy held prominence. In fact, even in 1947, a report published that year provided convincing evidence that college graduates made more money, indicating that a clear path to success resulted from college graduation.[47]

Although women and equality were virtually missing from the discussion about democracy and equality in the report by the 1947 President's Commission on Higher Education, World War II had an impact on the lives of women on campuses, one that led to some gains in the post-World War II period. As Charles Dorn shows, focusing on the University of California Berkeley while drawing upon examples from other institutions, when the white men left, the white women entered the leadership roles previously reserved for the most part for men. Following the return of men, women retained some of the leadership positions, such as editor of the student newspaper.[48]

Finally, while elements of access occurred during World War II and thereafter, national interests framed by white men and women continued efforts to exclude. Perhaps most notable, ensuring exclusion from higher education in the most basic way, the internment of Japanese Americans meant that their educational efforts were within those internment camps, through powerful means but not through formal educational organizations recognized by accrediting agencies.[49]

VIETNAM

It seemed to be a time of protest, beginning with protests against segregation and increasingly confrontational protests against the Vietnam War (discussed in Chapter 6 on students). It was also a time of significant shifts in enrollments, brought about in part by the nation's experience in Vietnam and in part by an increasing commitment to providing broader access to colleges and universities; discussed both in this section and the latter issue of increased access again in Chapter 8 on exclusion and stratification. In addition, the nation's involvement in Vietnam reinforced the relationships between academic science and the federal government. Finally, and curiously, the Vietnam War brought about skepticism toward colleges and universities, a skepticism that undergirded eventual efforts to ensure that public institutions of higher education had less public financial support and colleges and universities focused on efficiency.

Shortly after the veterans returned from service in World War II, the nation experienced what is called the Baby Boom, an extraordinary rate of growth in the number of babies born each year. Initially, of course, the population growth put a strain on the nation's schools, starting in the mid-1950s and continuing to the late 1960s and early 1970s. By the late 1950s, colleges and universities began to experience the pressure on enrollments, and the growth of college enrollments became extraordinary, as did the growth of institutions of higher education. For example, for a while at the end of the 1960s, states were establishing community colleges at the average of one per week. Enrollment growths at four-year colleges, especially at public institutions, were equally remarkable. According to the *Digest of Educational Statistics*, there were about 2.3 million students enrolled at colleges and universities in 1947, 4.1 million in 1961, and 8.5 million in 1970; hence in two decades, college and university enrollment essentially doubled each decade. Part of the reason for the enrollment growth was the male student response, particularly among white men, to the nation's Selective Service exclusion from the draft of men enrolled in college. There was also a declared war that had a direct impact on enrollment, the War on Poverty, which President Lyndon Baines Johnson declared in 1964. He saw education as one of the key means for eradicating poverty, and proposed legislation that went far beyond the G.I. Bill and the National Defense Education Act because the only criterion for eligibility was family or student income. Federal funding for scholarships and loans accelerated in 1965 with the passage of the Higher Education Act authorizing 1.2 billion dollars in support for higher education, including loans and grants; lower-income students found new ways to afford college.[50] This law represents the first full-scale use of federal dollars to provide financial assistance to students in higher education, without targeting them on the basis of national defense interests or service to the nation, and the enormity of the financial commitment (more than the amount authorized to support public schools in the Elementary and Secondary Education Act of 1965 despite the far larger number of students, teachers, and administrators in public schools) offered a convincing statement as to the federal commitment to supporting higher education.

Access, however, is not simply a matter of enrollment numbers, although it is highly important to remember the numbers in order to inform the meaning of access. (Obviously, the fact that very few African Americans enrolled in higher education in the pre-Civil War era means that the nature of their experience differs from increases in their enrollment in the post-Civil War era.) During the Vietnam War protests, women, especially white women, increasingly found voice in their desire to have futures that culminated in more than lives as mothers and wives. The post-World War II articulation of the limits and possibilities of white middle-class women arguably began with Betty Friedan's 1963 *The Feminist Mystique*. Its arguments were within the context of the white middle class, given that African American women were already working and did not need liberation to work, but it framed such an understanding of women as equal and capable that one might, indeed, suggest that the understanding is ovarian rather than seminal. Furthermore, her arguments found support in the theoretical landscape of higher education, resulting in the development of courses that examined women as full participants in the shaping of the society, the polity, and the economy. The Vietnam war and the protests accelerated the rise of feminism (which would become feminisms) on college and university campuses in the late 1960s because women participating in the anti-war activities often found that they were asked to vote and then asked to make the coffee and cookies rather than working in leadership roles during the conduct of protests.[51] Those developments signaled a shift in social attitudes, yet there were political attitudes and instrumental values of the past in regard to higher education that continued.

While the federal government had identified the importance of science, especially in its practical application, to the advancement of national interests, federal support of academic science grew to unprecedented amounts in the Vietnam years. Discussion of research universities in this time period occurs in a later chapter, providing the reader with the long traditions of research beginning in the mid-1800s and the power of research dollars to shape universities in the post-World War II period. For the purposes of this chapter, it is important that readers understand that the federal commitment to research, particularly in the natural and physical sciences, shaped universities in substantial ways. Universities experienced even greater separation (in what was already an important distance) between undergraduate life and graduate life than prior to World War II, with the latter focused on research and external funding.[52]

Two enduring consequences of World War II, the development of a national sense of the worth of college enrollments beyond the traditional students of mostly white middle-class or upper-class families and the importance of science in advancing national interests, were of great importance during the Vietnam years. Enrollment growth of nearly unbelievable proportions coupled with investments in research that opened graduate programs at a remarkable level of expansion began the creation of what one university president called, in borrowing a term from another writer, the multiversity. Having become all things to all people, the U.S. university seemed to be fulfilling the goals of advancing national interests on a variety of fronts, even though, as the president noted, the only shared grievance among faculty members was that there was not enough parking.[53]

"THE SHIBBOLETH OF ACADEMIC FREEDOM":[54] THE COLD WAR, THE WAR ON TERROR

One consequence of allowing war to define citizenship and leadership was the application of restraints on academic freedom; this section's title includes a quote from the *New York Times* in 1917, lauding the trustees of Columbia University for dismissing

Charles Beard, whom the *Times* considered to be someone who would advance "radicalism and socialism" under the guise of academic freedom. Such restraint continued in the early 2000s, While those issues certainly arose during declared wars of on-the-ground combat, the warlike atmosphere of the late 1940s and the early 2000s—the former in regard to the intensely combative relationship between the United States and the Union of Soviet Socialist Republics (USSR), the latter in regard to terrorist attacks and deadly responses—are highly illustrative of the subtle yet powerful ways in which nations (in this case, the United States) expect all citizens to be patriotic, exhibiting in fact a form of patriotism that is suspicious if not exclusionary in regard to others.

In February 1951, Senator Joseph P. McCarthy of Wisconsin delivered a speech in Charleston, West Virginia charging that there were nearly 200 Communists employed in the State Department. His claim galvanized support for anti-Communism that had been building since the end of World War II, and the fears of the Cold War (including the Chinese Communist takeover of the nation in 1948 and a nuclear winter resulting from atomic warfare between the United States and the Union of Soviet Socialist Republics that would end life on the planet except for, perhaps, roaches) lasted, in terms of intensity, until late 1954 when the U.S. Senate, in a rare moment, censured Senator McCarthy. Prior to McCarthy's claims, there had been two major instances of fear about Communist faculty members and their potential for disruption of university life and their ability to use university resources to persuade others, especially students, to become Communists. The first incident occurred at the University of Washington and resulted in the dismissal of three faculty members; the second incident at the University of California (which at the time consisted of two campuses, one at Berkeley and one at Los Angeles), which resulted in the dismissal of 51 faculty members. The California case is notable not only because of the large-scale dismissal but also because it highlighted an instrument of the state, the loyalty oath. The Board of Regents at the University had mandated that all faculty members sign a loyalty oath swearing that they were not members of any group attempting to overthrow the government, and 51 professors refused to sign the oath. While some relented, 29 continued their refusal and remained dismissed. This incident also marked the beginning of a long period in which the AAUP avoided any confrontation with colleges and universities over issues of academic freedom, although many professors throughout the nation suffered harassment or dismissal because of past or present political interests or activity.[55] It was a time when the phrase "Are you now or have you even been a member of the Communist Party" became widespread, a phrase that lasted well into the 1960s and was used to damn anyone based on political activity or political party membership, however weak or strong that interest.[56] The constraints on faculty members, and to a lesser degree administrators and students, were often subtle; there were, however, times when the constraints were direct, as in the case of the Association of American of Universities, the group of leading research universities, which in 1953 issued a public statement calling for the outright dismissal of any faculty member even suspected of Communist activity.[57]

The attacks, however, were more than attacks on political activity. In a broad and damaging sense, a sense of Americanism permeated the investigation of educators throughout the nation. Southern anti-segregationists often falsely linked desegregation activists to Communism, as occurred at Fisk University in the late 1940s and early 1950s. The president of Fisk, Charles Johnson, who firmly advocated for equal rights based on a rational, social scientific approach, made the difficult (and later, in reflection, wrong) decision to dismiss an activist professor who encouraged demonstrations against racism and segregation and was also questioned by the infamous House Un-American Activities Committee. At UCLA a professor with accused same-sex identity was investigated for her links to Communism. She was one of only two women who were full professors at the institution, but the administration, despite a recommendation from a faculty committee to support her, dismissed her. In West Virginia, an art professor from New York City was assailed for her Bohemian ways, and the American Legion was instrumental in her dismissal from the university because she was anti-American.[58] Citizenship definitions took form in a highly prescriptive set of norms, as white and heterosexual identities were reinforced as the only appropriate behaviors and values.

Concern about the safety of the nation escalated in October 1957, when the USSR launched a satellite, Sputnik, into orbit around the Earth. Radio stations in the United States as well as the much smaller number of broadcast television stations, played tapes of the satellite's beeping transmissions back to the USSR. Public outcry and Congressional demand resulted in the rapid 1958 passage of the National Defense Education Act (NDEA). The Act provided monies to support the study of mathematics and the science as well as critical areas (for example, languages such as Russian but also loosely defined in terms of area studies of different parts of the globe), and it generated another set of unprecedented funds for the support of higher education, although once again targeted at specific populations such as scientists and college students preparing to be teachers in the schools. Yet again, the federal government became more deeply involved in supporting higher education, including the acceleration of federal agency programs and administration in order to manage the money. In addition, it required that anyone receiving funds from the Act sign an oath of loyalty to the government (which some states, such as Georgia and Alabama, still require for employees in public institutions of higher education), yet again highlighting the specific definition of citizenship in the democracy. In this instance the AAUP coordinated a long effort to remove the oath; the Association's efforts were notable if only for the fact that it coordinated a fight against the oath.[59]

Although the fall of the USSR in the 1980s marked the end of one undeclared war, the deaths of U.S. citizens and members of the armed services at that time and later in the simmering conflict between the United States and a variety of Islamic groups led to another undeclared war, marked by the attacks on the World Trade Center towers in September 2001. It was one of the defining moments for the seemingly invincible United States, one not unlike the Japanese attack on Pearl Harbor on December 7, 1941, with the conclusion that the nation's soil had been violated. Yet again, the person not of Western European heritage became suspect, but this time the suspicion was fueled by national media and social network outlets that discovered those who were not American.

Not American meant not only born different, but also those who spoke out against U.S. activities that led to the attacks on the World Trade Center were under investigation. In 1940 the American Association of University Professors issued its *Statement on Principles of Academic Freedom and Tenure*, resulting from six years of negotiation with the Association of American Colleges. The statement defined academic freedom as full freedom to conduct and publish research and to teach with full freedom in regard to their subject, although avoiding controversial issues outside their subjects. It also cautioned professors about extramural utterances,

> When they speak or write as citizens, they should be free from institutional censorship or discipline, but their special position in the community imposes special obligations. As scholars and educational officers, they should remember that the public may judge their profession and their institution by their utterances. Hence they should at all times be accurate, should exercise appropriate restraint, should show respect for the opinions of others, and should make every effort to indicate that they are not speaking for the institution.[60]

A case that illustrates the complex nature of academic freedom is that of Ward Churchill, a professor at the University of Colorado Boulder. Professor Churchill wrote a scathing indictment of U.S. foreign policy and the work of corporations and their employees the day after the attacks, arguing that the attacks were justified. His indictment was not an academic publication, nor did it identify his institution, and it remained nearly hidden for years. Eventually it came to public attention when he was invited to speak at a small college in New York, and the outrage among conservatives as well as the caution among moderates and liberals led, according to a jury decision in Colorado, to his investigation for research misconduct at the University of Colorado that led to his termination. Although there was no direct link between his essay and his research, the jury concluded that the investigation would have not occurred if he had not come to such prominence because of his essay. The judge over-turned the jury's decision, and Ward Churchill's appeal was denied by the state's supreme court. The boundaries between the freedom to speak freely in the classroom or in academic settings (whether they are publications and presentations) and outside those arenas are unclear.[61] What is clear is that being deemed an American is typically of utmost necessity during times of war according to varied and powerful social and political forces.

THE TRIBAL COLLEGES

It would be wrong to ignore the centuries of war against the native tribes of North America, and specifically that part of the hemisphere named by Western Europeans and colonized, repeatedly brutally, by them and for them, as the United States. For that matter, while Dartmouth, Harvard, and William and Mary were attempting to colonize young American Indian men, the American Indian Wars (the plural is instructive) were underway, and an honest review of the armed conflicts between Western settlers and Natives indicates that they did not end until the 1880s (with such important exceptions as the 1973 events at Wounded Knee).[62] There were early efforts to educate members of the tribes during the colonial era, and as early as the late 1700s, the U.S. Congress passed a law for the education of the Cherokees in farming. By the late 1800s there was some support among Whites for the higher education of Native Americans, support evidenced by efforts to enroll them at Hampton Institute, a Black college, although that experiment failed, in great part because there was fear of racial mixing and subsequent societal acceptance of Native Americans; the numbers of Native American students remained small over the decades after the 1870s. On occasion a tribe would initiate efforts to secure higher education for its youth, as occurred with the Choctaw Nation from the 1830s to the early 1900s. The 1830

Treaty of Dancing Rabbit Creek authorized the forced expatriation of all Choctaws from Mississippi to Oklahoma; the tribe's leaders were committed to securing a white education for its youth in recognition of the need to know the white man ways of governance and administration, and some of its youth had already attended college. Through a variety of programs over the decades, the Choctaws identified youth for college attendance and provided financial support for them to do so. In reflection of the challenges experienced by American Indian youth at colonial colleges, many of those young men and women did not complete college, but of equal import is the fact that among those who finished college, many returned home and became leaders, in contrast to so many white youth who left home for college and did not return. While these leaders reflected the European nature of their higher education, they also reflected the importance of their tribal identity.[63] At times, however, respect for tribal identities resulted in the formation of colleges that combined Christian and American Indian perspectives. For example, Bacone College (OK) began in 1880, established by the American Baptist Home Mission Society, has long served the Cherokee and the Muscogee Creek Indian tribes. Its faculty and graduates have included many prominent Native Americans, and it has held to its tradition of Christian education and the preservation of American Indian cultures. Nevertheless, the overall picture is clear in regard to U.S. higher education and American Indians.

One overview of the history of American Indian postsecondary enrollment notes that by 1932, only 52 American Indians had graduated from postsecondary institutions in the period from 1636 to 1932. In erratic and minimalist form thereafter, the higher education of American Indians (the term used today by many Indian studies scholars, including radical ones, to identify the cultural rather than the political issues), continued to be typically Western in institution and expectation. While the numbers of Native students increased in the post-World War II era, they remained small, and today the percentage of American Indian students enrolled in U.S. postsecondary institutions remains at 1 percent, a number that has been relatively constant for decades. As many scholars in recent decades have argued, by and large only tribal colleges make a concerted effort to bridge students' native cultures and the expectations of Western civilization.[64] Native Americans have sustained a history in the twentieth century, developing most rapidly in the post-World War II period, of providing higher education to the members of their cultures, but with little recognition from accrediting agencies for differences and often with sparse funding.[65] In the 1960s and 1970s, leaders in the Native American community began establishing tribal colleges (typically community colleges) in a deliberate attempt to contest assimilation into the white culture and affirm tribal cultures, an effort paralleling the civil rights movement. Both securing charters and funding (of both buildings and equipment as well as salaries and financial support for students) proved challenging, but the leaders of the tribal college movement persisted and succeeded. As of the writing of this book, there were 32 tribal colleges.

It is well worth contemplating the meaning of attempts to assimilate those who were first here in what centuries later would become, named by others, North America. It is also instructive to examine the foundational characteristics of efforts to establish colleges serving specific populations, efforts that are at once separatist and reflective of assumed central norms of U.S. society.

CONCLUSION

Through the centuries in efforts to win wars, from the colonies to the modern era, institutions of higher education and their participants ignored, or struggled with, or intensified, meanings of citizenship. Higher education occupied an increasingly central role in defining those meanings, and while it also increasingly provided means to some form of citizenship to more and more groups, it sustained both overt and subtle mechanisms to offer more central meanings for some groups than others. In terms of socioeconomic class, gender, race and ethnicity, and sexual identity, access to higher education and its benefits were reflective of exclusion and stratification.

DISCUSSION QUESTIONS

1. Who has benefited in what ways from college and university participation in efforts to win wars?
2. Why has war had such an effect on definitions of citizenship and who is a citizen in what ways?
3. Why would participation in efforts to win wars result in increased opportunities for government and private monies for financial aid?

NOTES

1 In political terms, it was the Vietnam conflict, since the United States never officially declared war on what was at the time North Vietnam. While that is an important characteristic of the period, and no small cause for student demonstrations of the time, the fact remains that tens of thousands died. I offer this note in respect for Howard Zinn, who was an outspoken critic of the Vietnam conflict.

2 I could easily argue, unfortunately, that the federal act, No Child Left Behind, has all the marks of a federal ministry of education that controls all schools, as of yet there is no such act for colleges and universities, although the multiple efforts of federal agencies to ensure compliance on matters as broad-ranging as student drug use and ethical research projects has increasingly led to federal control of higher education.

3 Barbara Solomon, *In the Company of Educated Women: A History of Women and Higher Education in America* (New Haven, CT: Yale University Press, 1985), p. 7.

4 Linda K. Kerber, "Daughters of Columbia: Educating Women for the Republic, 1787–1805," in *The Hofstadter Aegis: A Memorial*, ed. Stanley Elkins and Eric McKitrick (New York: Alfred A. Knopf, 1974), 36–59.

5 David Madsen, *The National University, Enduring Dream of the USA* (Detroit: Wayne State University Press, 1966).

6 Richard Hofstadter and Walter P. Metzger, *The Development of Academic Freedom in the United States* (New York: Columbia University Press, 1955).

7 Margaret A. Nash, "'A Salutary Rivalry': The Growth of Higher Education for Women in Oxford, Ohio, 1855–1867," *History of Higher Education Annual 1996* 16: 27.

8 Christie Anne Farnham, *The Education of the Southern Belle: Higher Education and Student Socialization in the Antebellum South* (New York: New York University Press, 1994), 182–184.

9 Ronald E. Butchart, "Mission Matters: Mount Holyoke, Oberlin, and the Schooling of Southern Blacks, 1861–1917," *History of Education Quarterly* 42 (Spring 2002): 1–17.

10 David Levering Lewis, *W. E. B. Du Bois: Biography of a Race, 1868–1919* (New York: Owl Books 1994); Michael Bieze, *Booker T. Washington and the Art of Self-Representation* (New York: Peter Lang, 2008); on the use of white philanthropy to appear to promote practical education while advancing the liberal arts, see Wayne Urban, *Black Scholar: Horace Mann Bond, 1904–1972* (Athens: University of Georgia Press, 2008).

11 James P. Anderson, *The Education of Blacks in the South, 1860–1935* (Chapel Hill: University of North Carolina Press, 1988).

12 Joseph M. Stetar, "In Search of a Direction: Southern Higher Education After the Civil War," *History of Education Quarterly* 25 (Autumn 1985): 341–367 on the curriculum. On architecture, see both Stetar and Michael David Cohen, *Reconstructing the Campus: Higher Education and the American Civil War* (Charlottesville: University of Virginia Press, 2012). Cohen's work is an important step toward understanding the impact of the Civil War on U.S. higher education on both the North and the South.

13 Michael David Cohen, *Reconstructing the Campus: Higher Education and the American Civil War* (Chancellorsville: University of Virginia Press, 2012).

14 Harold Wechsler, *The Qualified Student: A History of Selective College Admission in America* (New York: John Wiley & Sons, 1977); Marcia G. Synnott, *The Half-Opened Door: Discrimination and Admissions at Harvard, Yale, and Princeton* (Westport, CT: Greenwood, 1979); David O. Levine, *The American College and the Culture of Aspiration, 1915–1940* (Ithaca, NY: Cornell University Press, 1986).

15 Carol S. Gruber, *Mars and Minerva: World War I and the Uses of Higher Learning in America* (Baton Rouge: Louisiana State University Press, 1975).

16 Joel H. Spring, "Psychologists and the War: The Meaning of Intelligence in the Alpha and Beta Tests," *History of Education Quarterly* 12 (Spring 1972): 3–15.

17 John L. Rury, "Race, Region, and Education: An Analysis of Black and White Scores on the 1917 Army Alpha Intelligence Test," *Journal of Negro Education* 57 (Winter 1988): 51–65; Christopher P. Loss, *Between*

Citizens and the State: The Politics of American Higher Education in the 20th Century (Princeton: Princeton University Press, 2012).

18   Carol S. Gruber, *Mars and Minerva: World War I and the Uses of Higher Learning in America* (Baton Rouge: Louisiana State University Press, 1975), p. 213.

19   James Wallace, *Twins in a Two-Room Schoolhouse* (CreateSpace Independent Publishing Platform, 2012).

20   Paul A.C. Koistinen, "The 'Industrial–Military Complex' in Historical Perspective: The InterWar Years," *Journal of American History*, 56 (March 1970): 819–839. See also Earl A. Molander, "Historical Antecedents of Military–Industrial Criticism," *Military Affairs* 40 (April 1976), 60, on specific criticism of the relationship of industry to militarism in World War I. On the Civil War, see Ben Baack and Edward Ray, "The Political Economy of the Origins of the Military–Industrial Complex in the United States," *Journal of Economic History*, 45 (June 1985): 369–375.

21   Rebecca Lowen, "Transforming the University: Administrators, Physicists, and Industrial and Federal Patronage at Stanford, 1935–49," *History of Education Quarterly* 30 (Fall 1991): 365–388.

22   Mary Ann Dzuback, *Robert Maynard Hutchins: Portrait of an Educator* (Chicago: University of Chicago Press, 1991), 216–218.

23   Vannevar Bush, *Science, the Endless Frontier* (Washington, DC: U.S. Government Printing Office, 1945).

24   Francis J. Brown, "Education and Military Defense," *Educational Record* 22 (July 1941), 414.

25   Francis J. Brown, "Education and Military Defense," *Educational Record* 22 (July 1941): 425–426.

26   Ralph A. Sentman, "The Program of Voluntary Education in the Armed Services," in *Higher Education Under War Conditions*, ed. John Dale Russell (Chicago: University of Chicago Press, 1943), 4–5.

27   Ralph A. Sentman, "The Program of Voluntary Education in the Armed Services," in *Higher Education Under War Conditions*, ed. John Dale Russell (Chicago: University of Chicago Press, 1943), 6–7.

28   Earl J. McGrath, "The Off-Duty Education Program of the United States Navy," *Educational Record* 25 (January 1944), 37 on future education, 45 on counseling.

29   Earl J. McGrath, "The Off-Duty Education Program of the United States Navy," *Educational Record* 25 (January 1944): 43. On passage of the G.I. Bill and African Americans, see Milton Greenberg, *The G.I. Bill: The Law That Changed America* (New York: Lickle Publishing, 1997), 16. This aspect of the bill's political history is missing from other works on passage of the G.I. Bill.

30   E.F. Lindquist, "The Use of Tests in the Accreditation of Military Experience and in the Educational Placement of War Veterans," *Educational Record* 25 (October 1944): 358–364.

31   John W. Nason, "What Have We Learned?" *Journal of Higher Education* 15 (June 1944): 29–296.

32   Rupert Wilkinson, *Aiding Students, Buying Students: Financial Aid in America* (Nashville, TN: Vanderbilt University Press, 2005); Jana Nidiffer and Jeffrey P. Bouman, "'The University of the Poor': The University of Michigan's Transition from Admitting Impoverished Students to Studying Poverty, 1870–1910," *American Educational Research Journal* 41(Spring 2004): 35–67.

33   Kevin P. Bower, "'A favored child of the state': Federal Student Aid at Ohio Colleges and Universities, 1934–1943," *History of Education Quarterly* 44 (September 2004): 364–387.

34   Daniel A. Clark, "'The Two Joes Meet–Joe College, Joe Veteran': The G.I. Bill, College Education, and Postwar American Culture," *History of Education Quarterly* 38 (Summer 1998): 165–189. Helen Lefokowitz Horowitz, *Campus Life: Undergraduate Cultures from the End of the Eighteenth Century to the Present* (Chicago: University of Chicago Press, 1988), 184–187.

35   Robert C. Serow, "Policy as Symbol: Title II of the 1944 G.I. Bill Review of Higher Education," *Review of Higher Education* 27, no. 4 (Summer 2004): 481–499; Douglas Craddock, "War, Civil Rights, and Higher Education: African American Vietnam Veterans, The Civil Rights Era, And The G.I. Bill"

(Ed.D. dissertation, University of Alabama, 2017); Christopher P. Loss, *Between Citizens and the State: The Politics of American Higher Education in the 20th Century* (Princeton: Princeton University Press, 2012).

36   *An Apartment for Peggy*, William Perlberg, producer, George Seaton, director, starring Jeanne Crain and William Holden, 1948.

37   Bernard C. Malty, *Strength for the Fight: A History of Black Americans in the Military* (New York: Free Press, 1986); John Dittmer, *Local People: The Struggle for Civil Rights in Mississippi* (Urbana: University of Illinois Press, 1994); Mary L. Dudziak, *Cold War and Civil Rights: Race and the Image of American Democracy* (Princeton: Princeton University Press, 2000).

38   President Dwight D. Eisenhower avoided the issue of education and civil rights, repeatedly procrastinating on enforcing the 1954 and 1955 Brown decisions by the U.S. Supreme Court, and implementing desegregation of Central High School in Little Rock Arkansas only because of his commitment to the U.S. Constitution. See Stanley I. Kutter, "Eisenhower, the Judiciary, and Desegregation: Some Reflections," *Eisenhower: A Centenary Assessment*, ed. Günter Bischoff and Stephen E. Ambrose (Baton Rouge: Louisiana State University Press, 1995), 89. Former Secretary of Health, Education, and Welfare Oveta Culp Hobby exhibited a similar reticence, requesting that the military delay integrating the remaining segregated schools on military bases despite Eisenhower's deadline of September 1955; see Clarence Mitchell, "The Status of Racial Integration in the Armed Services," *Journal of Negro Education*, 23 (Summer 1954): 210. Eisenhower consulted with Hobby about the Little Rock situation—although she had stepped down as HEW Secretary in 1955—and she recommended caution. See Stephen E. Ambrose, *Eisenhower: The President*, vol. 2 (New York: Simon & Schuster, 1984), 423.

39   *Organizing Higher Education for National Defense* (Washington, DC: American Council on Education, 1941), 56.

40   See Walter Francis White, *A Man Called White: The Autobiography of Walter White* (New York, Viking Press, 1948), 330, 331. See also Robert H. Ferrell, *Harry S. Truman: A Life* (Columbia: University of Missouri Press, 1994), 292–293.

41   President's Committee on Civil Rights, *To Secure These Rights: The Report of the President's Committee on Civil Rights* (New York: Simon & Schuster, 1947), 15–16 on groups, 6–9 on four rights.

42   President's Committee on Civil Rights, *To Secure These Rights: The Report of the President's Committee on Civil Rights* (New York: Simon & Schuster, 1947), 63 on Jews, 66 on liberal arts colleges, application questions, and Jews and Blacks, 67 and 72 on medical schools and health care.

43   James D. Anderson, "Race, Meritocracy, and the American Academy during the Immediate Post-World War II Era," *History of Education Quarterly* 33 (Summer 1993): 151–175.

44   Charles S. Padgett, "'Without Hysteria or Unnecessary Disturbance': Desegregation at Spring Hill College, Mobile, Alabama, 1948–1954," *History of Education Quarterly* 41 (Summer 2001): 167–188.

45   Linda M. Perkins, "The First Black Talent Identification Program: The National Scholarship Service and Fund for Negro Students, 1947–1968," *Perspectives on the History of Higher Education* 29 (2012): 173–197.

46   *Higher Education for American Democracy: A Report of the President's Commission on Higher Education*, vol. 1: "Education for a Better Nation and World" (New York: Harper & Brothers, 1948), 8–9.

47   Philo A. Hutcheson, "The 1947 President's Commission on Higher Education and the National Rhetoric on Higher Education Policy," *History of Higher Education Annual 2002* 22 (2003): 91–107; Helen Lefokowitz Horowitz, *Campus Life: Undergraduate Cultures from the End of the Eighteenth Century to the Present* (Chicago: University of Chicago Press, 1988), 187 on the report regarding economic success after college.

48   Charles Dorn, "'A Woman's World': The University of California, Berkeley, During the Second World War," *History of Education Quarterly* 48 (November 2008): 534–564.

49   Eileen H. Tamura, "Value Messages Collide with Reality: Joseph Kurihara and the Power of Informal Education," *History of Education Quarterly* 50 (February 2010): 1–33.

50   Dongbin Kim and John L. Rury, "The Changing Profile of College Access: The Truman Commission and the Enrollment Patterns in the Postwar Era, *History of Education Quarterly* 47 (August 2007): 302–327; Rupert Wilkinson, *Aiding Students, Buying Students: Financial Aid in America* (Nashville, TN: Vanderbilt University Press, 2005).

51   Linda Eisenmann, *Higher Education for Women in Postwar America, 1945–1965* (Baltimore: Johns Hopkins University Press, 2006).

52   Roger Geiger, *To Advance Knowledge: The Growth of American Universities, 1900–1940* (New York: Oxford University Press, 1986) and Roger L. Geiger, *Research and Relevant Knowledge: American Research Universities Since World War II* (Stanford: Stanford University Press, 2004).

53   Clark Kerr, *The Uses of the University* (Cambridge, MA: Harvard University Press, 1963).

54   "The *New York Times* Comments on Beard's Resignation, 1917," in *American Higher Education: A Documentary History*, vol. 2, ed. Richard Hofstadter and Wilson Smith (Chicago: University of Chicago Press, 1961), 886.

55   Jane Sanders, *Cold War on the Campus: Academic Freedom at the University of Washington, 1946–1964*. (Seattle: University of Washington Press, 1979); David P. Gardner, *The California Oath Controversy*. Berkeley: University of California Press, 1967).

56   Ellen W. Schrecker, *No Ivory Tower: McCarthyism and the Universities* (New York: Oxford University Press, 1986).

57   Harold Taylor, "The Dismissal of Fifth Amendment Professors," *The Annals of the American Academy of Political and Social Sciences* 300 (July 1955): 79–86; Sigmund Diamond, *Compromised Campus: The Collaboration of Universities with the Intelligence Community, 1945–1955* (New York: Oxford University Press, 1992); Philo Hutcheson, "McCarthyism and the Professoriate: A Historiographic Nightmare?" *Higher Education: The Handbook of Theory and Research*, vol. 12, ed. John C. Smart (New York: Agathon Press, 1997), 435–460.

58   Marybeth Gasman, "Scylla and Charybdis: Navigating the Waters of Academic Freedom at Fisk University During Charles S. Johnson's Administration (1946–1956)," *American Educational Research Journal* 36 (Winter 1999): 739–758; Kathleen Weiler, "The Case of Martha Deane: Sexuality and Power at Cold War UCLA," *History of Education Quarterly* 47 (November 2007): 470–496; Charles H. McCormick, *This Nest of Vipers: McCarthyism and Higher Education in the Mundel Affair, 1951–52* (Urbana: University of Illinois Press, 1989).

59   Wayne Urban, More Than Science and Sputnik: The National Defense Education Act of 1958 (Tuscaloosa: University of Alabama Press, 2010); Philo A. Hutcheson, *A Professional Professoriate: Unionization, Bureaucratization, and the AAUP* (Nashville: Vanderbilt University Press, 2000), 55, on the AAUP and the loyalty oath.

60   www.aaup.org/report/1940-statement-principles-academic-freedom-and-tenure (retrieved December 13, 2018).

61   Ward Churchill, "The Myth of Academic Freedom: Experiencing the Application of Liberal Principle in a Neoconservative Era," in *Works and Days: Academic Freedom and Intellectual Activism in the Post-9/11 University*, 26–27 (2008–2009): 139–230. See the entire collection of essays in the two volumes of this journal for a variety of perspectives on academic freedom and its interpretations in the past and present.

62   As an example of an early effort to illuminate these tragedies, I recommend Dee Brown, *Bury My Heart at Wounded Knee*. Any edition will do.

63   John Ehle, *Trail of Tears: The Rise and Fall of the Cherokee Nation* (New York: Anchor Books Doubleday, reprint edition 1988).

64   Donal F. Lindsey, *Indians at Hampton Institute, 1877–1923* (Urbana: University of Illinois Press, 1995); Steven Crum, "The Choctaw Nation: Changing the Appearance of American Higher Education, 1830–1907," *History of Education Quarterly* 47 (February 2007): 49–68; Bryan McKinley Jones Brayboy, Angelina E. Castagno, and Jessica A. Solyom, "Introduction," in *Postsecondary Education for American Indian and Alaska Natives*, ed. Bryan McKinley Jones Brayboy, Amy J. Fann, Angelina E. Castagno, and Jessica A. Solyom (San Francisco: John Wiley & Sons, 2012), 6–10. It is instructive that the authors identify those who drafted parts of this manuscript rather than the scholarly practice of identifying authors. This approach raises the important questions, who is the author and how do we define that person?

65   Michael Olivas, "Indian, Chicano, and Puerto Rican Colleges: Status and Issues," *Bilingual Review* 9 (January/April 1982): 36–58.

6

SEX AND LOVE! BEER! FOOTBALL!

And Other Important Student Activities

The range of student activities today is quite amazing, reflecting a myriad of interests on the part of students, faculty members, administrators, and graduates. Indeed, at the University of Alabama there is a club sport for people who fish, a sport with national intercollegiate competition. Interests as wide-ranging as diversity and chess have their clubs on campuses across the nation. This chapter offers an overview of student life from the colonial colleges to the development of so-called major sports, especially football, in the 1990s and early 2000s. In an extension of the previous examination about the rise of deans of women and men, there is also discussion of student services administrators.

One function of historians, one not always welcomed, is the exposure of historical myths. (This is not necessarily a popular act, as in the case of stating that Christopher Columbus did not discover the Americas—he was preceded by thousands of years—and adding that among other things, he and his crew brought European diseases to the natives.) There is a long-standing myth about the history of student affairs personnel, one so powerful that even after students complete a history of higher education course with required readings on the actual, documented history, in ensuing papers students continue to make the same mythical claim. Again and again scholars and higher education administrators state that student services arose as a result of faculty interest in research. Wrong.

In 1937, a committee of the American Council on Education (ACE) published what is now a well-recognized and often-cited report among student services personnel, *The Student Personnel Point of View*. On the first page of the report, the committee members stated:

> A long and honorable history stands behind this point of view. Until the last three decades of the nineteenth century interest in the whole student dominated the thinking of the great majority of the leaders and faculty members of American colleges. The impact of a number of social forces upon American society following the Civil War, however, directed the interest of most of the strong personalities of our colleges and universities away from the needs of the individual student to an emphasis, through scientific research, upon the extension of the boundaries of knowledge. The pressures upon faculty members to contribute to this growth of knowledge shifted the direction of their thinking to a preoccupation with subject matter and to a neglect of the student as an individual.[1]

There is no citation for this claim. Nor can there be. While there was indeed an important rise of interest in the possibilities of research and scholarship in the late 1800s and early 1900s (a history discussed in detail in the following chapter on research universities), it was not even close to widespread. Consider the Midwest in the 1800s as discussed in Chapter 3; the large number of small colleges had few if any resources for faculty research in the natural and physical sciences, nor did teaching expectations allow for substantial time for scholarship in any of the disciplines and fields of study. Almost all land grant universities had small enrollments, and most of them were unable to meet the expectations for practical science because both staffing and research knowledge in the basic sciences were limited. In the Northeast, it is too easy to ignore patterns of resistance to research—and not simply at small institutions, but also at universities such as Yale and Princeton, whose presidents had sustained and sometimes heated public arguments with the president of Harvard University (an advocate of expanding the elective system, which reinforced research by allowing for specialization) that he had enjoyed as an undergraduate at Harvard in the early 1850s.[2] The Yale and Princeton presidents, in contrast, advocated a focus on undergraduate education and the whole student.[3]

In addition, the report added, "These officers were appointed first to relieve administrators and faculties of problems of discipline."[4] To some degree this is an accurate claim, but it has its limitations. As Jana Nidiffer has illustrated, the early deans of women were appointed in order to work with women students on a number of issues, in great part because male administrators and faculty members had little sense of what to do with women. Their responsibilities included at the outset such duties as housing for women and academic advising as well as discipline. Robert Schwartz notes that although the early deans of men had responsibility for discipline, they were also responsible for the development of character (which could assist them in avoiding discipline but also meant that they worked with students who were already self-disciplined). Nidiffer, Schwartz, and Helen Horowitz all make it clear that most of the early deans of men or women typically came from the faculty (or in the case of deans of women newly appointed to their positions, they often negotiated for faculty appointments). More telling, as Eleanor Schetlin argues in an old but noteworthy article, these deans often came from a Progressive tradition. They were faculty members who believed in the development of the whole person, a highly important goal for Progressive educators, and their commitment was not the result of faculty research interests among colleagues.[5] Often these positions then and thereafter were far more the result of new populations on campuses or increasing in size on campuses—initially, white women—as well as the development of a more secular, broader interpretation of the whole person. The interpretation of the whole person has held many different meanings since the late 1800s, but disciplining students remains a challenge.

It is clear that faculty members were long loath to engage in student discipline review and action—a tradition that continues today for both faculty and staff members. It is no easy matter to dismiss a student. Veysey says of the late 1800s that despite the extensive codification of rules of conduct, "practice often proved far less stringent than theory." This attitude is highlighted in the Yale Report of 1828, in which the authors stated that the college had a responsibility to act as the parent for its students, using "kind and persuasive influence," although admitting, "There may be those whom nothing but the arm of law can reach." Faculty members were distancing themselves from discipline well before the rise of research, assigning much of that responsibility at Yale, for example, to tutors, young faculty members with temporary appointments. In fact, the practice of granting forgiveness to those who confessed their transgressions, an artful way of avoiding the vicissitudes of discipline, or in the case of expulsions, lessening the effect of the punishment by allowing readmission after one semester and a confession, dates back to the 1700s, as Kathryn Moore documented in her examination of Harvard's treatment of rule-breaking students. It did not take the rise of research and scholarship for faculty members to turn away from discipline, it took centuries of distasteful experience with making decisions about disciplinary cases, particularly given what Veysey termed, in quoting a 1910 letter, "that awful chasm,'" between students and professors, a chasm deepened by persistent cheating, well documented by scholars and a reminder that the academic evaluation systems instituted at colleges in the late 1700s and early 1800s were far more important to the faculty and president than to students.[6] A slightly more forgiving but equally telling appraisal of student life comes from an ethnographic examination of students at Rutgers in the 1980s; a junior male student declared, "'Class is the tediousness that the student body goes through between weekends.'"[7] Another common student tradition serves as a reminder that not all is academic at colleges and universities, including at ones that enroll high-achieving students, well-organized student pranks at different institutions—both Caltech and MIT seem to be at the forefront of such efforts. One of the most visible was in celebration of the 100th anniversary of Hollywood, when Caltech students changed the world-famous sign to read, "CALTECH."[8] Regardless of organized extracurricular activities, discussed below, students have long pursued informal activities, and this chapter focuses on sex and love as well as beer. Football and other organized activities receive attention later in the chapter.

SEX AND LOVE

A book on undergraduate students at Rutgers in the 1980s has two refreshing and blunt chapters, a topic often discussed in terms of wellness among campus staff and faculty members but hardly ever in terms of its reality: "Sex" and "Sex in College." The opening of the chapter on sex notes, in the words of a senior, that if he had spent as much time thinking about studying as much as he had sex, he would have been on the Dean's List. Despite the centrality of sex and love in the lives of young adults on college and university campuses, little has been written about those experiences, although there is a developing body of historical knowledge about same-sex relationships on campuses. Even for what is one of the earliest regulations about sex and gender, the 1745 rule at Yale prohibiting, in a long list of forbidden actions, "wearing woman's apparel," there is no stated reason for why that particular prohibition was necessary. What is clear, however, is that institutions of higher education were concerned about sexual activities; the same rules dictated that students guilty of fornication would be expelled.[9] Such a regulation indicates institutional concern about students and sex, and a later example shows that such concern was based on student behavior. As an odd example, Lexington, Kentucky was the home of a nationally known madame in the late 1800s and early 1900s; it appears likely that many young men at the University of Kentucky and Transylvania University experienced their first sexual encounters at one of her homes. Even the novelist Thomas Wolfe, in his semi-autobiographical novel, *Look Homeward, Angel*, notes just such an experience for the protagonist, a college student at the time.

Increasing enrollments of women students reshaped the sexual activities on campuses to some degree. Historical examinations of the advent of women students on coeducational campuses often note a transition from lone voyagers (not just faculty members, but students too) to participants in the dating rituals between men and women students, replete with faculty controls over holding hands, dancing, and other forms of public displays. Women students were often stereotyped as seeking the Mrs. Degree, not even necessarily planning to finish college but rather to find a husband. That expectation was evident at both coeducational institutions and women's colleges, and even in cases at coeducational institutions where there was some support for women in campus, problems could arise, as Lynn Gordon notes about the University of Chicago:

> Men and women had separate student activities, with the men dominating campus life, but the hostility men students directed toward women at California, Cornell, Rochester, Wesleyan, and Stanford did not exist at Chicago. And yet, when Chicago's male faculty became upset over women's prominence on their campus, they turned to further separatism as the answer and voted for classroom segregation.[10]

Not only was there coeducational involvement in extracurricular activities at normal schools and some private colleges in the Midwest, but also there were romantic relationships, or the early stages of romance; in the case of the former, it seems to have occurred as the institutions more and more resembled four-year colleges and universities. Discussion about women and their experiences on coeducational campuses often highlights their separation from male students in many activities. For example, while coeducation was on the rise in the postbellum era and often women students experienced marginalization, there were exceptions, such as occurred at Carleton and St. Olaf Colleges in Minnesota, which both opened as coeducational institutions in 1867 and 1875, respectively. While men were more likely to enroll in the classical division at Carleton and in the college division at St. Olaf and some elements of the extracurriculum were divided by gender—such as croquet at St. Olaf (as curious as that might seem)—other activities such as the student newspaper had both men and women. Only at Carleton, however, were women students substantially involved in the political debates sponsored by literary societies. Dances were of course coeducational, but at a time when single men and women faced many restrictions on public displays that even approached affection, such as holding hands, indicating the possibility of romances between men and women students.[11]

Heterosexual relationships had a different dimension in the South well into the 1900s, however, with chaperones common at dances and in the case of one white women's college, the requirement in the 1920s that a young man would have to meet the dean of women before he could visit a student. At some of those institutions, dances were not permitted until the 1930s (reminding those who know the South of the quip that Southern Baptists disdained sex because it was too much like dancing while lying down). Not surprisingly, women students were not allowed to drink, although the prohibition occasionally resulted in rebellion, including in one instance a series of eggnog parties in the mid-1920s. More than intellectual development, the deans of women favored social growth, preserving the image of the Southern Belle given their deep-rooted fears as the South industrialized and the African American intellectual movement gained momentum as part of the Harlem Renaissance.[12] Perhaps even more concerning than preserving a region's definition of a woman were same-sex relationships.

Sexual identity is hidden under the centuries, although by the early 1900s, increasing use of definitions that identified same-sex relationships began to shape college student life and institutional responses. Previously, particularly among white women, what are now sometimes called homosocial relationships, whether among students at Southern white women's colleges or faculty members at Northern white women's colleges (the Wellesley marriages), were generally accepted, but the developing identification of homosexual relationships starting in the late 1800s had no such acceptance. The increasing identification of same-sex sexual relationships resulted not only in the classification and definition of those as a psychiatric disorder until 1986, but also college and university efforts to uncover those relationships, particularly among men, and to punish them. Two examples, at Harvard and later at three state universities, show the extent and the determination of administrators and faculty members to halt same-sex affection.

The 1920 suicide of a Harvard freshman, whose suicide note identified himself as gay, led to a secret investigation ordered by the president, A. Lawrence Lowell, and a purge of gay students who had dormitory parties with each other and men from outside the Harvard community. As a result of the investigation, another student committed suicide, and it ruined the lives of many other students.[13] Later, during World War II and shortly thereafter, administrators at the University of Texas, the University of Wisconsin, and the University of Missouri not only identified gay men or, consonant with the vague identification of un-American evident in McCarthyism, men who were suspected of homosexual behaviors. In this case, the mechanism of discipline is important; the authorities at Texas expelled students and faculty members suspected of homosexual activity. Wisconsin ensured that there were criminal investigations through the police for those men known to be homosexual and psychiatric assessments accompanied by university administrative review for those men suspected of homosexuality, some of whom were expelled, never to receive a degree. In the case of Missouri, following the dismissal of a faculty member for being a leader of a "homosexual 'ring,'" student services administrators visited the University of Wisconsin and concluded that a committee whose membership included professors and a psychiatrist would allow the institution to deal with what it saw as an ongoing problem. One young man, Richard Jackson, drew the attention of the committee. His activities were suspect, as was his family background (his father had left the home when Jackson was younger, his mother was accused of having mental problems), and the committee had him expelled. In a very important example, Jackson and his mother fought the decision, and although they did not change the committee members' minds, the principles of their arguments are telling. Consistent with the higher ideals of democracy, such as occurred with the Double V movement, as Nash and Silverman highlight, "They argued that the real threats to democracy were spurious charges, and too much power and control in the wrong people's hands going unquestioned."[14]

Such concerns drew the attention of more than college authorities. An examination of fraternities at elite institutions concluded that their members attempted to affirm their heterosexuality by having sex with women, whether welcomed or forced. They also sought means to exclude gay men, an effort that was not entirely successful.[15]

Troubling all of these values and behaviors is the question of love, or who loves whom. Patrick Dilley's book, *Queer Man on Campus* offers a typology of identities that range from anonymous sex to loving relationships, arguing against the view that homosexual identity develops in a singular manner, instead arguing for a range not dissimilar from heterosexual relationships. One substantial difference was the need for anonymity, since peers, faculty members, and administrators were fully capable of such disapproval that the student would face not just scorn and isolation, but all too often dismissal, as noted above, although restrictions on heterosexual interactions persisted well into the 1960s at some institutions, with women students having a curfew for both weeknights and weekend nights. The questions about love and sex for same-sex relationships receive illuminating attention in a student's conference paper. As Lizzie Emerson argues in "What's Sex Got to Do with It: Reconsidering Women's Relationships with Women on College Campuses in the Late Nineteenth and Early Twentieth Centuries," framing the woman-to-woman relationships as homosocial rather than as acts of love relegates that relationship to either a temporary status or to one of lesser commitment.[16] Students have different sexual identities and different loving identities, and college campuses are a place where they explore those identities. Campuses are also a place where drinking beer happens, unfortunately all too often connected with behavior problems.

BEER

Beer and its varied relatives (wine, alcohol, illegal drugs, prescription drugs) have long been a favorite of college and university students. The roots of student drinking for the United States are as old as higher education in the British colonies; one of Harvard's early buildings was a brewery (based on the societal reasoning that God created alcohol and Jesus drank wine), and the first headmaster (a position later named president), Nathaniel Eaton, lost his position in great part because the food was bad and there was no beer for the students. The tradition of student drinking actually dates back to the medieval universities; in what is clearly an early rendition of an orientation manual for German university students, from 1480, among the many issues addressed is how a student learns academic lessons and also learns to discuss "the quality of beer in university towns."[17]

Although beer was accepted, harder drink was not, and the Yale Laws of 1745 indicated fines for any students bringing onto campus or frequenting taverns with "any quantity of Rum, Wine, Brandy or other strong Liquor [*sic*]."[18] Almost a century later, West Point had its own problem with strong liquor, known as the Eggnog Riot. The Academy superintendent, Colonel Sylvanus Thayer (who had overseen the recruitment of the mathematics professors whose pedagogy emphasized both academic knowledge and character), forbade alcohol on campus in 1826. In college-student fashion, shortly before Christmas cadets smuggled alcohol onto campus in order to make eggnog. After imbibing an apparently sufficient quantity, the cadets rioted, breaking furniture and even drawing swords (with no injuries), and the Academy expelled 19 of them. Drinking continued to be an important student activity in early 1800s and thereafter.

An in-depth examination of student drinking by Michael Hevel, focused on the period from the 1820s to the 1930s, reveals that college student drinking tended to be similar to societal expectations about who should drink. In addition, while colleges and universities at times disciplined students, the punishment was rarely severe, despite health problems and destructive behavior (including interference with academic performance). Finally, drinking had a great deal to do with privilege, evident in both white fraternities and white male students in general. One author asserts that by the middle of the 1900s, those fraternity men who drank the most were considered to be "the most accomplished and the most masculine," and Hevel notes that the portrayal of drinking in college novels mirrored race (white) and gender (men), and the practice of drinking among white men, particularly those of privilege, were followed by white women and white men of lesser means (class).[19]

In more recent years, college student drinking appears to be more widespread. As a student wrote for his dissertation, on the day after GameDay at campuses with revenue-producing football, the grounds are strewn with empty beer cans, liquor bottles, and trash (one might add, perhaps used condoms too), a far cry from the heady declarations of academic pursuits and contributing to the global good.[20]

FOOTBALL

Students are not necessarily calm participants in their non-academic pursuits. Raucous student activities date back to the Middle Ages, and the tradition continued in the colonies. Early food riots occurred at Harvard, and it is likely that the first student protest in the colonial era was the Butter Riot at Harvard in 1766 when students in protest of rancid butter walked off campus and dined in town. A salient example of student enthusiasm and institutional response in the Early Republic occurred at the University of Pennsylvania, when the provost introduced grades in order to control student misbehaviors by rewarding competition and good performance. During the nineteenth century, college faculties and presidents sought different means to capture the enthusiasm of students and channel it into more civilized activities. As interest in the well-balanced citizen, free of the excesses clearly visible in uneducated populations, increased, so too did the interest in organized athletics. Manliness, as well as the challenges that women's athletics faced and offered, became important and provided control over unorganized physical activity such as the class contests that involved physical violence, noted in the Introduction.[21] One remarkably curious example fully illustrates the coexistence of academics and athletics on campuses.

There are two large public universities in Berkeley, California, existing on the same campus at the same time. One is called Berkeley, a high-profile academic institution, in some areas unbelievably selective in undergraduate admissions and with many highly regarded and internationally recognized academic graduate programs. The other is called Cal, and it has Division I athletics with teams that have often done well in such sports as football, men's basketball, and especially women's softball. Sports broadcasters almost never, if ever, refer to Berkeley. Academics rarely refer to Cal. There is perhaps no better example of how football and other revenue-producing (interestingly, typically called "major") college sports are manifestations of a deep divide within institutions of higher education. Roger Geiger has captured one highly important reason for this divide, a reminder of the more utilitarian nature of the operations of colleges and universities, noting that in the early 1900s, enrollment growth at large universities meant they were able to fund operations at both the undergraduate and the specialized, less revenue-productive, graduate levels. Loyal graduates also meant increased political support and alumni/alumnae giving, and it is clearly arguable that loyalty increasingly found a strong base in intercollegiate athletics.[22]

Football likely began with a Rutgers–Princeton game in 1869, but that game bore little resemblance to the contemporary version. Walter Camp, head coach at Yale, was instrumental in developing rules for the U.S. version of what had been an English schoolboys' game similar to rugby; by 1880 the game included the line of scrimmage and the snap from center. The early decades of the game were rugged, at times brutal, and there was a now infamous meeting called by President Theodore Roosevelt in 1905, with representatives from Yale, Princeton, and Harvard, to reprimand them for the violent nature of the sport. Deaths were not all that uncommon, and the paucity of rules also meant that players included faculty members and paid athletes. Despite those conditions, college football was becoming very popular, overtaking older sports such as crew as the nation's favorite, and by 1910, Yale's annual revenue from football was nearly $73,000. Camp's approach at Yale was professional, with daily coaches' meetings and a clear hierarchy of coaches; he likened success in football to success in modern business.[23] Football led the way in terms of popularity and financial gain, while other organized sports became increasingly popular and available.

Athletics were important for college women, although at some institutions expectations about their femininity created boundaries. A historical examination of athletics at 13 women's colleges in the South offers the conclusion that with the exception of Sweet Briar College in Virginia, the other 12 (in Virginia, North Carolina, South

Carolina, and Georgia) did not begin intercollegiate athletics competition until the late twentieth century. The two institutions deepest in the South, Agnes Scott College (Decatur, Georgia) and Wesleyan College (Macon, Georgia) did not start intercollegiate conference play until the end of the twentieth century. According to the author, "Factors such as a dominant patriarchy, strongly emphasized traditional behaviors for women, and even the resistance of physical educators played a significant role in the entry of women's colleges into highly competitive athletics."[24] Young women at other institutions such as normal schools in Wisconsin in the late 1800s approached intercollegiate athletics with more institutional support. And Massachusetts women apparently played basketball with vigor; James Naismith, inventor of basketball, refereed an early college women's basketball game and supposedly declared that a player had questioned his ancestry. Athletic enthusiasm took hold across a variety of colleges and universities.

In the early 2000s, it might seem impossible to think of a Saturday afternoon on campus without a marching band playing rousing songs as fans—in many cases numbering over 100,000—walk to a stadium to watch a college football game. Such events as Homecoming, inviting alumni and alumnae to return to campus and celebrate memories of their college years, typically center on a home football game (colleges and universities without football teams may well use a basketball game in similar fashion). Preparations for home football games at institutions with highly ranked teams can begin days before the game, involve hundreds of staff members, and indeed, dot the campus with portable toilets. Tailgating, the art and craft of providing food, beverage, and entertainment before, during, and after the game, has become immensely popular. Even at small colleges, Saturdays in the fall often represent the enthusiasm of and for football. Two troubling characteristics deserve attention in this matter. First, there is a Division I conference that does not allow its member institutions to offer athletic scholarships. It is the Ivy League, despite the rough beginnings in the 1800s at some of those institutions. (It is ironic that generally people refer to the Ivy League in terms of the academic prestige of its members, even though it began in 1954 as an intercollegiate athletic conference, suggesting another form of the duality evident in the Berkeley-Cal naming.) With no athletics scholarships, those institutions are most clearly offering amateur athletics, but it is important to know that the origin of the definition of amateur for the modern Olympics was those who did not work with their hands.[25] Second, as disquieting as the notion of who can afford to be amateur is the century-old problem of reforming revenue-producing college sports. As John Thelin carefully details in *Games Colleges Play*, from the late 1920s to the 1990s a seemingly endless number of national commissions issued reports on how to reform major sports, a process with a sense of renewed urgency in the 1950s when television slowly made its way onto playing fields and into people's homes as well as into revenue streams and institutional popularity.[26] The mass of rules now affecting intercollegiate athletics, coaches, and athletics departments is one of the consequences of those reports, but it does seem that for every reform, another problem in another area arises as in the 2010s, when the Federal Bureau of Investigation became involved in investigating criminal activity involving corporate athletic gear at some institutions with revenue-producing sports, resulting in indictments.

By the end of the 1800s, concern about middle-class status included the goal of manliness. The middle class could not allow the rough-and-ready image of the man because it was not respectable, and the goal of a man who was of sound mind and in good shape, known for decades as (in Latin) *mens sana in corpore sano*. Physical fitness became an important goal, furthering goals of healthy behaviors and, administrators and faculty members hoped, dampening the brutal enthusiasm of young men often exhibited on campuses in the 1800s; both intercollegiate athletics and physical exercise for all men were important. At the University of North Carolina in the early 1900s, when it was consciously preparing itself as a modern university, "the emerging ideal of white American masculinity as physically robust, powerful, and scientifically engineered had taken root."[27] Manliness and prestige went hand in hand, starting in the late 1800s and early 1900s, for many college administrators and faculty members. Furthermore, the question of who is manly and in what ways is an insistent problem. A deeply troubling illustration of this question appears in an examination of the rise of intercollegiate athletics at black colleges between World War I and World War II. Leaders at many of those institutions as well as leaders in the African American communities nationally and regionally saw athletics as a space where there were opportunities to further dialogues about equality between African Americans and Whites. In addition, participation in sports would provide opportunities for the development of the whole person, a well-balanced physical body and the discipline and cooperation considered to be part of participation in organized sports (as opposed to the mayhem of beating each other bloody). Even magazine editors as notable as W.E.B. Du Bois advocated athletic competition. Nevertheless, while white educators and journalists trumpeted the virtues of manliness, balance, and character as the result of such competition, black athletes were not decorated as such but rather faced "allusions to survival in some distant jungle or to a distinctive anatomy and physiology." (Not surprisingly, black colleges also recruited athletes as the white colleges had, ignoring academic credentials, for example, in order to field a competitive team; those institutions were quite aware of the prestige available with winning teams.) Patrick Miller concludes his article with a telling statement, "there is substantial reason to be skeptical about the efficacy of sport to overcome the formidable prejudices that continue to clutter the social landscape." Yet winning and race had other dimensions as well, reminding the astute observer that these events are not simple matters to be read in a straight line. For example, the Mississippi State men's basketball team's successes in the early 1960s challenged what was called "the unwritten law," the understanding in Mississippi that any public institution's white intercollegiate team that competed with teams with African Americans would lose state funding. The team and the coach and their supporters eventually succeeded in competing in the national tournament, against a team with African Americans; while it lost the game, Mississippi took another step toward desegregation through a winning intercollegiate team, although it was a small step. Furthermore, some authors argue that revenue-producing sports have opened some doors for minoritized populations, especially African Americans.[28]

In addition, winning had another meaning, the increase in visibility as a means to prestige. The development of football at California State Colleges in the early 1950s is instructive. Even when a president was resistant to adding football, local boosters and students and some professors pushed hard enough that the president would acquiesce, and the institution would adopt intercollegiate football. Furthermore, it was not simply the adoption of football, as conference membership mattered as well—in both the case of the sport and the conference, supporters argued that visibility and fundraising would improve with the addition of the sport and entrance into the right conference.[29] In terms of fundraising, the connections between having a sport and being able to increase donations are unclear, unless the institution has a consistently winning Division I record in revenue-producing sports, and as a result, for decades only about 20 percent of Division I institutions make money on intercollegiate athletics. In terms of visibility, the increasing prominence of television not only accentuated the financial temptations evident in the FBI investigations but also the recognition of many colleges and universities; in 2018–2019 there were 40 college football bowl games, even though many were sparsely attended.

Football as well as men's basketball continue to dominate the public imagination about colleges and universities, while sports such as women's softball have developed their own widespread and enthusiastic fans. The rise of the Subway Alumni, Notre Dame fans who had not attended the institution, began after Notre Dame's defeat of Army in a 1919 football game; at times institutions were even more deliberate about the rise of visibility and prestige, as when officials at the University of Georgia decided to play Yale in football in 1927. Georgia's victory over the Northern football powerhouse resulted in national recognition, and boosters of institutions of higher education continue to demand more participation and winning. In regard to the revenue-producing sports, they are not without their foibles; even the Marx Brothers recognized the problems of college football and eligibility rules in their 1932 movie, *Horse Feathers*.

OTHER IMPORTANT STUDENT ACTIVITIES

Beginning with literary and debate societies in the earliest years of U.S. higher education, students have organized into formal organizations to express their interests and, in many cases, establish identities. Historians of higher education continue to note the lack of research on students and their organizations, although the literature is slowly growing. The following discussion on student protests, student government, and on-campus life in dormitories and fraternities and sororities offers some clear characteristics of the history of students.

Students have long found means to identify themselves in campus organizations in a variety of ways. In the 1800s, many students took seriously the academic possibilities of the extracurriculum, forming debating and literary societies that were independent of the classroom and, often, the faculty. Initially for white men, and then for white women and African Americans, these societies allowed students to discuss and debate events of the day. The rise of black college debating societies is informative, as their members established an equality of intellect with white debaters. Students attempting to engage contemporary issues had, however, at times had less substantial meanings at medieval universities.

Student riots, often town-gown riots, were not uncommon in the Middle Ages, and often enough the exuberance was centered in displeasure with local lodging and food and turned violent; one account indicates that town-gown riots in Oxford resulted in deaths.[30] Such outcomes did not disappear over the centuries, although food fights have usually been of far less intensity in the United States. Although Thomas Jefferson wished for a state university that would educate the most talented gentlemen of the state of Virginia, in the 1820s, student duels and even assaults on professors there were commonplace. The same occurred at the University of Alabama. Even where violence against fellow students or professors did not occur, student disruptions of institutional life occurred. The Second Great Awakening, beginning in the late 1700s and continuing into the 1820s, resulted in revivals on campuses, even on occasion shutting down the institution. Student political activism in the United States has roots in the Early Republic, with the reminder that the events at Dartmouth College included a battle, with axes, between students and professors. Protests such as these protests, whether in the distant or recent past, are important reminders that very often students are creating their identities, and often those are identities they want to shape in and against the context of other powerful identities at the center of the institution or society. In fact, the demise of *in loco parentis* began with a U.S. Supreme Court decision in 1961, *Dixon v. Alabama*, which had nothing to do with such matters as underage drinking on campus or such social matters. The president of Alabama State College expelled six black students for participating in civil rights demonstrations but claimed he expelled them for other reasons. The U.S. Supreme Court ruled that the six students had the right of due process, and the dismissal had violated their rights. (Thurgood Marshall, a lead attorney in many NAACP civil rights cases and eventually a U.S. Supreme Court justice, was one of the attorneys for the students.) Such historical incidents are not, as should be evident to anyone learning the history of higher education through the reading of this book, simply place-name-date crap. They speak to larger issues in higher education, both past and present. Re-thinking the meaning of *in loco parentis* leads to a more reflective stance on the work of student services personnel as well as the meanings of student life. *In loco parentis* stood upon a paternalism in this case that had to do with race and not simply the authority of the parent.

A heavy-handed perspective on black college presidents is that they were quick to silence protest when in fact they often found ways to develop resistance through such efforts as speakers and quiet subversion. While some faced unrelenting pressure to keep students in line, a threat with special weight for presidents of public black colleges, others were even forthright in their efforts to encourage students to participate in civil rights protests, most notably Willa Player at Bennett College in Greensboro, North Carolina, who even told the young women jailed for their activities that they should stay in jail to illustrate the principles of their protests and brought the students their homework—this at an institution that prided itself on developing Bennett Belles. The Bennett students' efforts included organizing for the famous 1960 Greensboro sit-in at the Woolworth's lunch counter. (Of note here is the fact that the 1960 Greensboro protest was not the first such sit-in; for example, Wichita, Kansas, had just such a demonstration in 1958.) In cases where administrators and professors were not consistently supportive, as was the case at Spelman College, nevertheless a small number of students participated in civil rights demonstrations in the late 1950s and 1960s, a few even being arrested. At some black colleges, presidents found ways to support reflection and discussion about equality through the extracurriculum: Benjamin Mays was adept at using guest speakers to encourage Morehouse College students to think about, and act upon, means to equality.[31]

Some student organizational types have offered students both the opportunity to establish an identity and, at times, to protest for broader recognition of that identity. For example, the first chartered student organization for gay men developed at Columbia in 1967, and some of its members were committed to protest as a means to establish their identity; nevertheless, some institutions (including the University of Missouri in the mid-1970s) attempted to shutter those groups.[32] Protests by same-sex students took on perhaps an unwitting attire of the past and the 1745 Yale laws; after decades of drag as performance (including skits and theatre productions for men as women at men's colleges and women as men at women's colleges) beginning in the early 1900s, it metamorphosized into protest in the late 1960s and 1970s.[33] At times the protests regarding identity resulted in presidential change, as occurred at Gallaudet University. In one week in 1988, students led protests against the selection of a hearing president at the only institution of higher education for hard-of-hearing and deaf students in the United States. They attracted national media and Congressional attention given the institution's location in Washington, DC, and they employed some artful ways of protest, such as driving school buses to the University's gated entrance, shutting the gates, and deflating the bus tires to block the entrance to the campus. As a result of their well-organized protests, the governing board agreed to appoint a deaf president.[34] There is also a remarkable video online that includes a shot of bewildered DC police officers trying to communicate with the deaf students while the students gleefully use American Sign Language with each other.

At times a minoritized population would develop an organization focused more on networking in order to further recognition of its identity. An early Mexican American organization at colleges and universities—public and private, two-year and four-year—occurred in southern California, the Mexican American movement from mid-1930s to 1950. Roots of the group were in meetings encouraged by the YMCA in an effort to work with Mexican Americans in their communities. The college organization established a sense of place on campuses through meetings and a newspaper (*The Mexican Voice*) that provided the opportunity for young Mexican American men and women college students to discuss possibilities for opportunities in Mexican American communities and culture. This activity happened "a generation before Mexican American professors, students, and activists pushed for and established the first Department of Chicano Studies at California State University at Los Angeles in 1968."[35] The early movement leading to a more formal place on a campus is characteristic of these efforts to establish an identity.

The most visible of student protests in the post-World War II era occurred from the mid-1960s to the early 1970s. While their origin on some campuses had more to do with the civil rights movement or, in the case of University of California, Berkeley, with university administrators such as Clark Kerr placing restrictions on free speech and assembly, much of the activity was in response to the nation's war in Vietnam. In other instances, students organized in ways reflective of the Mexican American movement in the 1950s, establishing identity and then moving toward protest leading to formal organizations. Disabled students at the University of California, Berkeley, came together in 1968, and in what echoes the claims of Dartmouth students in the early 1800s, they "found themselves positioned at the collision between institutional paternalism and personal freedom, living a tenuous balance between social control and self-determination." Facing a campus with virtually no access for disabled students, such as those using wheelchairs, they pressured administrators, especially those in direct contact with students, in the midst of the radical student protests at Berkeley in the 1960s, although they did not form coalitions with those protestors (attempts at such coalitions among protestors did not usually succeed for long). They focused on establishing control of disability rights, seeking a means to avoid the dehumanization that they experienced in the everyday routines established for them by nondisabled university employees and government officials. Their activism led to a federal grant and a student fee that resulted in a program for disabled students, and in addition their work eventually resulted in President Jimmy Carter finally issuing regulations for Section 504 of the 1973 Federal Educational Privacy and Rights Act, the section that provided advocacy and a grievance process for the disabled in educational institutions.[36] Asian American students at the University of California Los Angeles (UCLA) began their organizational efforts by establishing a newspaper, *Gidra*, in 1969. It contested the stereotypes of Asian Americans are unfeeling and "taciturn," and as members of a "model minority" (despite that naming, Asian American students at Ivy League institutions in the 1980s experienced discrimination much like Jews had in the early 1900s, the latter discussed in more detail regarding medical school admission and then the research universities). Reflecting on what had happened with their identities in the process of Americanization, the students drew upon ideas from the Black Power movement of the late 1960s (discussed shortly) but developed their broad ethnic identity, including the recognition of the multiple identities in the naming of Asian American while also recognizing the power of unity, a drive that led to the establishment of Asian American studies programs. They also identified with the Vietnamese in the midst of the war on their soil, contesting U.S. involvement in the war, and like other similar groups, evidenced the expansion of identities beyond the black–white construction. Another example of the focus on education and connections with the community occurred among Vietnamese American students in California in the 1980s and 1990s.[37] The discussion of the Mexican American movement also reflects establishing identity beyond the black–white conception of majority–minority relations, and that effort was part of a larger effort to create a place on campuses across the nation. While African Americans had been developing black colleges for a century and had long been part of the legal meanings of the federal and some states governments, for the most part Latinx did not have that identification except in immigration legislation, a situation that began to change during the administration of President Lyndon Baines Johnson, who had taught for a year at a segregated school for Mexican Americans. Latinx students acted upon their developing identity in the mid-1960s, primarily but not only in the Southwest as part of the larger movement and at a time when, in a sentence that seems to span across gender, race and ethnicity, and socioeconomic class,

> Not content to accept the glacial pace of reform efforts in Washington, Latino activists pushed elected leaders and appointees within the Johnson and Nixon administrations for a national agenda focused on a variety of political, economic, and social issues, including higher education.

Benefits from the activism included increased college attendance among Latinx. Yet as the authors noted, the gains that began in the 1960s slowed in the 2000s, a reminder that progress is most certainly not linear or continuously progressive. Furthermore, the late development of Hispanic-Serving Institutions as well as the opportunities offered by community colleges that have low transfer rates, to four-year institutions that are the primary avenue to adult success, has inhibited the expansion of opportunity.[38]

Events at Columbia University in the spring of 1968 illustrate the complexities of student protests. The university decided to build a gymnasium in a park that local African American residents used, and Columbia students protested that decision through the actions of two student groups, the white Students for a Democratic Society and the Student Afro-American Society. The white students sought to radicalize their peers, an important step in organizing protests against the Vietnam War and what they called the Establishment, and the Student Afro-American Society focused on affirming its connections with the neighborhood African Americans; the two groups began to shut down campus operations by occupying a university building. The Student Afro-American Society members forced the white student protestors out, however, establishing their occupation as a counter to the university's decision in effect to occupy the local park, and after some indecision, the white protestors occupied the offices of President Kirk. When Columbia halted construction of the gym, the black protestors left their building peacefully, but in contrast, the white protestors ruined the president's offices. Although other black student protests often had a great deal to do with institutions' educational policies, including eventually successful demands to establish black studies programs, the Columbia black students directly engaged the local black community and gained the support of nationally known African American protest leaders such as H. Rap Brown. Rather than creating a radical community, as the members of the Students for Democratic Society hoped, the black student protestors at Columbia recognized their connections with the community, reflective of the efforts of black and white students in the civil rights movement protests earlier in the decade. Despite calls for other consequences, by and large both groups of protestors faced few sanctions.[39] The apparent solidarity of African American students at Columbia was not necessarily characteristic of African American student societies across the nation's campuses, as Joy Ann Williamson documented in *Black Power on Campus* and her examination of African American students at the University of Illinois in the late 1960s and early 1970s, which is also reminds readers that such activism was evident in the 1920s when students at Fisk University protested yet another appointment of a white man as president. Those students did succeed at convincing the University to recruit more African American students, to establish a campus center and a research program, but not in establishing an African American studies program.[40] Across a number of communities, progress seemed to be coming in efforts to gain not just access but also engagement in curriculum and other matters.

Deadly consequences, however, faced white students at Kent State University and black students at Jackson State University in 1970 (as had African American students previously at North Carolina A&T University, Southern University, and South Carolina State), and the anti-war protests, and protests in general, lost most of their momentum after the deaths at the hands of the National Guard in the case of Kent State and state patrol officers at Jackson State. Smaller organized groups continue to pursue such goals as access and fuller engagement, often with success such as recognition among and for gender identities, but the organizing of large-scale highly activist (or even confrontational) movements has by and large dissipated.

In less violent matters, such activities as student government have a long tradition at U.S. colleges and universities, beginning either at William and Mary in the late 1700s or the University of Virginia in the 1820s. (Prior to that time, colonial colleges by and large did not allow for any form of student government.) Their origins were spread across a variety of student organizations, such as "literary and debating societies, as well as honor societies and class officers," and they serve as a good example of what students sought in formal activities. (So too would student newspapers, as well as other areas of student interest.) Each provided students with opportunities for combination and supplemented or extended the curriculum into student life, and following the American Revolution, students increasingly declared that they too had rights, as occurred at the literary society at Dartmouth in the 1810s, many times as a statement in opposition to the multiple institutional rules they faced as students, rules that often were intended to dictate the conduct of their lives for the entire day and night. Honors organizations began in the late 1700s and by the early 1800s they were becoming increasingly formal; there were occasions when the organization would petition for control of student discipline and there were even student-led discipline tribunals at some institutions, based on honor codes. As literary and debating societies began to fade, replaced by fraternities and then sororities, students also sought participation in honors organizations, often encouraged by college administrators. By the late 1800s student forms of self-government were widespread, even including separate organizations for women on coeducational four-year campuses; women and men students at Wisconsin normal schools, as noted earlier, participated in such activities together. As enrollments grew in the early 1900s, students were no longer able to meet as a whole, and the process of electing representatives began, starting with the rise of the system classifying students as freshmen (first-year students), sophomores, juniors, and seniors in the late 1800s, which often included electing class officers and having systems of honors, discipline, and efforts to recommend institutional processes to the administration. Officers in the senior class began to receive recognition as the most influential students, but further enrollment growth and the growth of other student activities resulted in even more fragmentation among students, and by the mid-1920s, class officers were no longer as influential as they had been. Student councils, with officers and representatives elected at large rather than by class, developed throughout the early 1900s and became the center of representation of student interests to the institution. By the 1950s, the president of the student government was often recognized by administrators and faculty members as the voice of the students and served on multiple college-wide committees, a pattern that remains in place today. Throughout these centuries, presidents and faculty members, and then later deans of women and deans of men, increasingly encouraged the student government activities, recognizing them as another means to educate students in self-government and leadership.[41]

Student government, however, unfortunately had its dark side after World War II. From 1947 to 1967, the Central Intelligence Agency secretly collaborated with members of the National Student Association (at the time, the largest national student organization) and provided funding to the organization in order to identify suspected Communists and to promote liberal patriotic ideals. The relationship ended when a magazine, *Ramparts*, exposed the relationship and forced the federal government to end the arrangement.[42] The fervor of anti-Communism meant that even liberal students seeking democratic forms of self-government would compromise principles, inheriting centuries of student life, in order to keep the nation "American." While some parts of student life have had long traditions, others such as living on campus are actually more recent developments.

One important part of student experiences in higher education is residential life, formerly known as living in the dorm (a phrase still common among undergraduates); campus housing issues have included fraternity and sorority life. In California, junior colleges in less-populated areas in the early 1900s often provided housing, but for two-year and four-year institutions of higher education in more urban areas, large percentages of the students were commuters (typically for junior colleges in those areas, there was no campus housing at all). Presidents also recognized that attracting students from afar required dormitories, as occurred at the University of Washington, but more commonly, problems of funding curtailed any interest in building residence halls. Fraternities provided an alternative to institutional funding, and despite some efforts to ban them (at the University of Michigan and the University of California, for example), their provision of housing was useful.[43]

Many literary and debate societies, curiously, became social fraternities and later social sororities, marking a shift of student interests from participation in self-education to social life. The beginning of the transition from literary societies to white Greek groups likely occurred at Union College (New York) in the late 1820s, rapidly followed by similar developments in the Northeast and then in the Midwest. Reflective of both the student combinations that troubled the University of Pennsylvania as well as the rebellious nature of the Dartmouth literary societies, these new groups afforded students "a small, select band pledged to secrecy," and fraternity campaigns to secure elected student leadership positions likely resulted in the demise of literary and debating societies. Southern institutions of higher education were less likely to see a similar conversion, perhaps because they drew students heavily from well-to-do parts of the society, and those students had no such pressing need for a secret combination that separated them from the president, faculty members, and other students, although the groups became increasingly more important even on those campuses. Where there was a need to separate, fraternity members typically viewed outsiders as either barbarians or as GDIs (God Damn Independents). Part of the separation involved traditional ideas about who belonged in higher education, and in the early twentieth century, fraternities increasingly excluded Jews and Catholics, as white male Protestant notions about manliness continued to dominate colleges and universities.[44] Not only Jews and Catholics organized their own fraternities, but also so too did African Americans. The rise of sororities represented a more complex relationship with the fraternities, as their separation was often a partial one.

White sororities also focused on developing the womanly woman, although one clear contradiction was the ways in which they offered a space for women only while they espoused middle-class ideals about white women. For much of the twentieth century the groups prepared "members for conventional, white, middle-class womanhood and their emphasis on physical appeal undermined positive aspects of the women's-only space, as it fostered a competitive and controlling environment." Specific instructions about how to appear womanly, similar to the expectations of white Southern deans of women, began in the 1920s, while maintaining relationships with white fraternities as part of their influence on campus.

All too often fraternities and sororities are lumped into a single analytical frame, but black fraternities and sororities occupy a substantially different world. Much of the difference results from the segregationist world of this nation; while the issue of who was first appears in this context too (either Alpha Phi Alpha fraternity at Cornell or Kappa Alpha Psi at Indiana University in the early 1900s), the groups began as a means to create community on an often hostile campus (the history of racism at white fraternities such as Kappa Alpha is an example of the problem of hostility), establishing their traditions as African Americans. The most important difference from white Greek groups is that they have provided, and continue to provide, a means to racial uplift not simply through volunteer projects during college but in addition, in terms of lifelong membership. Whether a member of Alpha Kapp Alpha or Delta Sigma (the two oldest black sororities), a black woman is always a member even after graduation, and the volunteer and financial contributions to the African American community are part of her life. There is also clear evidence that the groups offered opportunity for leadership growth on white campuses for black students.[45]

Students did not need Greek groups, however, to separate themselves from others. As Harold Wechsler argues, separations by socioeconomic class were as old as the colonial colleges, and separation by gender was a given beginning in the 1800s. Jews began arriving on campuses in greater numbers in the early 1900s, and they too faced exclusion; one response was the creation of Jewish fraternities that increasingly resembled the activities of white Protestant fraternities. In addition, students from well-to-do families often turned to expensive off-campus housing, a movement that student services administrators accepted and institutions tolerated because of "the acceptance of tuition from those students more prone to pranks than piety and more often in attendance for social than academic reasons."[46]

One now commonplace characteristic of on-campus living that occurred in the late 1960s and early 1970s was the shift to coeducational dormitories. Initially colleges and universities implemented dormitories that were coeducational by floor and then ones that were (and are) coeducational on the floor. Such arrangements furthered both students' and student services administrators' perspective of the importance of institutionally sponsored activities in residence halls, establishing another way for the personal growth valued by student services. Some of the more visible separations among students—by gender, race and ethnicity, or socioeconomic class, for example, shifted toward a state of friendliness.[47] Increasingly, student services administrators moved to address this new whole person, and perhaps more appropriately, new whole people.

Discussion of deans of women in the South from the early 1900s to the 1960s reveals a range of goals, very much part of the idea of developing the whole person. They worked toward establishing places on campus for women, including dormitories, and for their full participation in academic and extracurricular activities, and they encouraged some young women to pursue careers. They also sought to ensure participation in athletics; the range of activities in academic and non-academic terms is a reminder of the importance of the development of the whole person.[48]

Lucy Diggs Slowe, identified as a lone voyager in Geraldine Clifford's book, served as the dean of women at Howard University from 1922 to 1937. Her efforts were in the context of a domineering, often outspoken president, Mordecai Johnson, who showed little support for a woman in the role of dean; she began her work at Howard with Johnson's predecessor, agreeing to the position as a faculty member and an administrator. Prior to her appointment in 1922, in 1917 she participated in a three-day Howard celebration of 50 years of progress for African Americans, and that commitment to African American life continued in her role as a dean of women. She also evidenced the professional growth noted by Jana Nidiffer in regard to white deans of women in the Midwest, researching the best possible ways to encourage student growth and belonging to the National Association of Deans of Women. She also established the National Association for College Women, an organization for women graduates of black colleges and universities, another black college organization that emphasized the importance of racial uplift activities for black college graduates. She also steadfastly advocated for the development of the whole woman; students needed to develop their talents in full in view of the race and gender problems of society; one place for their development was in campus housing, and she was eventually successful in securing that housing at Howard. She also saw student government as an effective means for individual development, highlighting the possibilities of moral as well as leadership growth. Finally, she pushed for financial support of women, perhaps because of her own financial demands as an undergraduate. The range of her activities evidences the very sort of professional approach that white deans of women emphasized.[49]

The challenge of the present for student services administrators rests on the past and the present. As Amy Well Dolan and Sara Kaiser noted, a critical demand for those administrators is how to be mindful of the traditional behaviors and values while engaging the new populations, seeming to arrive in person or identity on a regular basis. A 2016 analysis of student services articles by Michael Hevel reveals that in the past 20 years, the administrators have increasingly discussed, conducted research about, and implemented programs to engage a remarkably diverse population.[50] Centuries of traditions remain on campuses, often signaling issues in regard to gender, race and ethnicity, and socioeconomic class, and more recently, sexual identities as well as disabilities, yet there remains concerted efforts to create community.

CONCLUSION

Fundamentally, to understand U.S. higher education and its history, it is important to know who the students are as well as how they like to spend their time; they are the ones who renew the institutions with their arrival each year. Efforts to enrich them in the classroom or in extracurricular activities are central to the life of a college or university, but it helps to be thoughtful of how they experience higher education, how they view their undergraduate experience. However absurd it may seem, a personal favorite movie is *Dead Man on Campus*, which offers a persistent student story that an anthropologist had also found on the campus of Rutgers University, one I had heard too many years ago as director of an academic advising office, and students continue the myth according to my daughter in college: if a student's roommate commits suicide, the dean automatically gives the student a 4.0 for the term. It is not true. Veysey's 1965 description of the relationship between faculty members and students (echoing to a much lesser degree the relationship between student services staff members but fully echoing the relationship between central administration and students) remains appropriate in some ways, an awful chasm. Yet student services administrators are not simply aware of all of these challenges but also seek ways to address them. To return to the beginning of this chapter, throughout the stories of students' lives are the lives of student services administrators. While rules as detailed at those at colonial colleges with stated risks of expulsion are far less common, it is true that more rules, rather than fewer, are the norm. The explosion of enrollments starting in the late 1800s beyond the traditional white Protestant students resulted in a myriad of ways of developing the whole person, although not always without problematic consequences. And as the institutions developed in the 1900s, particularly after World War II, they also adapted to a new mission, research and scholarship, one substantially different from student life. Ironically, the mythical reason for the rise of student services in the late 1800s and early 1900s increasingly became a reality, particularly at large universities in the 1960s and thereafter. A common quote until the early 2000s among historians of higher education celebrated personal instruction and attention: college is Mark Hopkins on one end of a log and a student on the other, now a process all too often in larger institutions offered not by professors who face lecture halls with 300 or more students, assisted by teaching assistants, but by student services administrators. (Hopkins was president of Williams College, Massachusetts, from 1836 to 1872.) The enrollment growth of the post-World War II period and, finally, faculty interest in research, shifted faculty interest away from direct involvement in student development at the multitude of large institutions.

DISCUSSION QUESTIONS

1. What do student combinations (formal or informal) mean in terms of college and university efforts to educate the whole person?
2. Which groups of students have participated in what ways in formal and informal extracurricular activities?

NOTES

1 *The Student Personnel Point of View* (Washington, DC: American Council on Education, 1937), 1.

2 Hugh Hawkins, *Between Harvard and American: The Educational Leadership of Charles W. Eliot* (New York: Oxford University Press, 1972); Laurence Veysey, *The Emergence of the American University* (Chicago: University of Chicago Press, 1965); Frederick Rudolph, *The American College and University: A History* (Athens: University of Georgia Press, 1962); John S. Brubacher and Willis Rudy, *Higher Education in Transition: A History of American Colleges and Universities*, 4th ed. (New York: Routledge Press, 2017).

3 W.B. Carnochan, *The Battleground of the Curriculum: Liberal Education and American Experience* (Stanford: Stanford University Press, 1993).

4 *The Student Personnel Point of View* (Washington, DC: American Council on Education, 1937), 2.

5 Jana Nidiffer, *Pioneering Deans of Women: More Than Wise and Pious Matrons* (New York: Teachers College Press, 2000); Robert A. Schwartz, "Reconceptualizing the Leadership Roles of Women in Higher Education: A Brief History on the Importance of Deans of Women," *Journal of Higher Education* 68, no 5 (September–October 1997): 502–522; Helen Horowitz, *Campus Life: Undergraduate Cultures from the End of the Eighteenth Century to the Present* (Chicago: University of Chicago Press, 1987); Eleanor M. Schetlin, "Myths of the Student Personnel Point of View," *Journal of Higher Education* 40, no. 1 (January 1969): 58–63.

6 Laurence Veysey, *The Emergence of the American University* (Chicago: University of Chicago Press, 1965), p. 35 on faculty aversion to discipline, pp. 294–302 on the chasm and cheating, "Yale Report of 1828," p. 9; Kathryn McDaniel Moore, "Freedom and Constraint in Eighteenth Century Harvard," *Journal of Higher Education* 17, no. 6 (November/December 1976): 640–659.

7 Michael Moffat, *Coming of Age in New Jersey: College and American Culture* (New Brunswick: Rutgers University Press, 1989).

8 Ted Jou, "A Brief History of Caltech Pranks," in *Essays on Caltech Student Government History*, http://donut.caltech.edu/w/images/7/7a/Jou02_E.pdf (retrieved December 16, 2018).

9 "Yale Laws of 1745," in *American Higher Education History: A Documentary History*, ed. Richard Hofstadter and Wilson Smith (Chicago: University of Chicago Press, 1961), 56–57.

10 Lynn D. Gordon, *Gender and Higher Education in the Progressive Era* (New Haven, CT: Yale University Press, 1990).

11 Michael David Cohen, "'What Gender Is Lex?' Women, Men, and Power Relations in Colleges of the Nineteenth Century," *Perspectives on the History of Higher Education* 24 (2005): 41–90.

12 Amy Thompson McCandless, "Preserving the Pedestal: Restrictions on Social Life at Southern Colleges for Women, 1920–1940," *History of Higher Education Annual 1987* 7: 45–68.

13 William Wright, *Harvard's Secret Court: The Savage 1920 Purge of Campus Homosexuals* (New York: St. Martin's Press, 2005).

14 Margaret A. Nash and Jennifer A.R. Silverman, "'An Indelible Mark': Gay Purges in Higher Education in the 1940s," *History of Education Quarterly* 55, no. 4 (November 2015): 455.

15 Nicholas L. Syrett, *The Company He Keeps: A History of White College Fraternities* (Chapel Hill: University of North Carolina Press, 2009).

16 Patrick Dilley, *Queer Man on Campus: A History of Non-Heterosexual College Men, 1945–2000* (New York: Routledge, 2002); Lizzie Smith Emerson, "What's Sex Got to Do with It: Reconsidering Women's Relationships with Women on College Campuses in the Late Nineteenth and Early Twentieth Centuries," Southern History of Education Society, March 23, 2018, Gainesville, Florida.

17   Charles Homer Haskins, *The Rise of Universities* (Ithaca, NY: Cornell University Press, 1923).

18   "Yale Laws of 1745," in *American Higher Education History: A Documentary History*, ed. Richard Hofstadter and Wilson Smith (Chicago: University of Chicago Press, 1961), 57.

19   Michael S. Hevel, "'Betwixt Brewings': A History of College Students and Alcohol" (Ph.D. dissertation, University of Iowa, 2011); Nicholas L. Syrett, *The Company He Keeps: A History of White College Fraternities* (Chapel Hill: University of North Carolina Press, 2009), 241.

20   Michael Fulford, "Failing at College Football Reform: An Analysis of the Jan Kemp Trial at the University of Georgia" (Ph.D. dissertation, Georgia State University, 2008).

21   David S. Churchill, "Making Broad Shoulders: Body-Building and Physical Culture in Chicago 1890–1920," *History of Education Quarterly* 48, no. 3 (August 2008): 341–370.

22   Roger L. Geiger, *To Advance Knowledge: The Growth of American Research Universities, 1900–1940* (New York: Oxford University Press, 1986); Brian M. Ingrassia, *The Rise of Gridiron University: Higher Education's Uneasy Alliance with Big-time Football* (Lawrence: University Press of Kansas, 2012).

23   David L. Westby and Allen Sack, "The Commercialization and Functional Rationalization of College Football: Its Origins," *Journal of Higher Education* 47 (November–December 1976): 625–647.

24   Caryl Martin, "'Dutiful Daughters' & Rowdy Women: A Historical Examination of Athletics at Southern Women's Colleges" (Ph.D. dissertation, Georgia State University, 2000).

25   Allen Guttmann, *The Olympics: A History of the Modern Games*, 2nd ed. (Urbana: University of Illinois Press, 2002).

26   John R. Thelin, *Games Colleges Play: Scandal and Reform in Intercollegiate Athletics* (Baltimore: Johns Hopkins University Press, 1994).

27   Charles Holden, "Manliness and the Culture of Self-Improvement: The University of North Carolina in the 1890s," *History of Education Quarterly* 58, no. 1 (February 2018): 122–151.

28   Patrick B. Miller, "To 'Bring the Race along Rapidly': Sport, Student Culture, and Educational Missions at Historically Black Colleges during the Interwar Years," *History of Education Quarterly* 35, no. 2 (Summer 1995): 111–133; Thomas Aiello, "The Heritage Fallacy: Race, Loyalty, and the First Grambling-Southern Football Game," *History of Education Quarterly* 50, no. 4 (November 2010): 488–512; Russell J. Henderson, "The 1963 Mississippi State University Basketball Controversy and the Repeal of the Unwritten Law: 'Something more than the game will be lost,'" *Journal of Southern History* 63, no. 4 (November 1997): 827–854; Lane Demas, *Integrating the Gridiron: Black Civil Rights and American College Football* (New Brunswick: Rutgers University Press, 2010).

29   Marc A. VanOverbeke, "Out of the Quietness, a Clamor: 'We Want Football!' The California State Colleges, Educational Opportunity, and Athletics," *History of Education Quarterly* 53, no. 4 (November 2013): 431–454.

30   Charles Homer Haskins, *The Rise of Universities* (Ithaca, NY: Cornell University Press, 1923).

31   Sharon Height, "Protest, Faith, and Race and Gender: Student Experiences at Bennett College for Black Women, 1960–2000" (Ph.D. dissertation, University of Alabama, 2018); Harry G. Lefever, *Undaunted by the Fight: Spelman College and the Civil Rights Movement, 1957–1967* (Macon, GA: Mercer University Press, 2005); Philo Hutcheson, Marybeth Gasman, and Kijua Sanders-McMurtry, "Race and Equality in the Academy: Rethinking Higher Education Actors and the Struggle for Equality in the Post-World War II Period," *Journal of Higher Education* 82, no. 2 (March–April 2011): 121–153.

32   Erin Niederberger, "The Gay Lib Controversy: Social Change Versus Social Norms at the University of Missouri," *Artifacts: A Journal of Undergraduate Writing* 14 (April 2016): 1–10. Brett Beemyn, "The Silence

Is Broken: A History of the First Lesbian, Gay, and Bisexual College Student Groups," *Journal of the History of Sexuality* 12, no. 3 (April 2003): 205–223.

33   Margaret A. Nash, Danielle C. Mireles, and Amanda Scott-Williams, "'Mattie Matix' and Prodigal Princes: A Brief History of Drag on College Campuses from the Nineteenth Century to the 1940s," in *Rethinking Campus Life: New Perspectives on the History of College Students in the United States*, ed. Christine A. Ogren and Marc VanOverbeke (New York: Springer International, Kindle edition).

34   John B. Christiansen and Sharon N. Barnartt. *Deaf President Now! The 1988 Revolution at Gallaudet University* (Washington, DC: Gallaudet University Press, 1995).

35   Christopher Tudico, "The Mexican American Movement," in *Rethinking Campus Life: New Perspectives on the History of College Students in the United States*, ed. Christine A. Ogren and Marc VanOverbeke (New York: Springer International Publishing, Kindle Edition).

36   Scot Danforth, "Becoming the Rolling Quads: Disability Politics at the University of California, Berkeley, in the 1960s," *History of Education Quarterly* 58, no. 4 (November 2018): 506–536.

37   Thai-Huy Nguyen and Marybeth Gasman, "Activism, Identity and Service: The Influence of the Asian American Movement on the Educational Experiences of College Students," *History of Education* 44, no. 3 (January 2015): 339–54; Jerome Karabel, *The Chosen: The Hidden History of Admission and Exclusion at Harvard, Yale, and Princeton* (New York: Houghton Mifflin Harcourt, 2005); Thai-Huy Nguyen and Marybeth Gasman, "Culture and Allegiance Among Vietnamese Students and Their Organizations at University California, Irvine: 1980–1990," *Teachers College Record* 117, no. 5 (May 2015): 1–22.

38   Victoria-Maria MacDonald, John M. Botti, and Lisa Hoffman Clark, "From Visibility to Autonomy: Latinos and Higher Education in the U.S., 1965–2005," *Harvard Educational Review* 77, no. 4 (Winter 2007): 474–504.

39   Stefan Bradley, "'Gym Crow Must Go!' Black Student Activism at Columbia University, 1967–1968," *Journal of African American History* 88, no. 2 (Spring 2003): 163–181.

40   Joy Ann Williamson, *Black Power on Campus: The University of Illinois, 1965–75* (Urbana: University of Illinois Press, 2003).

41   Walter May, "Student Governance: A Qualitative Study of Leadership in a Student Government Association" (Ph.D. dissertation, Georgia State University, 2009).

42   Karen M. Paget, *Patriotic Betrayal: The Inside Story of the CIA's Secret Campaign to Enroll American Students in the Crusade Against Communism* (New Haven, CT: Yale University Press, 2015).

43   Lester F. Goodchild, Richard W. Jonsen, Patty Limerick, and David A. Longanecker, eds., *Higher Education in the American West: Regional History and State Contexts, 1818–2010* (New York: Palgrave Macmillan, 2014).

44   Helen Lefkowitz Horowitz, *Campus Life: Undergraduate Cultures from the End of the Eighteenth Century to the Present* (Chicago: University of Chicago Press, 1987); Nicholas L. Syrett, *The Company He Keeps: A History of White College Fraternities* (Chapel Hill: University of North Carolina Press, 2009).

45   Walter Kimbrough, *Black Greek 101: The Culture, Customs, and Challenges of Black Fraternities and Sororities* (Madison, WI: Fairleigh Dickinson University Press, 2003); Walter Kimbrough and Philo Hutcheson, "The Impact of Membership in Black Greek-Letter Organizations on Black Students' Involvement in Collegiate Activities and Their Development of Leadership Skills," *Journal of Negro Education* 67, no. 2 (Spring 1998): 96–105.

46   Harold S. Wechsler, "An Academic Gresham's Law: Group Repulsion as a Theme in American Higher Education," *Teachers College Record* 82, no. 4 (Summer 1981): 567–588.

47 Michael Moffat, *Coming of Age in New Jersey: College and American Culture* (New Brunswick: Rutgers University Press, 1989).

48 Carolyn Terry Bashaw, *"Stalwart Women": A Historical Analysis of Deans of Women in the South* (New York: Teachers College Press, 1999).

49 Lisa Rasheed, "Lucy Diggs Slowe, Howard University Dean of Women, 1922–1937: Educator, Administrator, Activist" (Ph.D. dissertation, Georgia State University, 2010).

50 Amy Wells Dolan and Sara R. Kaiser, "The History of Student Life in American Higher Education," in *Today's College Students: A Reader*, ed. Pietro A. Sasso and Joseph. L. DeVitis (New York: Peter Lang, 2015), 225–240; Michael S. Hevel, "Toward a History of Student Affairs: A Synthesis of Research, 1996–2015," *Journal of College Student Development* 57, no. 7 (October 2016): 844–862.

7

THE RESEARCH UNIVERSITY, REVISED

Many histories of higher education attend to the research university, an institutional type with high visibility and considerable influence. This chapter revisits those institutions.

Well into the late 1800s, college and university educators easily and eagerly argued that knowledge and faith were interdependent—or in the words of the motto of Beloit College, *Scientia vera cum fide pura*. Scientific truth with pure faith. Faith, however, increasingly faced a powerful challenger, research. Before embarking on a review of the development of research universities in the United States, it is necessary to discuss the origins of research as we know it today and its organizational basis.

All of that can be summarized in a brief phrase: In the beginning was the University of Berlin. Wilhelm von Humboldt led the Prussian education offices in the early nineteenth century, and in 1810 he established the University of Berlin, the first institution of higher education emphasizing research and scholarship in the developing Western tradition (key elements of the research ethos, such as publishing papers, was already a part of the lives of some German academics, especially at the universities at Göttingen and Halle as early as the late 1700s). Relatively quickly aspiring academics from the United States went to Germany to study for their advanced degrees, where they learned fundamentals of research in the humanities, natural and physical science, and the developing social sciences. Philology and theology were early disciplinary leaders in the development of scholarship and research, further splintering the unity of knowledge based on the Bible as scholars sought ways to verify the historical aspects of the Bible and developed different ways of knowing. Not just the search for knowledge, but also teaching experienced changes in the United States as a result of the German university. In contrast to such standard practices as the recitation and disputation in the instruction of undergraduates, German professors' pedagogical mainstays were the seminar and the laboratory, innovations at the time. Equally important, the Germans emphasized three aspects of research—*Wissenschaft, Lerhfreiheit*, and *Lernfreiheit*, the first two of which would provide foundations for the development of disciplinary and professorial frameworks in the United States, foundations that endure in the twenty-first century.

Wissenschaft was the German term for scientific inquiry, and here science does not mean the forms of objective inquiry efforts highlighted by the natural and physical sciences and attempted by the social sciences as pursued in the United States. Rather, it is a rational, formalized approach to inquiry; many U.S. academics, however, took it to mean an objective approach. As a means to illustrating the difference between *Wissenschaft* and objectivism, U.S. historians returning home after graduate education in Germany broadly interpreted their work as purely objective, establishing facts that led to conclusions, in the words of one historian, creating a building brick by brick. By the 1930s, however, such leading historians as Charles Beard and Carl Becker challenged those conceptions, arguing that subjectivity played a critical role in historical study, an argument that divided the historical profession for decades. In contrast, the context for *Wissenschaft* was Idealism, a German philosophical approach that explained the material world from the perspective of consciousness and the mind. Consciousness and not facts explained the world. In addition, the German university rested on the German educational effort known as *Bildungkultur*; throughout the primary and secondary schooling of German youth, instruction included lessons on the importance of the German view. *Wissenschaft* rested on *Bildungkultur* and was not, therefore, simply a statement of the facts. It was rigorous advanced study, with the expectation that Germans were the one to lead the world in understanding the world. The translation into the United States followed a more objectivist, empirical stance.

It also had tremendously important implications in terms of the curriculum as separate departments with faculty members pursuing different lines of inquiry resulted in the slow dissolution of the use of the formerly central text, the Bible, and the development of an elective system, given that specialized research resulted in specialization of knowledge even at the undergraduate level. One of the most comprehensive challenges to the Bible as explanatory text came, however, not from Germany but from England with the publication of *On the Origin of Species* by Charles Darwin in 1859. The book has two illuminating characteristics, one of which was sharply different from German research. In the first case, it refuted the earlier scientific ideas about species change resulting from transmutation by clearly showing that species adapted to their environments. The second, often overlooked, is that *On the Origin of Species* did not result from laboratory research as was common in Germany but from Darwin's observations of changes over time. Nevertheless, the impact is clear, as his work refuted not only claims of transmutation but also the deep-seated beliefs about the creation of the world and its inhabitants in the Bible. The splintering of knowledge resulting from German research and Darwin's arguments began the creation of specialized subjects of inquiry since the central narrative of the nature of the world increasingly became narratives by disciplines; psychology evolved from philosophy with the establishment of a psychology laboratory at a German university in the late 1870s, for example, providing separate, disciplinary explanations for human behavior. By the early 1900s, a handful of U.S. universities were beginning their ascendancy as one of the most dominant groups of research institutions, if not the most dominant, in terms of scholarship and research in the world. While the institutional process resulted from the efforts of presidents and professors, the pursuit of research was a process led by professors.

RESEARCH UNIVERSITIES: THE INSTITUTIONS

The first research university in the United States was in a Southern state. The Johns Hopkins University began in 1871 in Baltimore, Maryland (although arguably Maryland is a Border State, given its role in the Civil War, on the drive south on Interstate 81 in Pennsylvania into Maryland, there is a road sign that says, simply, Mason-Dixon Line—or at least, it was there as late as 2010). The institutional beginning of the research university was not in the Northeast, although Yale awarded the first doctorate, six of them, in 1861; Yale was not an institution, however, that embraced scholarly and research activities until many decades later. The Johns Hopkins University instituted research opportunities through a number of activities, including the appointment of research-oriented professors, the development of academic journals, and laboratories (although the initial use of the instructional laboratory likely began at Rensselaer Polytechnic Institute in the mid-1820s).[1]

Equally important, despite inaccurate historical claims about the advent of the elective system and its initiation at Harvard under the presidency of Charles W. Eliot, the elective system was underway at the University of Virginia in the mid-1820s. The development of the elective system as an institution-wide effort began at the University of Virginia, designed by Thomas Jefferson with the expectation that the new college student was mature enough to elect courses across the university until he decided upon which school of study in several areas, "ancient languages, modern languages, mathematics, natural philosophy, natural history, anatomy and medicine, moral philosophy, and law," at which time elective choices ceased. The first advocate for electives in the Northeast, a modern languages instructor at Harvard named George Ticknor—one of the first U.S. professors to study in Germany—maintained a friendship with Jefferson. Upon Ticknor's return from study in Germany, he began to advocate for the elective system at Harvard. Despite initial partial successes, due to faculty opposition, eventually President Kirkland of Harvard modified the system so it was optional across departments.[2] In fact, Eliot was himself a product of a partial elective system as a chemistry major at Harvard; rather clearly, then, he did not initiate the system but rather popularized it with a zeal punctuated by essays, books, speeches, and a forceful effort at Harvard to implement the system so completely that for part of his presidency, the entire curriculum consisted of electives. There is no question that he was the primary advocate of the elective system for decades, but those were decades later than the first attempt to have such a curriculum.[3]

Hence common arguments about the development of the research university and its curricular core, the elective system, highlight in fact a later period when the northern, midwestern, and western universities, and to a lesser degree and typically later, some of the liberal arts colleges, embraced the research ethos in a manner that resulted in long-term growth for both enrollment and revenue among the universities.

Reinforcing the institutional drive for research university status was the Association of American Universities (AAU), established in 1900. The 14 founding institutions intended to highlight the Ph.D., particularly in comparison with the previously popular European Ph.D. In 1908 the institutions established membership rules, which explicitly included the requirement that the institution offer a post-baccalaureate professional program with the admission standard of a minimum of one year of college (a reminder that professionalization, given the common four years now required, is a historical process). Over the decades, university graduate professional programs increased their requirements for years of college as well as increasing the years of their programs.[4] By the early 2000s there were 62 members (out of the more than 4,000 institutions of higher education in the nation), and they received more than half of the research grants and graduated more than half of the doctoral students. In addition, most of the U.S. recipients of Nobel Prizes in recent years were at AAU institutions.

Sustaining these institutions financially was no easy matter. Although the public universities received support from the state governments, that support never fully funded those institutions, nor did the private institutions received consistent or sufficient support from their original denominations. In both cases the institutions turned to external support to add to the revenue created by tuition and their endowments, and increasingly presidents turned to fundraising as their primary goal. The period between the World War I and World War II was the period where the research-university presidents focused on private philanthropy, securing the place of a small number of research institutions.[5]

As professors and universities increasingly moved toward research, the process of establishing a research ethos became more a result of institutional decisions, as occurred at Stanford University's Physics Department in the 1930s and 1940s. There were also instances when universities with proud traditions of undergraduate education moved into a focus on research, such as Princeton University after World War II. While the institution had received national attention for the strength of its physics and mathematics programs prior to World War II, it had neither of the common professional programs in medicine and law. The Korean War, however, provided added momentum for the practical applications of science, and the Princeton aeronautical engineering program had established itself during World War II as a preeminent place for research on flight, and with the expansion of the faculty after the war, increased its technological expertise. Despite concerns about the loss of autonomy with industrial and government demands for control and the effect on undergraduate education, in some ways the Princeton faculty had already moved toward a research focus; students complained that professors were busy with research and less interested in teaching. (As a colleague in philosophy, Scott Pratt, remarked many years ago while working at the University of Minnesota, it is intriguing that professors speak of research opportunities and teaching loads.) In addition, the need for jets in the Korean War meant that the Armed Services want to support the physics and aeronautical engineering expertise at Princeton. Despite a standing resistance to classified research in which the findings were kept secret except for the sponsoring organization (whether commercial or governmental), the university administration found a solution by ensuring that the research was an exception and would be conducted on a newly acquired large parcel of land near the institution, separating the work from the university's main campus.

The sponsored research received large amounts of money in the 1950s—millions of dollars at a time when millions was substantial money, but in 1961 the new president, wary of the effect of much higher faculty salaries for professors in the sciences and engineering compared to those in the social sciences and humanities as well as the problems of classified research, commissioned an economics professor to examine the problem. His resulting extensive report, primarily based on university materials, argued that despite the salary issues (not only costly in terms of faculty relations but also in terms of the budget and dependence on government support), the institution gained financially from sponsored research and furthered its status as a prestigious university. Planning for research efforts was not imbued by rationality but rather by the circumstance of large amounts of money and the possibility of increased prestige.[6]

The Princeton example is instructive because it illustrates a highly important aspect of higher education in the United States, histories ranging from two-year to four-year to research institutions: systematic planning of any sort is by and large absent in their histories until the 1980s or latter. The rise of research universities had a great deal to do with institutional competition in a decentralized arena, and for those institutions specifically, a national market for professors; planning, for example in the context of national ministries of education in Europe, too easily results in sequences of academic changes that require layers of improvement and may inhibit innovation at the price of bureaucratic control. Despite the decentralized nature of U.S. higher education and its markets, nevertheless the institutions developed in similar form organizationally with a large undergraduate college and most often, a smaller graduate school, and in terms of the structure of academic rank in the tenure track, from assistant professor to associate professor to professor. From 1900 to 1950, the number of undergraduates at all U.S. institutions of higher education increased from about 238,000 students (which in 2018 could be as few as five institutions' enrollments) to 2,700,000 students. Much of the enrollment shift in that time period and thereafter occurred at public institutions; in the 1920s, Michigan and Wisconsin were smaller than Columbia and Chicago, obviously no longer the case. While a core of research universities developed prior to World War II, most of the growth occurred after that war as the nation increasingly looked to higher education to provide opportunities for the advancement of national interests.[7]

The arguments of Vannevar Bush at the close of World War II, advocating for an agency provided momentum for the 1950 establishment of the National Science Foundation (previously a West Virginia senator, Harvey Kilgore, had repeatedly proposed just such an agency). Now the National Science Foundation is a leading contributor on a global level to advancements in science. As Geiger has clearly shown, military interests served as prime source for funding university research in the post-World War II period; not just Chicago and Princeton, but other research universities benefitted as well, a powerful reminder of war's effect on research.[8]

The federal government's interest in funding basic research, or pure science, provided multiple opportunities for research universities starting in the early 1950s. In addition to the National Science Foundation, there were substantial and numerable opportunities for research support among a large number of federal agencies, although much of the growth focused on development (i.e., practical research) rather than pure research and was funded in industries such as defense contractors. The National Defense Education Act provided another impetus for the support of basic research across a variety of areas, and over the next few years representatives of the AAU, the National Academy of Sciences, and the American Association for the Advancement of Science successfully advocated, for federal funding of basic research.[9] The funding, however, by and large remained in the hands of the group of institutions that had secured the core of research activities in the 1920s; while a very few might slip or gain, the vast majority of those institutions maintained and increased their standing. Even state flagship universities might not have such research prestige; both the University of Georgia and Georgia Tech awarded only a handful of doctorates in the early 1960s.[10] By the mid-1960s, however, more populist politics were gaining momentum, as indicated by the War on Poverty (a war by any other name . . .) and the 1965 Higher Education Act, and President Johnson, who as Senate majority leader had helped to bring the 1958 NDEA to passage, argued that far too much federal research money was going to too few research universities (about half of the funds went to 20 universities). In the midst of a booming economy, the federal government expanded support, with the foundation of the National Endowment for the Humanities and the National Endowment for the Arts as well as the 1968 addition of the social sciences to National Science Foundation funding (previously, the National Institutes of Mental Health provided the bulk of the funding to psychology and sociology). Nevertheless, the preeminent research universities, well organized to secure the research dollars, continued to fare well, and while the federal research budget increased, the federal commitment to supporting higher education had far more rapid growth in support of campuses and students, beginning with the 1963 Higher Education Facilities Act and then the 1965 Higher Education Act. As Hugh Davis Graham and Nancy Diamond noted, "By 1968 federal assistance in some direct form reached 92 percent of the nation's 2,734 colleges and universities . . . Yet most institutions in most states received no research funding."[11]

An under-recognized and highly important advancement in U.S. higher education in the development of research universities was the establishment of professional schools. For example, for all of the misplaced credit given to Charles W. Eliot
for his efforts in regard to electives and graduate education, his work in graduate
professional education was certainly substantial and influential. College and university presidents at institutions with a research focus advanced the argument that
professions required the scientific knowledge (a term applied to law as well as to medicine) that only their institutions could provide. They also argued that the preparation
of professionals required a liberal arts education; being a professional was more than
simply acting on technical knowledge about the event or problem as it also required
an understanding of the context of the event or problem and an appreciation of societal good. Finally, they were confident that university-educated professionals would
be effective. One exception to the development of professional schools at universities was the independent divinity school, such as Andover Theological Seminary,
an institution that focused on educating New Light ministers (such as those leading
the Second Great Awakening that caused such problems at Yale) in opposition to
Unitarianism at Harvard. While Harvard's president, Charles W. Eliot saw those as
useful, he was sure that professional schools attached to universities would produce
the best and the brightest professionals. Eliot argued first and foremost for the liberal
arts as preparation for professional education in his 1869 inaugural address: "The
American university, Eliot predicted, would grow out of American soil, adapted
to the ambitions of 'the better educated classes,' and those ambitions increasingly
aimed at professional careers." He successfully contested the activities of the Harvard
medical and law school faculties in areas such as admission, prerequisites for admission in terms of courses, and the programs themselves. Daniel Coit Gilman, the first
president of the Johns Hopkins University, also focused on undergraduate preparation, a clear indication that the emphasis on an undergraduate liberal arts education
was becoming the standard for professional preparation. As the universities further
developed their graduate professional programs—increasing the years of college
preparation for admission and the years of actual professional preparation—the professional accrediting associations also played a key role in ensuring the increased
requirements (those who did not succeed could be expelled, as happened for
Vanderbilt and Mississippi in 1926 following review by the Association of American
Law Schools). Finally, universities, particularly those seeking acceptance by the
AAU, developed professional schools that were post-baccalaureate. One decided
consequence of these developments was the loss of white women and people of color,

a trend reversed starting in the 1970s, with the added curricular expectation of concern for the social, political, and economic contexts faced by clients.[12]

Led by private universities ranging from the Johns Hopkins University to Cornell (the latter of which also brought, at least briefly, an egalitarian spirit to the elective system for men and women) to the University of Chicago and public universities ranging from the Universities of Michigan, Wisconsin, and California, the drive to institutionalize the research ethos remains unabated. It has been and is, however, an ethos that must grapple with the meanings of a complex organization.

Research universities were not without critique in their early years, as in the case of Thorstein Veblen, who had developed the idea of conspicuous consumption in his popular book, *The Theory of the Leisure Class*, a sharp criticism of the wealthy, who made money and enjoyed expensive lives while laborers made products. Veblen, not surprisingly, found the increasingly bureaucratic research university to be counter to the possibilities of contemplative life that research-oriented professors needed to pursue. The core of his argument can be found on page 202 of his book, *The Higher Learning in America*, where he declares that the best step for universities to improve their efforts would be to dismiss the president and the governing board. This did not happen. Nevertheless, his arguments reflect both faculty members' widespread distrust of administrators (professors often remark that colleagues who go into administration have gone to the dark side) as well as the need for administrators at colleges and universities with the variety of demands in running a complex organization with multiple demands.

Laurence Veysey addressed bureaucratization of higher education occurring in the early 1900s. He notes in one of his later works, "The American University of 1900 was created less as a direct result of direct copying from German models than through unconscious borrowing from bureaucratic industrial norms and practices closer to home." Those norms allowed for the combination of basic research in the sciences, scholarship in the humanities, a liberal education for undergraduates, undergraduate student life, and differing faculty roles in research and teaching, coordinated by an increasingly large administration. An example of the coordinating effects of bureaucratization is the credit hour, as it somehow equates six weekly hours of laboratory and lecture in the sciences with three (or four) hours of weekly class time in English. In his discussion of Progressivism, Veysey only refers to the "efficiency craze"; obviously the craze had not even ended 50 years later as (in only one example) the ACE found several ways to efficiently develop, assess, and implement education for service personnel and veterans.[13] The research university and its faculty grapple with a bureaucratic organization supporting an ethos—research—that does not necessarily lend itself to efficiency. Whether a scholar is alone in her study examining the literature on reform of public health or is in the laboratory examining the relationship of charmed quarks to other quarks, she faces the need for organizational support at the same time that she is engaged in a set of reflective acts that can lose their quality when they are forced into specific outcomes completed by a specific time.

It also reflects institutional drive to achieve or increase prestige. William James, a turn-of-the-century philosopher, wrote an essay, "The Ph.D. Octopus," published in 1912, in which he excoriated colleges and universities for requiring new faculty members to have an earned doctorate. Whether it was a time of few U.S. graduate schools and the scarcity of those doctorates, thereby carrying with them "a sense of preciousness and honor," or today, when those degrees abound at both not-for-profit and for-profit institutions of higher education, respectability comes with "some kind of badge or diploma . . . stamped upon" the individual (in Frank Baum's 1900 book, does not the Wizard of Oz bestow a diploma on the Scarecrow?).[14] His assessment, however, does not deny the substantial gains in scholarship and research evident over the course of the twentieth century.

In addition, graduate programs are in part dependent on the undergraduate programs. As Roger Geiger argues, large undergraduate enrollments provide both tuition revenue and then later (one would hope) alumni and alumnae giving. Oddly, then, the activities discussed in the previous chapter have critical connections to the activities discussed in this one, although they are often disparate, even wildly different. Undergraduate students may decry heavy reading loads in courses, and graduate students may respect, even celebrate, them. Nor do graduate students often join social fraternities or sororities. An interesting aspect of this difference that also reflects the orientation of faculty members who focus on research, first articulated in the late 1950s by Alvin Gouldner. In great part, research-oriented faculty members connect intellectually with colleagues at other institutions, for example forming what one scholar called invisible colleges in an examination of such specialized fields as rural sociology, participating in academic conferences with colleagues from across the region or nation, and reading the work of colleagues at other institutions.[15] In contrast, faculty members focused on teaching are more likely to be primarily connected with their colleges or universities and the classroom activities for their courses. There is need, however, to be keep in mind the nuances of those differences, including the long-term commitment to campus service evidenced by a noticeable proportion of research-oriented faculty members as well as how teaching faculty members draw upon national research and scholarship to maintain currency in their teaching.[16]

The differences between undergraduate and graduate study reflect another consequence of the movement toward research institution status, the undergraduate curriculum as preparation for graduate study. For example, Catholic institutions of higher education faced substantial pressure to move away from their traditional undergraduate curriculum, and two instances illustrate this problem. For centuries the Catholics and classicists held a central place in the university, given the importance of the Catholic Church for centuries in Europe and the curricular place of Latin and Greek. While the two groups, in part because of the religious differences Catholicism and Protestantism, did not form a coalition, they shared opposition to the rise of the secular elective system. The modern world of bureaucratic efficiency and secularism was a challenge to the two groups, a challenge epitomized by the research university. Despite the virtues of the past that both Catholics and classicists espoused in different ways and updated in accordance with modern and research expectations, the modern higher education institutions pressured the traditional notions in terms of enrollments and new institutions (such as business schools) and both groups found ways to preserve their interpretations of virtue in such forms as the Western civilization courses for undergraduates. The diminished status of higher education for virtue has an interesting counter-example, the work of President James T. Laney at Emory University, who led the institution from 1978 to 1993. In Laney's first year, Robert Woodruff of the Coca-Cola family donated a then-unheard-of sum of $105 million to the university, and the institution slowly and carefully moved into research university status. Laney was an ordained Methodist minister, including serving as a Methodist missionary in South Korea in the late 1950s and early 1960s, and the matter of virtue was paramount to him. He held steadfast to that commitment and consistently gave speeches on campus (especially to undergraduates) and to external constituencies on the need for a moral compass. He led an institution of higher education into elite research status (the AAU accepted Emory as a member in 1995) while reminding students and other communities of the need for a moral perspective.[17] The more likely condition, however, is well represented by the major challenge faced by the Jesuit order in the first half of the twentieth century. One of the Catholic Church's more powerful religious orders, for centuries the Jesuits had used a specific undergraduate curriculum, the *Ratio Studiorum* with a focus on Latin and Greek. That curriculum began to face challenges starting in the early 1900s, in part because the rise of regional accrediting associations brought about more of a focus on standardized curricula and in part because the Association of American Universities (AAU) increasingly made clear the importance of preparing undergraduate students at institutions fully accredited by the regional associations. Over the course of decades, the influence of the regional accrediting associations and the AAU changed the Jesuit institutions, as new faculty members and programs increasingly reflected the expectations of the elective system and the institutions sought to model the programmatic aspects of the more secular research universities; the Jesuit institutions moved away from their European roots and accepted the modern U.S. research university model.[18]

The Southern regional accrediting association (Southern Association of Colleges and Schools, SACS) had an even more detrimental effect on two groups of institutions, colleges for white women and colleges for African Americans. SACS had two levels of accrediting, A and B, and only students from A-level institutions of higher education were deemed to have the level of collegiate education necessary to enter graduate or professional schools, a practice that remained robust into the 1930s. This was, of course, deeply problematic for students at the institutions without full accreditation, and in the case of students at black colleges, the accrediting stratification was coupled with the 1930s growth of courses in such areas as black history, black literature, and black sociology, topics unlikely to receive attention or even to be dismissed by admission committees at white universities with doctoral programs and professional schools.[19]

Problems of discrimination went beyond the undergraduate curriculum at these major universities. A pressing but often unasked question for these institutions remains their role in regard to not only individual instances of discrimination, but also patterns of discrimination. Whether the institutions are the highly regarded public universities of the Southeast and the Midwest or highly regarded private ones located in the Northeast where the rise of public state flagship universities occurred much later than in the Southeast or Midwest (often not until well into the post-World War II era), their signal role as the central institution of higher education in each state suggests a broad responsibility to all citizens. Notably, women seeking advanced degrees in the late 1800s and well into the 1900s were often able to find a place for study at a research university, including many of the major research universities. They often faced discrimination based on gender, including professors' expectation that they would fulfill a more traditional role of wife and mother as well as a dearth of academic employment opportunities except at women's colleges. The first full professor who was a woman at Columbia University was Marjorie Hope Nicholson, and she was not a proponent of social or political advancement of women: she was actually called the best man in her department.[20]

RESEARCH UNIVERSITIES: THE PROFESSORS

As college graduates aspiring to become professors increasingly looked to Germany in the late 1800s to earn their doctorates rather than serving as tutors at U.S. institutions of higher education to prepare themselves, research began its long movement toward ascendancy. As earlier examples and examples in this chapter show, often it was the faculty members who moved institutions toward research, at times encouraged by presidents, provosts, and deans but nevertheless forming the core of the institution's movement. Furthermore, these early researchers often highlighted their distance from the public and from such colleagues as those at the University of Wisconsin and at institutions such as Bryn Mawr who saw the social sciences as a place for instituting social change, eschewing the practical applications of the social sciences for theoretical and abstract investigations.[21] Nor were they interested in enrollment growth; that growth served the purposes of the administrators and professors interested in utility, but research-oriented professors wanted serious students, not the students (and their combinations) who had other reasons than academic achievement for their college enrollment.

The movement toward research status among four-year institutions had an impact beyond gender, race and ethnicity, and salary, as it was also the meaning of professional status that changed. Not only, as William James pointed out in the early 1900s the case that increasingly the earned doctorate was a requirement for a faculty appointment at four-year institutions, so too did the definition of an academic professional develop. Starting, perhaps, with Logan Wilson's 1942 work, *The Academic Man*, which examined professionalism at major universities, observers as well as administrators and faculty members turned to the model of the research university for a definition of an academic professional, an effort continued by such scholars as Talcott Parsons in the 1960s and Donald Light in the 1970s.[22] As the definitions developed, they focused more and more on research rather than teaching, with such attributes as expert knowledge and autonomy serving as key indicators of the profession. As a result, professors at institutions where teaching was the core activity, or in some cases the only activity for faculty members, were marginalized, both at small liberal arts colleges and community colleges. One solution for the small liberal arts college was to begin to emphasize research despite limited facilities and equipment for those disciplines requiring extensive infrastructure such as physics, as occurred at Beloit College in the 1980s. For community college faculty members, however, there was no such opportunity, although some scholars have identified professional markers for teaching for community college professors, using empirical evidence that clearly shows a set of powerful norms for professionalism and teaching.[23] Regardless of such findings, the research-productive, tenured, faculty member at the research university remains the iconic figure in academic professionalism, the core of the research university.

As these research institutions developed, they increased the expectations for faculty appointments. While norms of scholarship—such as the careful use of evidence that can be replicated by other scholars, whether it is matter of measuring sub-atomic particles or referencing historical events—are relatively clear and clearly attractive to a large group of aspiring academics, selection also matters in terms of gender, race and ethnicity, and socioeconomic class. Mentioned briefly earlier, James Anderson investigated interest in hiring African Americans for faculties at Northern white colleges and universities. An official of the General Education Board, in response to a request from the president of Black Mountain College (which in 1945 hired four African American professors), assembled a list of African American scholars, many with highly impressive *vitas* and proposed to about 600 presidents of Northern white institutions that they consider these candidates. It was a propitious time for his proposal given the rise of enrollments and the increase of African American scholars with advanced degrees, but only about 200 presidents responded, and only a few offered any support for his idea. A few pointed to African Americans on their campuses, in one instance even providing the example of interest in such appointments by indicating that an assistant director of a dining hall, African American, was a representation of the institutional interest in hiring African American professors. Far more common was to insist that the institution was committed to meritocracy and always wanted the best man (the gender naming of the time) for a position, a declaration contrary to the impressive list of African American scholars on the official's list. As Anderson argues, the events represented the limitations of meritocracy in a racist set of assumptions, stating,

> Institutional racism is a form of ethnic discrimination and exclusion through routine organizational policies and procedures that do not use ethnicity or color as the rationale for discrimination, but instead rely on nonracist rationales to effectively exclude members of ethnic minority.[24]

Black scholars faced an additional challenge in the South, where segregated campuses were the only form of higher education. Talented scholars such as Horace Mann Bond, with a Ph.D. from the University of Chicago and publications such as his 1939 book, *Negro Education in Alabama: A Study in Cotton and Steel*, were unable to secure teaching positions with adequate income because black colleges faced restricted funding that resulted in lower salaries for faculty members, and he chose administration, eventually becoming a college president with uneasy outcomes. Nor could African Americans earn doctorates at the racist Southern white institutions, so the General Education Board (GEB) and the Julius Rosenwald Fund funded advanced studies at Northern institutions for African Americans. Furthermore, in 1938 the U.S. Supreme Court ruled that the University of Missouri had to admit an African American candidate to its law school, in the *Gaines v. Canada* case brought by the Legal Defense Fund of the NAACP, part of the Fund's long-term project to desegregate educational institutions by starting with the most expensive form, post-baccalaureate studies. Southern states responded with scholarships for African Americans to study at Northern colleges and universities (begun by the University of Missouri in 1921, so the *Gaines* case accelerated those programs), thereby providing separate but equal education. GEB focused its efforts on improving public education and black colleges, while the Rosenwald Fund increasingly looked to developed talented scholars in the liberal arts. While the programs often suffered from paternalism, they also provided individual African Americans with opportunities to succeed as individuals and to further racial uplift; Horace Mann Bond, for example, received Rosenwald Fund support.[25]

The process of developing research university status lent itself to re-shaping the faculty in regard to advancement. Pursuing a line of inquiry resulting in presentation or publication quickly became a norm for professors at those institutions, and they also had concerns about their role in the governance of the institution and, particularly in the social sciences, the freedom to pursue their lines of inquiry. After six years of negotiation led by Ralph E. Himstead of the AAUP (who would later be fully complicit in the organization's failure to address academic freedom cases during McCarthyism), the AAUP and the Association of American Colleges (now the Association of American Colleges and Universities, reflecting the expansion of many liberal arts colleges into comprehensive university status, offering master's degrees as well as the baccalaureate) issued in 1940 the Statement of Principles on Academic Freedom and Tenure, commonly known now as the 1940 Statement. The Statement specified the now familiar seven years of pre-tenure for full-time faculty members, with a review at the end of the probationary period.[26] Fundamentally the Statement was an attempt to protect pre-tenure and tenured faculty members in terms of their academic freedom, and the probationary period ensured that the institution and the faculty would be able to have faculty members well qualified to serve in the roles, although as importantly noted earlier, the meaning of that service was problematic in terms of gender as well as race and ethnicity. Tenure provided essentially a life-time appointment, although institutions have dismissed tenured professors without the due process of review outlined in the 1940 Statement.

The group of faculty members known as contingent faculty, both full-time and part-time, represent another problematic condition of the professoriate. These professors are not pre-tenure or tenured, and their ranks have swelled since the 1970s as institutions of higher education choose to appoint faculty members who are not eligible for tenure (a costly appointment, worth close to a million dollars over the professor's lifetime appointment), whose primary responsibility is most often teaching.[27] Without tenure, these faculty members are at-will employees, whom the institution can dismiss without cause, especially a problematic condition for part-time contingent faculty members (who also often have no offices or institutionally provided computers and can be called to teach right before a semester starts).[28] Nevertheless, these appointments provide not only the institution with a potentially quick solution to, for example, enrollment declines but also replacements for research-oriented faculty members with reduced teaching loads in exchange for their research time or external funding supplanting part (or at times all) of their teaching responsibilities.

Research goals have also proven to be powerful in changing institutional goals. An examination of faculty hiring processes at two comprehensive universities (their highest degree is the master's) in the 1970s illustrates the increasing centrality of research among U.S. universities. These two institutions by and large experienced a succession of three hiring cohorts, the first to teach, the second to conduct research, and the third, broader in interests and demographic backgrounds, conducting research yet also more committed to issues of diversity and teaching diverse populations. As the institutions shifted their hiring focus, they also increased expectations for faculty productivity in research. An even clearer picture of the commanding position of research comes from salary research conducted by James Fairweather starting in the 1990s. His repeated analyses of criteria influencing merit-pay increases for faculty members show that measures of research (publications, teaching graduate students rather than undergraduate students) result in greater increases in merit pay than teaching. Most remarkable about his findings is that while such choices are understandable at research universities at any level, and perhaps not all that surprising at comprehensive universities, they are quite evident at four-year liberal arts colleges. Those institutions, with a long and well-touted commitment to teaching, have increasingly rewarded faculty members who engage in scholarship and research.[29]

Research has also had clear implications for gender as well as race and ethnicity. These implications became increasingly clear in the 1960s and 1970s, as the civil rights movement and the first wave of feminism had an impact, even starting points, on college and university campuses. A thorough review of the academic historical profession from its origins in the late 1800s to its status in the 1990s argues convincingly that the study of history splintered in that period (one might well argue that splintering is neither good nor bad) as graduate students and young faculty members investigated not just traditional forms of historical understanding such as diplomatic history but also the role of white women and African Americans in U.S. history, topics previously buried under white male assumptions about what matters as history.[30]

The benefits of recognition for research faculty members had an effect on colleagues' recognition both those professors and lesser-known professors, what Robert Merton called the Matthew Effect; Merton's analysis focused on scientists, based on previous empirical work done by Harriet Zuckerman. He extended her research by arguing that the efforts of Nobel Prize winners resulted in increased citations for their work even when other, less-recognized scientists had done similar work because other scientists tended to cite the more famous; further analysis, they often came from prestigious institutions as undergraduates, received their graduate degrees from similar institutions, and worked at those institutions, concentrating federal research and support at those same universities, reflecting more than a half century of elites in U.S. higher education. There is another important dimension, extending the interesting social characteristics of academic citation to other than the academically famous. The Matthew Effect was not simply a matter of Nobel Prize winners accruing citations, it was also an indicator of such issues as gender, race, and ethnicity. The African American scholars whose credentials were not deemed as meritocratic as white scholars by presidents of Northern white institutions were not cited by their white male colleagues for pursuing areas of inquiry in areas such as black literature or black history (the very reason for Carter G. Woodson to start the *Journal of Negro History* in order to ensure black history, an effort he furthered by establishing Negro History Week, now Black History Month); nor were white women investigating social science problems and offering solutions cited as the empirical approach to social science, with less attention to practical social science research, secured primacy in the social sciences, as noted in the discussion of Bryn Mawr and Wellesley social science professors. Here then is a powerful indicator of the politics of knowledge, that even in the absence of gender, and more broadly such characteristics as race and ethnicity; black history was an African American issue, and solving social problems was a woman's issue.[31]

It would be haphazard to argue for full autonomy accorded to research endeavors in view of the attacks on professors and their academic freedom in general and especially in times of war. Equally important, external efforts to re-create academic disciplines despite their seeming autonomy may be hidden, as is the case of the discipline of economics in the 1970s and the 1980s. Richard Hamilton and Lowell Hargens examined faculty political attitudes and their changes from a 1969 survey to a 1989 survey and found that overall, faculty political attitudes shifted toward the middle from the left, although the overall movement was not particularly strong. Nevertheless, as Everett Carl Ladd and Seymour Lipset highlighted in their 1976 book, *The Divided Academy*, disciplines and fields of study often reflect very different political attitudes; sociologists tend to be liberal or very liberal, while engineering professors tend to be conservative. A careful examination of an appendix in the Hamilton and Hargens' article shows that the most substantial shift in the social sciences occurred in economics. In 1969, 64.8 percent of the economics faculty members identified themselves as Left or Liberal; in 1984, 27.7 percent were Left or Liberal. This shift was not accidental or a mere function of aging or some other internal variable. Philip Kovacs' 2006 dissertation details the forces behind that shift. After Barry Goldwater's failed run for the presidency of the United States, Far Right politicians feared the demise of the Far Right, and William Simon (former Secretary of the Treasury) and Lewis Powell (who would become a Supreme Court Justice). In a 1971 memorandum, Powell feared not only the Far Left but more important, voices on college and university campuses, and among other goals, he suggested ensuring that conservative scholars would be on campuses. Simon (at the time, he was head of the Olin Foundation, well known for its conservative views) wrote a 1978 book in which he urged foundations to seek more financial support from business people to support researchers and professors with conservative capitalist points of view, stating, "The alliance between the theorists and men of action in the capitalist world is long overdue in America." Over the decades businesses and foundations have contributed hundreds of millions of dollars to support theorists in economics whose lines of inquiry support conservative economic policies.[32] Given the rise of free-market ideas most often articulated by University of Chicago economists

(Milton Friedman won the Nobel Prize in Economics in 1976, one of 12 connected with that university since 1974, many exploring free-market ideas), their work and the efforts of Powell, Simon, and wealthy donors and foundations indicate that internal and external mechanisms can combine to develop and sustain substantially different views within a discipline, or more deeply, to change the primary theories of a discipline. Research and academic specialization, then, is not independent of political ideas.

RESEARCH UNIVERSITIES: THE STUDENTS

The rise of academic specialization and the search for what might be called academic students had a profound effect on college admissions. Throughout the 1600s, 1700s, and 1800s, the president or the faculty or both were the direct arbiters of who would be admitted. Generally, institutions of higher education accepted all qualified students, particularly since there was no great demand for higher education, and often accepted students who were not fully qualified. After the Civil War, presidents and faculties shifted from oral examinations to written ones to evaluate applicants, but nevertheless the review was conducted of individual students, systematic only in each institution's definition of a qualified student who had read certain classical works and had some combination of other subjects "such as geography, history, and English literature." As noted, one solution was the preparatory department, and another was to admit students conditionally, a remarkably common response. For example, in "1907 over half of the freshmen matriculating at Harvard, Yale, Princeton, and Columbia had failed to meet their entrance requirements in one particular or another."[33] The certification system instituted at Michigan and Wisconsin had a parallel among some northeastern institutions, but as the demand for a higher education increased and as developing secondary schools saw little to their benefit to tailor their curricula to individual institutions' expectations, certification lost its appeal. The rise of social sciences and mass testing offered another possibility, and in the late 1800s several colleges and universities in the mid-Atlantic states developed a uniform assessment for English literature, and shortly thereafter the president of Columbia, Nicholas Murry Butler convinced the group to consider establishing a larger group, which became the College Entrance Examination Board. The College Board offered its first tests in 1901, albeit with only a small number of students and institutions of higher education participating; that group of institutions and others that followed suit were, for the most part, the older colleges and universities in the Northeast. At the same time, the Carnegie Foundation for the Advancement of Teaching, concerned about the distribution of large amounts of money donated by Andrew Carnegie in 1909 to fund faculty retirements, sought to standardize college preparation through the identification of a student's four years of secondary school, an effort that assisted the development of the differentiation between secondary schools and institutions of higher education. Actual selection of students typically began to occur after World War I, and while putatively the selectivity was based on academic achievement as determined by four years of secondary school and acceptable performance on a standardized test, other factors together played an important role.[34]

Changing expectations about student qualifications at professional schools, especially medical schools following the Flexner report of 1910, was one factor. As the president of the Carnegie Foundation, Henry Pritchett, argued in his introduction to the Flexner report, it had become clear that not only was there a need for better and fewer medical schools, but also "the needs of the public would equally require that we would have fewer physicians graduated each year, but that these should be better educated and better trained."[35]

Academic selectivity had, however, troubling conditions in regard to how institutions interpreted meritocracy, not only for faculty members or applicants to medical school but also for undergraduate students. As Harold Wechsler detailed in *The Qualified Student*, institutions such as Columbia and Harvard in the early 1900s developed means to select only a few of the identifiable minorities, in the case of those two institutions deliberately excluding Eastern European Jews because the presidents (Nicholas Murray Butler and Charles W. Eliot, respectively) wanted their institutions to develop leadership at the national level, leadership requiring a manliness evident, in their eyes, in white male Protestant students. This effort broadened and continued after World War I.[36] The means to achieve meritocratic selections expanded after World War II with the establishment of the Educational Testing Service (ETS), which merged the testing services of the College Board and the SAT, the Carnegie Foundation and the GRE, and the American Council on Education and the National Teacher Examination. That organization, as well as the younger ACT (which offered its first test in 1959), have attempted to open the meritocracy by using testing as a means to assess students beyond the variability of their secondary school preparation, but the problems of different scores for different populations, in terms of race and ethnicity but especially financial background, continue to sustain a meritocracy with unequal demographic characteristics.

Nor does admission to the institution mean full engagement or a welcoming environment, as shown by Cally Waite in her discussion of Oberlin in the late 1800s.

Problems with racism on campus has clearly been part of college life since early in the time when institutions of higher education began to admit American Indians, and then later, African Americans, and the research university has been part of the problem. A study of six midwestern research universities, five of which received and accepted the invitation to join the Association of American Universities (AAU) in the first decade of the 1900s, illustrates the depth of these problems over time. All six are the state flagship universities and early members of the AAU—Illinois (1908), Iowa (1909), Kansas (1909), Minnesota (1908), Nebraska (the one not in the AAU), and Wisconsin (1900)—and all enrolled African American students before 1900 except for the University of Illinois, graduating a total of 30 of them. The pattern from the early 1880s to the late 1930s is constant and clear for African Americans; while some white students accepted them, some had little to do with them, and the remaining participated in virulent racist acts, including wearing KKK robes or performing in blackface. Just as occurred for women at the University of Wisconsin in contrast to their widespread participation in extracurricular activities at Wisconsin normal schools, these students were often excluded from extracurricular groups. In fact, the KKK was a student organization at Illinois and Wisconsin in the 1910s, and had student support at Illinois, Iowa, and Minnesota in the 1920s, a period when the Klan was experiencing a resurgence nationally. Only University of Nebraska administrators made clear that they would not tolerate Klan activities on campus. Minstrel shows even held an annual place in Homecoming activities or other annual student events at all six universities. Black Greek-Letter fraternities and sororities provided support for some of the African American students, the first appearing at Kansas University in 1898 (earlier than the common statement that the first Black fraternity began at Indiana University in 1903), doing well in annual academic achievement rankings and in some instances providing homes, most helpful in those instances where racist landlords refused housing to African Americans. Yet even in those cases, the Greeks section of yearbooks often published caricatures of African Americans.[37]

There were also socioeconomic class issues, noted previously in the movement away from enrolling poor students and toward studying the poor. Furthermore, institutions of higher education often and consistently raised their tuition rates in the 1900s, prior to the extensive federal financial aid programs. While state universities may have a reputation for lower tuition rates (except for out-of-state students in recent decades), there was a notable growth of wealthy students among state flagship universities starting in the 1960s, a wealth accompanied by their change in selectivity.[38] In the early 1970s, for example, the University of Wisconsin-Madison faculty voted to change the admission criterion for class rank, so that Wisconsin high school students had to be in the top quarter of their senior class rather than only the top half.

CONCLUSION

In broader historical terms, there is the necessary reminder that these research universities, which hold the center in prestige, and a strong supporting mechanism, highly selective liberal arts colleges (which pride themselves on sending their graduates to graduate and professional schools), as well as the pervasive movement to have undergraduate research symposia every spring, support and advance multiple means that ensure that the meritocracy sustains. Exclusion and stratification are deeply characteristic of these institutional mechanisms.

DISCUSSION QUESTIONS

1. How did the rise of research transform the professoriate?
2. How did the rise of research affect students?

NOTES

1   Hugh Hawkins, *Pioneer: A History of the Johns Hopkins University* (Ithaca, NY: Cornell University Press, 1960).

2   John S. Brubacher and Willis Rudy, *Higher Education in Transition: A History of American Colleges and Universities*, 4th ed. (New York: Routledge, 2017).

3   Hugh Hawkins, *Between Harvard and America The Educational Leadership of Charles W. Eliot* (New York: Oxford University Press, 1972).

4   Hugh Hawkins, "American Universities and the Inclusion of Professional Schools," *History of Higher Education Annual* 13 (1993): 53–68.

5   Hugh Davis Graham and Nancy Diamond, *The Rise of American Research Universities: Elites and Challengers in the Postwar Era* (Baltimore: Johns Hopkins University Press, 1997).

6   Amy Sue Bix, "'Backing into Sponsored Research': Physics and Engineering at Princeton University," *History of Higher Education Annual* 13 (1993): 9–52

7   Hugh Davis Graham and Nancy Diamond, *The Rise of American Research Universities: Elites and Challengers in the Postwar Era* (Baltimore: Johns Hopkins University Press, 1997).

8   Roger L. Geiger, *Research and Relevant Knowledge: American Research Universities Since World War II* (Brunswick, NJ: Transaction Publishers, 2004).

9   Hugh Davis Graham and Nancy Diamond, *The Rise of American Research Universities: Elites and Challengers in the Postwar Era* (Baltimore: Johns Hopkins University Press, 1997).

10 Cameron Fincher, *Historical Development of the University System of Georgia, 1932–1990* (Athens: University of Georgia Institute of Higher Education, 1991).

11 Hugh Davis Graham and Nancy Diamond, *The Rise of American Research Universities: Elites and Challengers in the Postwar Era* (Baltimore: Johns Hopkins University Press: 1997).

12 Hugh Hawkins, "American Universities and the Inclusion of Professional Schools," *History of Higher Education Annual* 13 (1993): 53–68.

13 Laurence Veysey, *The Emergence of the American University* (Chicago: University of Chicago Press, 1965), 311–317 on bureaucratization and 116–118 on the efficiency craze; Laurence Veysey, "From Germany to America," *History of Education Quarterly* 13 (Winter 1973): 406.

14 William James, "The Ph.D. Octopus," in *Memories and Studies*, ed. William James (New York: Longmans, Green, & Company, 1912), 329–347.

15 Diana Crane, *Invisible Colleges: Diffusion of Knowledge in Scientific Communities* (Chicago: University of Chicago Press, 1975).

16 Alvin W. Gouldner, "Cosmopolitans and Locals: Toward an Analysis of Latent Social Roles—I," *Administrative Science Quarterly* 2 (December 1957): 281–306; Alvin W. Gouldner, "Cosmopolitans and Locals: Toward an Analysis of Latent Social Roles–II," *Administrative Science Quarterly* 2 (March 1958): 444–480.

17 F. Stuart Gulley, *The Academic President as Moral Leader* (Macon, GA: Mercer University Press, 2001).

18 Kathleen A. Mahoney and Caroline Winterer, "The Problem of the Past in the Modern University: Catholics and Classicists, 1860–1900," *History of Education Quarterly* 42 (Winter 2002): 517–543; Lester Goodchild, "The Turning Point in American Jesuit Higher Education: The Standardization Controversy Between the Jesuits and the North Central Association, 1915–1940," *History of Higher Education Annual* 6 (1986), 81–116.

19 Philo Hutcheson, "The University, Professionalization, and Race in the United States," in *Beyond the Lecture Hall: Universities and Community Engagement from the Middle Ages to the Present Day*, ed. Peter Cunningham, Susan Oosthuizan, and Peter Taylor (Cambridge, UK: University of Cambridge, Faculty of Education and Institute of Continuing Education, 2009), 103–115.

20 Mary Ann Dzuback, "Gender and the Politics of Knowledge," *History of Education Quarterly* 43 (Summer 2003): 171–195. Andrea Walton, "'Scholar,' 'Lady,' 'Best Man in the English Department'? Recalling the Career of Marjorie Hope Nicolson," *History of Education Quarterly* 40 (Summer 2000): 169–200.

21 Dorothy Ross, *The Origins of American Social Science* (New York: Cambridge University Press, 1991); Mary O. Furner, *Advocacy and Objectivity: A Crisis in the Professionalization of American Social Science, 1865–1905* (Lexington: University Press of Kentucky, 1975).

22 Logan Wilson, *The Academic Man* (New York: Oxford University Press, 1942); Talcott Parsons and Gerald Platt, "The American Academic Profession: A Pilot Study" (Washington, DC: National Science Foundation, 1968); Donald Light, Jr., "Introduction: The Structure of the Academic Professions," *Sociology of Education* 47, no. 1 (Winter 1974): 2–28.

23 Alan E. Bayer and John M. Braxton, "The Normative Structure of Community College Teaching: A Marker of Professionalism," *Journal of Higher Education* 69, no. 2 (March–April 1998): 187–205.

24 James D. Anderson, "Race, Meritocracy, and the American Academy During the Immediate Post-World War II Era," *History of Education Quarterly* 33 (Summer 1993): 151.

25 Wayne Urban, *Black Scholar: Horace Mann Bond, 1904–1972* (Athens: University of Georgia Press, 2008); Jayne R. Beilke, "The Politics of Opportunity: Philanthropic Fellowship Programs: Out-of-State Aid and Black Higher Education in the South," *History of Higher Education Annual* 17 (1997): 53–96.

26 Philo Hutcheson, *A Professional Professoriate: Unionization, Bureaucratization, and the AAUP* (Nashville, TN: Vanderbilt University Press, 2000).

27   Philo Hutcheson, "The Corrosion of Tenure: A Bibliography," *Thought and Action* 13 (Fall 1997): 89–106; Howard R. Bowen and Jack L. Schuster, *American Professors: A National Resource Imperiled* (New York: Oxford University Press, 1986).

28   John G. Cross and Edie N. Goldenberg, *The Toll Road to Contingency: Off-Track Profs: Nontenured Teachers in Higher Education* (Cambridge, MA: MIT Press, 2009); Judith M. Gappa and David W. Leslie, *The Invisible Faculty: Improving the Status of Part-Timers in Higher Education* (San Francisco: Jossey-Bass, 1994); Gina L. Sheeks and Philo A. Hutcheson, "How Departments Support Part-Time Faculty," *Thought & Action* 14, no. 2 (Fall 1998): 85–90; Gina Sheeks, "Feeling Connected: The Socialization of Part-Time Faculty Members at a Private Liberal Arts College" (Ph.D. dissertation, Georgia State University, 2003).

29   Dorothy E. Finnegan, "Segmentation in the Academic Labor Market: Hiring Cohorts in Comprehensive Universities," *Journal of Higher Education* 64, no. 6 (November–December 1993): 621–656; James S. Fairweather, "Academic Values and Faculty Rewards," *Review of Higher Education* 17, no. 1 (Fall 1993): 43–68.

30   Peter Novick, *That Noble Dream: The "Objectivity Question" and the American Historical Profession* (New York: Cambridge University Press, 1988).

31   Robert K. Merton, "The Matthew Effect in Science, II: Cumulative Advantage and the Symbolism of Intellectual Property," *Isis* 79 (December 1988): 606–623; Mary Ann Dzuback, "Women and Social Research at Bryn Mawr College, 1915–1940," *History of Education Quarterly* 33 (Winter 1993): 579–608; Mary Ann Dzuback, "Gender and the Politics of Knowledge," *History of Education Quarterly* 43 (Summer 2003): 171–195.

32   Richard F. Hamilton and Lowell L. Hargens, "The Politics of the Professors: Self-Identifications, 1969–1984," *Social Forces* 71 (March 1993): 603–627; Philip Kovacs, "Are Public Schools Worth Saving? If So, By Whom?" (Ph.D. dissertation, Georgia State University, 2006); William E. Simon, *A Time for Truth* (New York: Reader's Digest Press, 1978), 233.

33   John S. Brubacher and Willis Rudy, *Higher Education in Transition: A History of American Colleges and Universities*, 4th ed. (New York: Routledge, 2017).

34   W. Bruce Leslie, *Gentlemen and Scholars: College and Community in the "Age" of the University* (University Park: Pennsylvania State University Press, 1992); on 1907 admissions, see John S. Brubacher and Willis Rudy, *Higher Education in Transition: A History of American Colleges and Universities*, 4th ed. (New York: Routledge, 2017).

35   Henry S. Pritchett, "Introduction," in *Medical Education in the United States and Canada: A Report to the Carnegie Foundation for the Advancement of Teaching*, Abraham Flexner (New York: Carnegie Foundation for the Advancement of Teaching, Bulletin No. 4, 1910).

36   Harold S. Wechsler, *The Qualified Student: A History of Selective College Admission in America* (New York: Routledge, 2017); David O. Levine, *The American College and the Culture of Aspiration, 1915–1940* (Ithaca, NY: Cornell University Press, 1986).

37   Richard M. Breaux, "Nooses, Sheets, and Blackface: White Racial Anxiety and Black Student Presence at Six Midwest Flagship Universities, 1882–1937," *Perspectives on the History of Higher Education* 29 (2012): 43–73.

38   Rupert Wilkinson, *Aiding Students, Buying Students: Financial Aid in America* (Nashville, TN: Vanderbilt University Press, 2005).

8

FROM THE COLONIAL COLLEGES TO THE COLLEGES AND UNIVERSITIES OF TODAY

Processes of Exclusion and Stratification

As noted, even in their earliest years, colonial colleges enrolled scholarship boys, the serious boys, often from poor backgrounds, often intent on becoming ministers. Were these institutions inclusive? Although the distribution of class at those was far wider than suggested in the term "aristocracy" too often used in describing those colleges, as Cremin wrote, the poor was a much larger class relative to the middle or upper class than it is today, and the poor were by and large excluded. We also know that women were excluded, as were almost all African Americans. Frighteningly, one minoritized population, American Indians, that was enrolled at some of those colonial colleges by and large had harsh experiences. In some very important ways, those institutions did not have many issues of stratification because exclusion was a given.

That exclusion was and remains part of U.S. higher education is evident in the curricular meanings of the *ars liberalis*, the liberal arts. For those who could afford it, it was more than the sort of reflective thinking argued in the Yale Report; it served utilitarian purposes as preparation for professional advancement—at the time, in such terms as leadership in governing councils. Profession, of course, is very different now than it was then, but a liberal education remains a cornerstone in professional school admission criteria particularly for medicine and law. Furthermore, the most prestigious colleges and universities offer a liberal arts education with little if any offerings in utilitarian areas such as education, business, or social work.

Upon the advent of the Republic, there were nine colleges, all of which excluded on the basis of gender and were almost exclusively white, and mostly mercantile (as previously noted, the middle class developed in the latter part of the 1800s) and upper class. The colleges were fundamentally exclusionary.

In the first 50 years or so following the American Revolution, the spread of colleges was remarkable, and it is a growth that continued at different rates for decades and then accelerated in the 1950s and 1960s. In this process, the expansion often demarcates different populations by institution, as in the growth of white women's colleges and black colleges (including coeducational, the men's college, and eventually both of the women's colleges). In the cases where white women were accepted, they typically began as lone voyagers and often as their numbers grew, the social definition changed to heterosexual terms. For African Americans, as one Northern university president argued in the early 1900s, a few on campus was fine, but the Southern experience of millions of African Americans resulted in a different, exclusionary, response among white Southerners and would likely result in the same reaction among white Northerners. He saw promise in "self-help, educational endeavor, dependence upon white paternalism, and faith in the gradual process of cultural assimilation," representing a Northern white liberal expectation of the time.[1]

Exclusion might appear to shift when considering denominations and their need to admit students regardless of denomination, that it was no longer Puritans or Calvinists or Congregationalists excluding students of other denomination, but instead they were accepting Christian, or at least Protestant, students. To some degree, that is accurate. But opening higher education in terms of denomination actually meant only that more white men were able to go to college, because denominational colleges had to practice tolerance in order to sustain their enrollments. While this development leads to the expansion of the middle class—as does the foundation of state universities starting with Southern states and then in the midwestern and western ones, it is only a shift of exclusion in terms of denominational affiliation. The advent of institutions of higher education for white women and African Americans more fundamentally signaled the beginning of exclusion by institution type, a very different type of shift.

A richer understanding of the shifts in exclusion at the time obtains in considering gender. Seminaries, institutes, and academies for female students in the early 1800s and later represent more than some sort of secondary education; they resemble colleges too much to be seen as not being a form of higher education. Early women's colleges such as LaGrange Institute in Georgia and Mary Sharpe College in Tennessee moved into comparable college status in such matters as curriculum rather quickly. As argued earlier, even the rise of the normal schools starting with an entry age similar to Yale's 14 suggests an expansion of higher education based on gender; arguably, however, these institutions entered into a process of stratification as the Yale faculty proclaimed that their institution, rather than those focused on utilitarian goals, was the meaning of a college. Nevertheless, as broadly higher education began to include white women, exclusion on the basis of institutions continued, with institutions bearing the banner of college also proudly bearing the banner of all-male, almost without exception in the Northeast and the South. Exclusion, then, shifted toward stratification by institutional types beginning in the early 1800s.

Another form of stratification, within institutions, is evident in coeducation, which often occurred outside the traditionally prestigious colleges and universities of the North as well as private and public institutions in the South. Both private and public institutions of higher education in the Midwest and West either began as coeducational or admitted women starting in the 1800s, about a century before the Ivy League institutions and some public universities such as Rutgers University (1972) and the University of Virginia (1970) that were all-male began admitting women—often those midwestern and western institutions or the states prior to then had separate colleges for women. Those coeducational institutions therefore moved away from exclusion on the basis of gender, but access is not the same as engagement (a key term among many student services administrators), and the experiences of those women at formerly all-male institutions in the 1970s were often ones of marginalization and disdain, echoing the experiences of many college women on coeducational campuses in the Midwest or West in the 1800s, a form of social stratification. An examination of the experiences of women students at four colleges in the 1980s concludes that for the most part, women at the women's college (Wells) and the coordinate college (William Smith) had more positive collegiate experiences, although those at Hamilton and Middlebury (the latter began admitting women in the 1880s as a matter of financial expediency, a common enough event) reported more faculty encouragement in academic matters. Institutional stratification by selectivity, however, appeared to matter more in terms of career outcomes than the gendered nature of the college experience. Women at the most selective of the four institutions reported the highest levels of graduate degree attainment (doctorates, medical and law degrees), suggesting that academic selectivity has a powerful effect on graduates' attainments. In addition, the alumnae of all four institutions evidenced only minor differences in regard to their goals and attitudes, suggesting the weakened lines between public and private spheres.[2] While some institutions shifted away from institutional stratification, internal or social stratification sustained differences.

INTERTWINING EXCLUSION, INSTITUTIONAL STRATIFICATION, AND SOCIAL STRATIFICATION

While African Americans enrolled on occasion at U.S. institutions of higher education prior to the Civil War, it was in such small numbers as to suggest that they were not in large enough numbers to threaten the Whites. As African Americans began to enroll in larger numbers after the Civil War and in the early 1900s, particularly at black colleges beginning with Lincoln University (begun as Ashmun Institute) and Wilberforce College, other mechanisms of exclusion minoritized their participation, such as the closing of African American medical schools and the SACS designation of black colleges as holding secondary accreditation status. Exclusionary measures did not disappear, but rather became more nuanced and yet just as powerful.

An important example of the nature of exclusion by institutional type and control deserves discussion here. Those knowledgeable about desegregation at Southern colleges and universities nearly always offer comments about the violent nature of anti-desegregation protests at such institutions as the University of Georgia and the University of Alabama (for a deeply personal account, there is Charlayne Hunter-Gault, *In My Place*, about her experiences at the University of Georgia when she and Hamilton Holmes became the first two African American students to enroll there). Sometimes other, smaller, institutions such as Spring Hill College in Mobile, Alabama desegregated too. Furthermore, Melissa Kean authored an extensive work on the desegregation of preeminent private universities in the South, such as Vanderbilt and Tulane. In those cases, there was most certainly resistance to desegregation, but hardly ever at the level of large mobs threatening to murder young African American men or women. It is reasonable to argue that state flagship universities were the center of such virulent protests because they were just that, state flagship institutions, and the racist residents of the state could not abide by the thought that their primary institution would no longer be a bulwark of exclusion, the core of resistance to desegregation, whereas at such institutions as Spring Hill College, desegregation often occurred with little protest.[3] Excluding African Americans was a more important process at the highly visible state flagship universities than at other institutions; the seemingly most important institutions meant the most to Whites.

Exclusion and stratification occur even within institutions with traditions of opposition to exclusion. An examination of Tuskegee Institute focused on the transition from a chef-training program for men, "industrial and paternalistic," to a fully credentialed program in dietetics offers consideration of the role of gender in the African American community, in this instance a professionalizing role based on the American Dietetic Association, which was "nearly all-white and feminized." Despite those characteristics of the professional association, the Tuskegee professors also responded to the needs of African Americans, shaping a curriculum based less on traditional notions of white professionals as espoused in the Flexner report and more on African Americans and their "values, conduct, role conceptualization and how they went about their work." This work exemplifies the complexities of exclusion and stratification; the African American men at the Tuskegee program initially resisted the efforts of the African American women, yet the eventual outcome focused on the African American community even while conforming to the demands of a professional association. Even within a community with centuries of brutal oppression, divides are visible in such matters as gender within race, as Marybeth Gasman reminded readers many years ago.[4] So too, race divides occurred by gender, given that colleges for white women such as the Seven Sisters ranged from admission of African American women in the late 1800s and early 1900s to only doing so under pressure in the 1950s.[5]

One recent minoritized population's enrollment growth in higher education, Latinx students, exemplifies the increased role of the federal government as well as the still-developing understanding of minority student experiences on campuses. There is little historical scholarship on the higher education of Latinx students, although one examination evidences the patterns of discrimination experienced by those students, linked to discrimination against Mormons and Roman Catholics. The foundation of Colorado College was based, not surprisingly, in boosterism and Protestantism, the latter in that region carrying a clear message of anti-Mormonism and anti-Catholicism, although the college was open to both genders and all races and ethnicities. In the case of the Mormons, one pamphlet described them as a "'strangely Americanized Asiatic abomination,'" and Catholics were "'densely ignorant, grossly immoral, cruelly superstitious, and tyrannized by a band of Jesuits.'" Such sentiments were reflective of the man who was central in the college's early years and his New England roots.[6]

Aspects of exclusion also went beyond our current notions of race and ethnicity. A case in point is an examination of the admission of 14 private colleges in upstate New York in the fall of 1946, on the eve of the creation of the State University of New York (SUNY) in 1948. The institutions selected as few as 7 percent of the Jewish applicants (the same institution accepted 32 percent of non-Jewish applicants) and as many as 75 percent (the acceptance rate for non-Jewish students was 70 percent); for all 14 institutions, the average acceptance rate was 37 percent for Jews and 48 percent for non-Jews. There was only one institution with an acceptance rate for Jews higher than for non-Jews, and seven accepted 50 percent or far less of the Jewish applicants in contrast to the acceptance rate for non-Jewish students.[7] One way of ascertaining, or at least guessing, that a student was a Jew (even the common naming of Jewish is odd, since we never refer to Catholicish or Protestantish students) was to require a photograph, providing a way of determining whether or not an applicant was a Jew, based on crude portrayals, and as Charolotte Borst showed, medical schools used admission interviews during part of the years between World War I and World War II in order to make a similar determination.

This analysis, however, deserves nuance. While the Yale Report makes a clear claim as to who is best suited to the decision-making centers (local, state, regional, national) of the nation, the liberally educated, or more specifically, the classically educated, but the utilitarian all-male institutions (West Point, for example) saw their purpose as creating leaders too. In a very real sense, gender and race and ethnicity trumped socioeconomic class to some extent, as in both cases white men were identified as the leaders. Yet in other instances, socioeconomic class and race and ethnicity trumped gender because examining the women's institutions of higher education highlights class and race and ethnicity issues in some remarkable ways; the most salient example might be the Southern women's college before the Civil War and its goal of educating well-to-do young white women to have privileged lives on plantations, then after the Civil War they faced the burned plantation but were still at the top of the social hierarchy.

In regard to the slow movement toward coeducation in the midwestern and western state universities, perhaps, the story of social stratification accelerates and becomes more complicated. Obviously, men at all-male colleges divided on the basis of class, with scholarship boys doing work instead of paying tuition, including at some institutions serving tables at meals. Yet once women enter with men, how we define whom takes on new measures and the expectation of roles expands, as women feminized fields such as teaching; women were more serious students, but then women were also pretty and "deserving" (the quotation marks are deliberate) of men's attention. And women did not always pursue careers with the same focus as that of men, the power of societal expectations steering them toward family life in the private sphere. In a poignant title, "After College, What?" a scholar examined the lives of Wellesley graduates of the Class of 1897, and while some pursued careers, most did not, some combining volunteer work with life at home, others filling traditional private sphere roles in their homes.[8] Those pioneers who did pursue careers for their lifetimes were often, as Geraldine Clifford suggests, lone voyagers.

Yet of far deeper concern for this investigation than gender or race and ethnicity exclusion is socioeconomic class, as it has a remarkable meaning in the history of higher education. The education of middle- and upper-class women was often different from the education of lower-class women, either by institutional stratification or social stratification within an institution. In the case of the former, institutions of higher education that emphasized the liberal arts were a likely choice, whereas normal schools more typically enrolled lower- and middle-class women. Even more so than the founding of the U.S. Military Academy in 1802 (the professional class of the military officer seems to occupy a nearly separate world) and Rennselear Polytechnic Institute in 1824, already noted as important developments in U.S. higher education in the 1800s in terms of utilitarian education, white institutions of higher education whether for men, women, or coeducation explain class. If an institution educated or aspired to educate to the liberal arts, its constituency was more likely to be of higher socioeconomic class than if it were one that educated for work such as teaching. At times, in fact, socioeconomic class issues were more evident than choices of curriculum.

Institutions were admitting poor students in the 1800s, as shown by Jana Nidiffer and Jeffrey Bouman, but that effort fell prey, at least at one developing research university, to a shift in institutional goals and an emphasis on studying the poor rather than enrolling them. There was a seeming moment of possibility in the late 1800s, the expansion of opportunity regardless of gender (women's colleges and coeducational institutions) or race and ethnicity (black colleges and increased admission of African American students at white institutions), or socioeconomic class (the rise of access among state universities), and then the door closed down to a great degree. The Flexner report may be taken as a moment of such closure, despite the decided improvement of medical care that resulted from university preparation and a university-affiliated hospital, divides accentuated by nursing's ill-fated attempts to professionalize in a similar manner shortly after the publication of the Flexner report.

An important development in professional education occurred in law, beginning with the establishment of case study at Harvard Law School in the 1870s, widely imitated at other law schools; no longer was the aspiring lawyer an apprentice to a practicing lawyer with responsibilities for reading law books, but instead the aspiring lawyer needed to know case law, the precedents that could set the context for a legal determination. Law schools, however, did not fully move in the direction of medical school professionalization. As corporations grew in size and importance toward the end of the 1800s, the role of lawyers shifted from personal to corporate representation, and while a minority of candidates sitting in the bar in 1870 were law school graduates, by 1920, two-thirds were. In addition, only about 42 percent of law schools were full-time programs. In regard to institutional stratification, 19 of the part-time programs were affiliated with the YMCA, commonly located in urban areas, with several others affiliated with Catholic institutions of higher education, and initially faculty members were local practitioners for the most part—by the 1920s the schools were attracting more professors from more prestigious backgrounds. Some of the students were women, a few were African American (except in the South); many of the students came from the lower-income classes and after graduation practiced law locally. In contrast, the graduates of the more selective prestigious full-time programs typically worked on national and international issues. Some of these part-time schools continue today, and their graduates often work locally.[9]

The rise of junior colleges is another example of institutional stratification in higher education, although the nature of these institutions in historical and contemporary terms is not as simple as pure stratification. For example, many junior colleges developed extracurricular programs that resembled four-year colleges, and the parents of students attending junior colleges sent them there because they viewed the institutions as colleges. Nevertheless, part of the complexity of the roles of junior colleges was that some institutional leaders throughout the 1900s viewed the institutions (in the words of an Ivy League professor in a presentation in 2016) as subcolleges, seeming to perform the task of sifting through under-prepared students to find the most gifted, to paraphrase Thomas Jefferson. Junior colleges might have been a way of sifting, although four-year institutions often have had programs that were really no different from preparatory departments, indicating another form of stratification while providing tuition revenue.

At the very time when some states were developing junior colleges, presidents from what had been the colonial colleges led the effort to use standardized testing beginning in the early 1900s. Much of the purpose of the selectivity, despite the putative goal of searching broadly for talent, was to choose talented Protestant white men, echoing the growing quantitative identification of who was seemingly capable of being leaders at the national level. The process accelerated over the decades, and while the post-World War II period marked the beginning of mass higher education in the

United States, the variety of standardized tests and the concomitant characteristics of testing success by race and ethnicity and especially socioeconomic class emphasize the power of testing to exclude and stratify through the mechanism of admission selectivity. One aspect of the meaning of this form of selectivity is that it furthered the movement toward recruitment of students nationally, expanding access, albeit into selective colleges and universities.

The development and maintenance of mass higher education following the World War II period illustrates the nature of exclusion and stratification in important ways. An oft-cited piece of information about that beginning is from the 1947 President's Commission on Higher Education report, indicating that 51 percent of the population was likely capable of succeeding in post-secondary education. That common figure, however, is not the only estimate offered by the Commission; its estimate that 36 percent of the population could succeed at a four-year institution speaks volumes to the assumption about who ought to go where. It would serve the reader well to remember that most of the veterans who took advantage of the 1944 G.I. Bill were either previously enrolled or would have been likely to enroll at a college. The nation celebrates the access offered by the G.I. Bill although analyses of the students who went to college using the Bill belie that celebration. One characteristic of stratification in U.S. higher education is the more limited opportunities for access and for engagement, and the diminished access for white women and African Americans in terms of the G.I. Bill is a salient example. There is no denying the stunning growth of undergraduate populations in the post-World War II era, both in terms of sheer size and diversification, as Dongbin Kim and John Rury documented in an extensive quantitative analysis of enrollments. Women increasingly entered higher education from 1939–1940 to 1979–1980, becoming the majority by 1979–1980, and the percentage of students of color tripled from 5 to 15 percent. As the authors noted, "Going to college became a relatively commonplace experience."[10] Nevertheless, this book makes clear that the experiences of so many who are not white, male, middle class, and heterosexual form a reminder that access is not engagement; nor does it mean access to the governing councils or professional prestige.

Furthermore, real opportunities occurred for the elite universities—massive federal funding and substantial enrollment growth, coupled with powerful mechanisms for selection, i.e., standardized test scores; the mechanisms, however, are deeply tied to racial, ethnic, and class backgrounds. One unremitting piece of evidence about success on standardized tests, such as the ACT and the SAT, is that the most powerful correlation with test scores is family income. Despite federal financial assistance, students from lower-income homes had less access when their standardized test scores did not meet the expectations of highly selective institutions of higher education, a matter further complicated as the federal government shifted from grants to loans, particularly starting in the 1980s. Students from lower-income homes had less chance of admission and were more likely to incur loan indebtedness. Students from higher-income homes had a greater likelihood of admission and faced fewer financial challenges.

Elite university students also enjoyed the opportunities for further advancement available at their institutions. Students at selective liberal arts colleges also received the benefits of elite status, especially highly selective liberal arts colleges, institutions that often prepared undergraduates for professional education at the elite universities and as Bruce Leslie showed, created a college culture for middle- and upper-class white men.[11] The institutions eventually became coeducational and somewhat diverse in terms of race and ethnicity, and as a result, exclusion shifted toward institutional stratification, mass higher education having its effect of including a much broader range of students; yet experiences within the institution and within the elite are still exclusionary. There has remained continued division within and across institutions of higher education, exemplified by the curricular divisions beginning in the early 1800s—first-generation students so often majoring in practical fields, the children of college-educated students often going to elite colleges and universities and then the elite professional schools or into networks of the elite. Even within the elite institutions, Harvard students as recently as the late 1980s chanted at Ivy League games when their team was losing, "Hey hey, it's okay, you'll be working for us some day." Perhaps they did not bother chanting at games against institutions outside the Ivy League. At least as disturbing, if not more so, is the case of the Yale dean who recently posted restaurant reviews suggesting that one local Japanese restaurant offered food suitable only for white trash.

The gendered aspects of teacher education over the century also deserve attention in this analysis of exclusion and stratification. While missing the clinical aspects that now impose state and bureaucratic expectations on teacher-preparation professors and students, nevertheless the medieval university emphasized the importance of male teachers, evident in the degree title of *ius ubique docendi* (the right to teach anywhere). The normal school, beginning in the 1830s and spreading throughout the nation in the remainder of the century, was a teacher-preparation program for women more often than not. It would be foolhardy to compare two programs across several centuries, but it is instructive that a gendered conception of who belonged as a teacher was accompanied by a diminished prestige while offering increased access. Normal schools offered access to higher education for students from lower-income backgrounds, as the previous examples of Wisconsin normal schools and the Illinois State Normal University show. For white ethnic women, normal schools (known as training schools in New York City) again provided access. In New York City, large numbers of Jewish women studied at the training schools for teachers in the early 1900s; in Providence, Irish women formed a large part of the teaching force beginning in the late 1800s. In both cases, their ethnic identities were problematic during the late 1800s and early 1900s.[12] In the case of Jews, although the *New York Times* was Jewish-owned, job advertisements often indicated they were for Christians only, while for the Irish, in many northeastern city newspapers, the acronym NINA was part of job advertisements, No Irish Need Apply.

Stratification for teachers was a matter of institutional stratification, not just differences in the prestige of teaching. While it is popular to point at exaggerated numbers of dead colleges, a broader comprehension of the nature of institutional transformation is more informative and accurate. For example, normal schools did not, by and large, die. They metamorphosized into state colleges and then state universities. (A quick look at a four-year or comprehensive state university's website and the institution's history often reveals the normal school as the origin of the institution.) A good example is Troy University (Alabama), which began in 1887 as a normal school to educate white teachers, expanding its teacher-education program in 1924 with the establishment of a lab school (an outgrowth of the Progressive education movement at the University of Chicago begun by John Dewey in the early 1900s, heavily based on the work of Francis Parker and Ella Flagg Young among others). In 1929, the Alabama State Board of Education (then responsible for public institutions of higher education) re-named the institution as Troy State Teachers College; following the remarkable expansion of enrollment following World War II, the College expanded its offerings into other fields such as business, and in 1957 the Board of Education changed the name to Troy State College. In 1967 the institution became Troy State University, and in 1982 the name changed to Troy University. The most thorough review of these institutions remains a 1969 book, *Colleges of the Forgotten Americans*, which examines three institutions' changes and growth over the decades, documenting their change from teacher-education institutions in the expansion of their curricula in the liberal arts and undergraduate professional preparation such as business. Of particular note is the drive among administrators and professors to raise the prestige of the institution, or as one professor noted, to play in the Rose Bowl (a reminder that the effort to establish revenue-producing football, as was the case at California State Colleges in the 1950s, has a great deal to do with institutional prestige).[13] Nevertheless, in terms of research productivity, student selectivity, or football prowess, universities such as the University of Alabama and Berkeley or Cal remain substantially different from those characteristics at Troy (even given its football team's victory over a revenue-producing football team in 2017). As students in my history of higher education classes often hear, it is a good idea to remember that institutions at the top of prestige do not often lessen their efforts to remain at the top.

California offers a critical example of institutional stratification in its development of a plan for public higher education. As a result of the state's long commitment to public education and public higher education, a higher education enrollment substantially higher than the rest of the nation with a concomitant large number of public junior colleges and public colleges and universities, and a series of state policy reports on higher education beginning in the early 1930s, by the 1950s the state recognized that it needed to address how it would sustain its large public higher education system. It developed the 1960 Master Plan, which assigned roles to three types of institutions: the universities (such as Berkeley and UCLA) for research; the colleges (now universities, by the early 2000s offering the Ed.D.) for teaching; and the community colleges for access. Remarkably, initially all three types of institutions were tuition-free for California residents, as the differentiation was not cost but admission selectivity, with the universities being the most selective, the colleges less so, and the community colleges were essentially open-access institutions, accepting anyone who could benefit from higher education. While a highly efficient system for such a large group of institutions, the Plan also assured stratification, furthered by the fiscal austerity of the 1970s that unfortunately forced the 1978 Proposition 13 (yes, that was the number) and allowed the institutions to charge fees of one form or another. Hence, even in attempts to ensure the accessibility of higher education, systems of exclusion and stratification were at work.[14]

Elements of social stratification can be manifest or subtle as two examples indicate. In the first case, there were the decided efforts to flunk out students at state universities in the 1950s and 1960s, and in the second case there are the processes of advising students at two-year institutions in regard to their choice of degree. In 1960, in Burton Clark's article, "The 'Cooling-Out' Function in Higher Education," he pointed out that state universities admitted large numbers of students and systematically flunked them out; a 1958 report indicated that the attrition rate for first-year students was about 25 percent and by the end of the sophomore year, about 40 percent had left. (One popular story about deans at state universities in the 1950s and 1960s was that at the orientation each fall, they would tell students to look to the student at their left and to their right because by the end of the year only one of them would be left. This idea is baffling, since if everyone looked to the left and the right, then it seems that only the students on the aisle had a chance of persisting.) The public junior college, as it was known at the time, had a different mechanism for culling students; Clark found at a California junior college that advising students based on their standardized test results, performance in classes, and in some cases, a course for new students orienting them to their roles at the institution, served as the basis for moving students away from the academic track to the career track.[15]

One means to increased selectivity, or at least shifting an institution's academic profile of undergraduates, has been the use of merit aid, a process that accelerated in the 1970s and has not seemed to slow. Institutions direct these scholarship monies not toward needy students as such but toward students who have performed well in secondary school and on standardized tests. As a result, students from lower incomes have less available funding, and academic achievers receive benefits.[16] In like manner, offering free tuition to students whose family incomes are less than $70,000 while only 4 percent of its students receive Pell Grants, as occurred at the University of Pennsylvania in the early 2000s, creates stratification by socioeconomic class. Those students with fewer financial resources may well choose other institutions of higher education, but those are unlikely to be institutions with high levels of prestige.

Organizational differences such as faculty roles highlight stratification as well. The American Federation of Teachers (AFT) was instrumental in organizing the first post-secondary institution's faculty as a formal bargaining unit recognized by a state labor relations board, the Milwaukee Vocational School faculty in 1963. The AFT was a relatively radical labor union, in contrast with the professional norms of the AAUP. Collective bargaining slowly took hold among faculties, especially those at public two-year and four-year colleges, promoted by the AFT, the National Education Association, and eventually the AAUP, and always only in those states that had enabling legislation or at private colleges and universities under the jurisdiction of the National Labor Relations Board. Faculty union growth accelerated in the late 1960s and 1970s, but it slowed considerably in 1980, when the U.S. Supreme Court ruled that faculty members at Yeshiva University, a private institution, had managerial responsibilities and, therefore, were not employees who could unionize. Curiously, the decision marked a divide between faculty members as employees who could unionize and faculty members whose professional responsibilities in such matters as admission policies and curricular decisions assigned them a different role, representing a very powerful difference between faculties at institutions serving a range of students and the elite institutions. Another divide in faculties, particularly at four-year institutions, is the rise of contingent faculty members, including the rise of part-time, or adjunct, faculty members. Continuously since the early 1900s, however, tenured faculty members at more prestigious institutions of higher education have tended to have more involvement in governance, curriculum, and establishing admission criteria, creating a class structure in faculties across the nation, across and within colleges and universities.[17]

CONCLUSION

Despite structural and intentional characteristics of exclusion and stratification in U.S. higher education in the twentieth century, it would be an error to assume that communities facing fewer opportunities in the context of traditional expectations about college simply accepted their presumed stations in life. Two examples provide ample illustration of this argument.

White women too found ways to contest their place in higher education in the nation, as Linda Eisenmann shows in *Higher Education for Women in Postwar America, 1945–1965*. While such widely read documents as the report by the 1947 President's Commission on Higher Education celebrated the possibilities of people of color entering and succeeding at colleges and universities, naming, much less recognizing women (white and of color), was a rarity. The end of World War II brought surging enrollments to higher education, for the most part male enrollments, as well as the return of men to careers. Women did not, however, simply return home; they found a home especially in some institutions' continuing education programs in the 1950s and early 1960s, where they sought to expand white women's lives beyond traditional roles in marriage and the family. Their efforts extended to the Commission on the Education of Women of the American Council on Education, to the American Association of University Women, the former National Association of Deans of Women, and the 1962–1963 President's Commission on the Status of Women established by President John F. Kennedy. Furthermore, there was some development of research about the lives of women, by women scholars, at this time, and arguably the hallmark for the empowerment of middle-class white women, Betty Friedan's 1963 work, *The Feminine Mystique*, was an outgrowth of these efforts. Most important, Eisenmann makes clear that the 1950s were not a silent decade for women, instead they organized and wrote and likely set the stage for the rise of women's activism in the late 1960s, albeit more for white women than women of color.[18]

Most certainly the wealthiest colleges and universities, based on their endowments, separate themselves from the rest of the institutions. Although Massachusetts had provided funds to support Harvard as late as the 1820s, President Eliot's effort to promote the institution as private doubtless reinforced donors' support; now even public universities have large-scale fundraising campaigns, especially important given dwindling state support in recent decades. Yet as scholars have reminded us, large parts of institutional wealth came from people with deeply racist beliefs (even in 2018, Harvard was quietly securing land with water rights in California, and it is worth asking who will have the money for access to that water).[19] Nevertheless, racist beliefs did not preclude private black colleges, for example, from developing means to secure their own funding, as in the case of the members of the UNCF. Marybeth Gasman's carefully researched work on the organization's history (it was originally called the United Negro College Fund, and readers may want to re-visit endnote 2 in the Introduction in regard to naming) clarifies the activism of black presidents of private black colleges to ensure their institution's health. Initiated by Frederick Douglass Paterson, president of Tuskegee, and Mary McLeod Bethune in 1944, the Fund's leaders were able to work with John D. Rockefeller, Sr., whose racist beliefs often led him to think that funding education for African Americans to control them was a better investment than funding liberal arts education for them. The presidents of the private black colleges increasingly used the monies they received from the Fund for curricula as well as extracurricular activities that celebrated equality, the humanity of the oppressed African American, and eventually, activism in the civil rights movement. Over the years, fewer and fewer UNCF staff members were white, more and more were African American, one remarkably appointment being Vernon Jordan, who headed the Fund only from 1970 to 1972, yet directed the campaign with the powerful slogan, "A Mind Is a Terrible Thing to Waste." The development and successes of the UNCF form a reminder of the possibilities of agency.[20]

Exclusion and stratification have taken many forms over the centuries of colonial and then U.S. higher education. Careful examination of those characteristics, however, finds neither immutable but rather likely to shift over time. It is clear that each shift results from either an attempt to exclude in broad or institutional form or to stratify by or within institutions as well as the efforts of those experiencing exclusion or stratification to establish their identities in higher education. What has remained stable as an idea while changing in operational terms is meritocracy, the focal point of the next, final, chapter.

DISCUSSION QUESTIONS

1. Why do institutional efforts at exclusion in U.S. higher education face challenges over time?
2. What are the consequences of stratification in U.S. higher education?

NOTES

1   Jennings L. Wagoner, Jr., "The American Compromise: Charles W. Eliot, Black Education, and the New South," in *Education and the Rise of the New South*, ed. Ronald K. Goodenow and Arthur O. White (Boston: G.K. Hall & Co., 1981), 26–46.

2   Leslie Miller-Bernal, *Separate by Degree: Women Students' Experiences in Single-Sex and Coeducational Colleges* (New York: Peter Lang, 2000).

3   Charlayne Hunter-Gault, *In My Place* (New York: Farrar Straus & Giroux, 1992); Melissa Kean, *Desegregating Private Higher Education in the South: Duke, Emory, Rice, Tulane, and Vanderbilt* (Baton Rouge: Louisiana State University Press, 2013); Charles S. Padgett, "'Without Hysteria or Unnecessary Disturbance': Desegregation at Spring Hill College, Mobile, Alabama, 1948–1954," *History of Education Quarterly* 41 (Summer 2001): 167–188.

4   Laurita Burley, "Reconceptualizing Profession: African American Women and Dietetics at Tuskegee Institute, 1936–1954" (Ph.D. dissertation, 2005); Marybeth Gasman, "Swept Under the Rug? A Historiography of Gender and Black Colleges," *American Educational Research Journal* 44, no. 4 (December 2007): 760–805.

5   Linda Perkins, "The African American Female Elite: The Early History of African American Women in the Seven Sister Colleges, 1880–1960," *Harvard Educational Review* 67, no. 4 (December 1997): 718–757.

6   Joe P. Dunn, "A Mission on the Frontier: Edward P. Tenney, Colorado College, the New West Education Commission, and the School Movement for Mormons and 'Mexicans,'" *History of Education Quarterly* 52, no. 4 (November 2012): 83–108.

7   David S. Berkowitz, *Inequality of Opportunity in Higher Education: A Study of Minority Group and Related Barriers to College Admission* (Albany, NY: Williams Press), 108, table 138.

8   Joyce Antler, "'After College, What?': New Graduates and the Family Claim," *American Quarterly* 32, no. 4 (Fall 1980): 409–434.

9   Dorothy Finnegan, "Raising the Bar: Standards, Access, and the YMCA Evening Law Schools, 1890–1940," *Journal of Legal Education* 55, nos. 1 and 2 (March/June 2005): 208–233.

10 Dongbin Kim and John L. Rury, "The Changing Profile of College Access: The Truman Commission and the Enrollment Patterns in the Postwar Era, *History of Education Quarterly* 47, no. 3 (August 2007): 302–327.

11 William Bruce Leslie, *Gentlemen and Scholars: College and Community in the "Age of the University," 1865–1917* (University Park: Pennsylvania State University Press, 1992).

12 Ruth Jacknow Markowitz, "Subway Scholars at Concrete Campuses: Daughters of Jewish Immigrants Prepare for the Teaching Profession, New York City, 1920–1940," *History of Higher Education Annual* 10 (1990): 31–50; Victoria-María MacDonald, "The Paradox of Bureaucratization: New Views on Progressive Era Teachers and the Development of a Woman's Profession," *History of Education Quarterly* 39, no. 4 (Winter 1999): 427–453.

13   Dendy Moseley, "Troy University Branch Expansion, 1965–2005: Kudzu U." (Ed.D. dissertation, University of Alabama, 2018); E. Alden Dunham, *Colleges of the Forgotten Americans: A Profile of State Colleges and Regional Universities* (New York: McGraw-Hill. 1969).

14   John Aubrey Douglass, *The California Idea and American Higher Education: 1850 to the 1960 Master Plan* (Stanford: Stanford University Press, 2007).

15   Burton R. Clark, "The 'Cooling-Out' Function in Higher Education," *American Journal of Sociology* 65, no. 6 (May 1960): 569–576.

16   Rupert Wilkinson, *Aiding Students, Buying Students: Financial Aid in America* (Nashville, TN: Vanderbilt University Press, 2005).

17   Philo A. Hutcheson, *A Professional Professoriate: Unionization, Bureaucratization, and the AAUP* (Nashville, TN: Vanderbilt University Press, 2000); Philo A. Hutcheson, "Faculty Tenure: Myth and Reality 1974 to 1992," *Thought and Action* 12, no. 1 (Spring 1996): 7–22; John G. Cross and Edie N. Goldenberg, *The Toll Road to Contingency: Off-Track Profs: Nontenured Teachers in Higher Education* (Cambridge, MA: MIT Press, 2009).

18   Linda Eisenmann, *Higher Education for Women in Postwar America, 1945–1965* (Baltimore: Johns Hopkins University Press, 2006).

19   Stephanie Y. Evans, *Black Women in the Ivory Tower, 1850–1954: An Intellectual History* (Gainesville: University Press of Florida, 2007); "Harvard Quietly Amasses California Vineyards—and the Water Underneath," www.msn.com/en-us/money/companies/harvard-quietly-amasses-california-vineyards-and-the-water-underneath/ar-BBQMqlo?li=BBnbfcN&ocid=mailsignout (retrieved December 18, 2018).

20   Marybeth Gasman, *Envisioning Black Colleges: A History of the United Negro College Fund* (Baltimore: Johns Hopkins University Press, 2007).

9

AN EPILOGUE ON THIS HISTORY OF U.S. HIGHER EDUCATION

Historical Dimensions of Meritocracy

In this chapter I will address meanings of history in U.S. higher education, then discuss how I see those meanings constructed over the past several decades, offer some discussion about where we have gaps and where even in seemingly well-addressed areas we need to know more, and examine what a colleague, Bruce Leslie, has called "useful history." In addition, there is substantial discussion of meritocracy in U.S. higher education. In all of this chapter, I am driven by an astounding novel in which the epilogue is prologue, *Invisible Man* by Ralph Ellison.

At times in the study of higher education, there seems to be some certainty in contemporary evaluations of the participants and institutions of higher education, as if those who write in contemporary terms do not realize that they themselves reflect history when, over the decades, they themselves change their arguments and when the institutions and participants who they study change. For example, the discussions in the study of diversity in higher education have changed greatly in the past 20 years; the past is never past. Discussing problematic conditions of diversity in higher education as if it were a post-World War II or post-1960s discussion omits the historical fact that American Indians are part of the portrait starting with the mid-1600s.

As Gerda Lerner (see the endnotes for the Introduction) argues, history matters, and even those who ignore history are subject to its influence. U.S. institutions of higher education have traditions that clearly stretch back to the Middle Ages in both academic and social lives, whether it is the liberal arts (readers of the Yale Report and its arguments for classical liberal education often note the similarity with contemporary discussions about the liberal arts) or students' common preference for beer. For generations in this country, colleges and universities have developed complex mechanisms, some obvious, some not, to manage enrollments not simply in terms of numbers but also in terms of demographics. Asking if we should have black colleges or women's colleges or tribal colleges or Hispanic-serving institutions today, is not a contemporary question, it is a historical one. Why did we establish those colleges? What purposes do they fulfill for their communities? What are the consequences of those decisions today? History is the opportunity to answer those questions.

Unfortunately, all too often students come to my course on the history of U.S. higher education ready for name-date-place crap, some sort of nonsense poem . . . "In 1492, Columbus sailed the ocean blue." Those reasonably acquainted with that history know that he did not discover the Americas, he was not the first European to land on the shores of the Americas, and his legacy for the natives was one of devastation. Howard Zinn grounds his history of the United States with the perspective of marginalized, oppressed, and brutalized populations, beginning with the systematic genocide of the Arawak Indians of Jamaica by Columbus and his men. Names, dates, and places fall by the wayside under the force of Zinn's narrative. Hence, whatever interpretative framework beyond name-date-place crap that I or other historians of higher education choose to use, it is inevitably challenged by common ways of understanding the history of higher education, memorizing this date (1862) or that individual's name (Justin Morrill). Even schoolteachers who love and teach secondary school history admit that they are held to the expectations of name-date-place crap and too often become entwined in such approaches, dutifully instructing students as to who did what when and where, foregoing the possibilities of how, much less why. The plethora of standardized tests reinforces such teaching, so it is the historian's responsibility to present the narratives of human lives in order to explain the past and possibly explicate present conditions.

Admittedly, historians have a distinct fondness for details, knowing the person, time, and place. Thus, it especially becomes the responsibility of historians educating those who will likely never become historians to understand humans in all their complexities without submerging the student under the weight of details. That is no easy task for those who love those details as historians so often do, for human affairs are carried out in details. Nevertheless, the fundamental nature of history rests on large pictures of human affairs and how we interpret them, whether that is in local, regional, or national frames in the United States or, equally important, different populations.

A second problem is the comprehension that anyone can teach history; after all, it is easy enough to recount names, dates, and places and ask students to insert them into papers so that all can majestically declare that the 1862 Morrill Land Grant Act is important. It is my fervent hope that this book has made clear that it is not the 1862 Act, it is the 1862 and 1890 Acts. Those two Acts established a legal system of public segregation, even in the former case by funding state institutions that would often eventually become rather wealthy and thus extend the power of segregation, that remains in force today not in legal terms but by maintenance of separate institutions with distinct effects on students as well as in terms of segregation on supposedly desegregated campuses, regardless of countless court decisions reaffirming equitable resources and diverse enrollments. For too long in too many places, non-historians have treated history as an act of memorization with dusty historians remembering dusty facts. It is incumbent upon the historian to engage others in the understanding that how we write histories is a manifestation of what we emphasize and what we omit or even ignore. It is also incumbent upon non-historians to recognize the limits of contemporary analysis. Over two centuries have passed since the University of Pennsylvania established a grading system seemingly built on meritocratic characteristics in order to maintain social control, yet today many a professor complains that students expect or even demand an A . . . or an A+. If they were well informed about the history of higher education, they might well argue that those demands are the result of student combinations, every bit as informal and every bit as powerful as those at the University of Pennsylvania in the early 1800s as students today combine in the effort to get a good job after graduation. There are obviously formal college and university efforts to support those goals (with historical roots in the work of the early deans of women . . . starting a century before STEM or STEAM or STREAM), but there is no question that students bring that desire to campus. And getting an A is important for serious students is important at all institutions; as Helen Horowitz observed, the competition to get good grades at elite institutions in order to get into top professional or graduate schools is keen.

It is important to remember that the details that those facts represent are important for an important set of reasons. History and historians resist theory not because there is no understanding of cause-and-effect relationships and abstract ideas but because, fundamentally, humans do not act theoretically. If that were the case, every strategic plan (an application of a theory of organizational behavior in its most rational form) would work every time for everybody. A case in point is an article by Philip Kotler and Patrick Murphy on the strategic planning process focused on increasing enrollment at Beloit College in the late 1970s and early 1980s. I was there, and the process was not at all as rational as they describe; we were scrambling just to get a reasonably sized first-year class after years of devastating enrollment decline. Even their chronology is inaccurate. For example, the cuts in the tenured faculty (done under the aegis of AAUP financial exigency procedures) occurred in 1974–1975 and were a drastic and immediate response to extreme drops in revenue, not as a result of a "resource audit" later that decade. In the admissions office at that time we knew that Chicago was only 90 miles away; we didn't conduct an analysis of "market opportunity" before focusing efforts on Chicago, we looked at a map and knew the large enrollment of Chicago-area students at Beloit that had been happening for many years. And, there is no mention of the decided effort begun in the period covered by Kotler and Murphy to return to concentrated recruitment in Wisconsin. I know, I am the one who led that drive and doubled the percentage of Wisconsin students in two years with a concomitant increase in the number of National Merit Scholars from Wisconsin.[1] Those historical facts were the reality of that time, not a theory of strategic planning. Or, as I often remark in class, we teach rationality, we do not practice it; the rationality of strategic plans appeal to the central administration and some faculty members, but the quotidian activities of students, professors, and administrators is often shaped by outcomes based on experiences of the moment and value-laden decisions, not rational effort, as a sociologist insightfully discussed nearly a century ago.[2] I have long enjoyed reminding students that humans are typically bundles of contradictions, ideologues and single-minded people notwithstanding. After all, law-and-order advocates drive well over the speed limit all over the nation every day. Theoretical abstractions do not explain such details, and even each revision of theory only brings it closer to the details while continuing to force inconvenient facts of human values and behaviors out of the way.

So how might someone thinking about the history of U.S. higher education make sense out of the details without being held to them bereft of context? Writing from the Midwest, South, and West about the development of higher education is one example. Another is that all too often even historians of higher education have casually assigned the rise of research universities to President Eliot's advocacy for the elective system and research at Harvard University. The details say otherwise given the elective system at the University of Virginia and the establishment of the Johns Hopkins University in a Southern city, and institutions such as Chicago and Wisconsin had impressive and influential research goals and achievements by the end of the 1800s. Hence, useful history might, in this case, cause us to reflect on who defines institutional influences from what perspectives and in so doing, creates a history. There is no denying that Harvard long influenced the development of research and scholarship, it was an early leader. Yet as Patricia Palmieri, Margaret Rossiter, and Mary Ann Dzuback have carefully and thoroughly documented, women's colleges in the Northeast had many scholars who developed rigorous lines of research, particularly but not only in the social sciences. And other scholars have pointed out that other old and wealthy men's colleges and universities of the Northeast showed little interest in pursuing research in the late 1800s and early 1900s, focusing instead on the development of the well-educated gentleman.[3] The flow of ideas, individuals, and institutions crossed not only gender and racial and ethnic lines starting in the 1800s, it also moved back and forth geographically. The *New Yorker* cover in this case ought to be more of a prism than a two-dimensional object; the source of influence here must necessarily be seen as more diffuse—which indeed might well explain the extent to which institutions throughout the nation took up the goal of research as an important definition of higher education while maintaining goals of liberal arts education and utilitarian education and to a lesser degree, stayed attuned to Western morals and beliefs (even today many a public college or university campus has nearby buildings occupied by denominational representatives).

RECONSIDERING THE HISTORIOGRAPHY OF
HIGHER EDUCATION

Given the diversity of colleges and universities starting in the late 1800s, one might well ask, how have research universities become the focus of so many historical inquiries, as well as topics for many contemporary investigations? One might well cast an eye on what are probably the earliest historical investigations of the influence of German universities, Charles Franklin Thwing's *A History of Higher Education in America* (1906) and *The American and the German University: One Hundred Years of History* (1928). The first work is more general in nature, of course, but in combination with the second, a reader is easily left with the sense that the glory of higher education, particularly the glory of the mind, results in the sort of scholarship and research made part of the institution at German universities and eagerly adapted in the United States, initially by a few institutions and then increasingly by many more. Thwing argued for personal and moral growth as well, but his quantitative analysis of U.S. scholars who studied in German highlights the influence of the research ethos. Subsequent work affirmed that influence, such as Richard Hofstadter's work as the first volume of *The Development of*

Academic Freedom in the United States (1955), a contribution later reprinted separately as *Academic Freedom in the Age of the College* (1961). Following an elegant articulation of the development of academic freedom at northern European universities in the Middle Ages, Hofstadter then takes aim at the small colleges of the 1800s, reducing them to the title of "oldtime colleges." Writing from the perspective of a history professor at Columbia University with a major history prize already on his *vita* and on the verge of winning his first of two Pulitzer Prizes, it may well be that Hofstadter saw the advantages of the research university without seeing the advantages of creating an educated state and regional elite. In like manner, Laurence Veysey highlighted the rise of utility and research—both leading to professional and graduate education—and placed liberal culture as something of a reactionary movement and dismissed community colleges in a footnote; Veysey earned his Ph.D. at the University of California-Berkeley. There is an old political science axiom, where you stand depends on where you sit. While only an axiom and not meant as hard and fast rule, it does not hurt to look at who is where to ask who writes what. This means too that I have been acutely aware of my outsider status in regard to gender, race and ethnicity, and socioeconomic class as I have written, revised, and rewritten this book. It is no easy matter to revise so substantially who is centered in broad histories of higher education.

This approach to understanding U.S. higher education creates a challenge for anyone interested in who attended for what reasons, who taught and conducted scholarship and research for what reasons, and who governed and administered for what reasons. For example, historians of higher education have long questioned, even resisted, the history of presidents, that singular approach of understanding these institutions by understanding a sole figure. Certainly, presidents are key figures who have an impact on their institutions, but that impact has its limits—unlikely to reach into racist talk in late-night conversations in dorm rooms, unlikely to change a culture of rape, unlikely to shift student expectations about career choices deeply contextualized by parent or family (either of those with meanings beyond genetic relationships), community, or prior schooling. Nor is presidential leadership at all likely to change the deeply rooted ways in which different groups work with and against each other. Yet often it is the presidential record that is most visible, a reminder that comprehensive history requires careful research.

Institutional behaviors may change under the guidance or direction of a president, but there are many factors involved. It is curious that so many scholars point at Charles W. Eliot and the many changes he instituted at Harvard without noting that he was president for 40 years there. One might well imagine either a lot of change or an increasingly stultifying atmosphere under such leadership longevity (the longest serving president of any U.S. college or university was Eliphalet Nott, president of Union College from 1804 to 1866, even serving simultaneously as president of Rensselaer Polytechnic Institute from 1829 to 1845; he receives far less attention than Eliot). Longevity considerations aside, in other ways the presidential record is not a clear statement about the institution. As many black college presidents observed, their institutions did not refuse a white applicant because of race; that said so well, but nevertheless white enrollments at black colleges have always been small with the exceptions of programs legally or politically mandated at black colleges in order to achieve that odd norm, racial balance. Histories of higher education based on presidential decisions and actions have their limits, despite the lure of finding the records of presidents far more extensive than other individuals in archives.

Knowing more historically about the institution and its presidents or a set of institutions offers a fuller comprehension of the meanings of human behaviors. It is important to raise questions both about the conduct of research as the primary goal of so many types of institutions (as reflected in annual merit pay increases) and the need to place those institutions at the center of historical narratives. They are certainly influential, but scholars of higher education and practitioners need to think about what sorts of meanings and conclusions derive from placing them at the center. Student selectivity immediately comes to mind. Who gets admitted, and equally important, what experiences do which students have once enrolled? A historian of higher education needs to be mindful of the fact that selective admissions indeed had a home in raising academic standards, but the definition of those standards repeatedly reflected social expectations about who was suitable for what education for what purposes and employed several means to achieve the assessment of suitability.

As a very different example, for-profit institutions have been part of the continent since the colonial era, in the 1970s and thereafter they grew at an astounding rate, in some years even being recognized as some of the best stock values on Wall Street. Their rapid rise first brought support from federal legislators and then well-founded criticism as their students assumed crushing loans. Yet condemning for-profit institutions as preying on students—which most certainly happened, at times at great personal cost to students—but ignoring that those privateering institutions benefited from the fact that not-for-profit colleges failed to engage those students is a failure of historical thinking. Why open-access and often reasonably priced institutions, particularly among two-year colleges in the post-World War II period, did not attract those individuals is a more substantial historical question, as is the institutional position that perhaps those students drawn to the for-profit colleges were not of sufficient quality and needed little attention from two-year and four-year not-for-profit institutions alike. That failure of institutional and scholarly perspective might have some slim justification because the not-for-profit institutions did not have the marketing funds for television advertising on the Jerry Springer show in many instances, but nevertheless a system of mass higher education left behind those students, and an insightful scholarly analysis would recognize that the meritocracy (scholars, of course, are deeply embedded in the meritocracy) need only feign concern about such students once they have been exploited.

SOME THOUGHTS CONCERNING MERITOCRACY

A more comprehensive view engaging meritocracy has more substance than the lives of presidents. The consequences of the divide between a literate class resulting from primary education and a privileged class resulting from higher education has yet to be fully considered, as best I know, by historians of higher education, although there are scholars in other fields who have in recent years addressed that fundamental issue. That divide also speaks to exclusion and stratification in higher education and the broad characteristics of those effects. In 1958 a British sociologist, Michael Young, wrote a short, sardonic monograph, *The Rise of the Meritocracy: An Essay on Education and Equality*. Drawing upon an earlier use of the term meritocracy, he expanded its meaning by writing his book as if it were 2034, casting an eye upon the steady, albeit uneven, development of a meritocratic society in the United Kingdom from the late 1800s to the 2030s. His work echoes in this historical text because Jeffersonian notions of raking the rubbish to find talent are today fundamentally "American" in the maintenance of the meritocracy even through its ongoing diversification.

While it is far too casual to follow without critique a scholar's analysis, Young's work is chilling for its insight into how we construct socioeconomic class today in the United States. His description of an uneven beginning of testing that sorted test-takers to the powerful use of testing in not only educational but also employment settings, Young highlights how the perceived objectivity of testing and meritocracy hides assumptions about equality of opportunity—who really has opportunity—assumptions far less evident as those in the hereditary forms of establishing differences and class. He writes that the elite in his scenario argued that meritocracy justifies income differences. Meritocracy in his futuristic description of the 2030s became the justification for socioeconomic classes; the well-educated elite rule, despite resistance from the proletariat.

Educational institutions find means of "appropriating and educating the able children of the lower classes while they are still young," his future reflected in our talent identification programs and reflecting Jefferson's argument.[4] Elite colleges and universities have long found ways to help the less fortunate, although the helping hand is slippery. Witness young American Indian men at Dartmouth, Harvard, and William and Mary. In view of the extraordinary selectivity of the elite colleges and universities today, with rejection rates of undergraduates as high as 95 percent, how, then, do we really achieve meritocracy with equality of opportunity? Does the single young mother in rural Nebraska have the equality of opportunity of a prep school graduate or a student at a suburban high school with both AP and International Baccalaureate courses? Class structures obtain by gender and race and ethnicity as well; only recently have white women had greater access to long-term careers with substantial incomes, and minoritized populations such as African Americans and Latinx consistently have less opportunity for more lucrative careers. In the case of all, single white mothers and people of color, they are greatly over-represented in lower income categories. The trajectories of those students (and far more important, the oft-hidden meritocracy embedded in the socioeconomic classes they occupy) is a lifetime event. It is not just what college or university a student enters, but also what if any professional school follows after college, what networks open as a result of alma mater and which remain nearly closed. The selection process with substantial relationships to gender, race and ethnicity, and socioeconomic class has serious long-term consequences. Herein, therefore, is the crux of my argument that I have written a social history in which intellectual history is central. The idea of meritocracy has driven U.S. colleges and universities for centuries, evident in the idea that young American Indian men would benefit from a Christian perspective, in the arguments of the Yale Report as to who was best suited for a liberal arts education, in the passage of the 1862 and 1890 Morrill Land Grant Acts and the continued affirmation of segregation, and accelerating throughout the 1900s to what seems now to be to be an absurd level of admission selectivity for some institutions. And for all the claims that these highly selective institutions look at all aspects of their applicants, it is most curious that again and again they report entering classes with remarkably high standardized test scores. The socioeconomic contract, then, the enduring relationship between institutions of higher education and their communities, has variable form, yet a very powerful and continuous form. Its unspoken words ensure that access, experience, and opportunities to build communities have different outcomes throughout the process of higher education and thereafter. In straightforward terms, as diversity has become more important and institutions of higher education—especially highly selective institutions—have developed increasingly sophisticated means for identifying diverse admission candidates, what the meritocracy is doing is developing means not to increase diversity for the good of diversity but in order to sustain and advance the meritocracy, reshaping the demographics of the meritocratic elite but not changing the fundamental nature and goals of the meritocracy. As Joseph Kett argues, notions of merit shifted from the individual in the Early Republic to the institutional definition accompanied by standardized testing, challenging the broader principles of the Enlightenment and the possibilities of progress for all peoples.[5] (Scholars in other fields have taken note of the contemporary nature of meritocracy in recent years; my arguments clarify the long history in higher education of moving toward an even more expanded yet refined meaning of meritocracy than simply only a few white men having access to college.) There are very real differences between the transfer of wealth and status and the introduction of new groups to increase the position of the meritocracy, and the latter approach has been the dominant form of institutional positioning for several decades. The Ivy Leagues came upon diversity in the 1960s; Christopher Loss notes with precision, "In 1967, Ivy League administrators reported their institutions were moving toward a new concept in admissions known as 'student diversity.'"[6] Higher education in the United States has long been diverse, but the institutional stratification of diversity in the context of meritocracy highlights the means for keeping some on and many off the pathways for the most success. Harvard's president, Charles W. Eliot insisted that "universities would train the elite." In his inaugural address he stated that Harvard graduates

> were properly considered part of an aristocracy—not "a stupid and pretentious caste founded on wealth, and birth," but rather one that sacrificed self for the public good and "carries off the honors and prizes of the learned professions." All professionals were not part of this aristocracy. One entered through the gateway of collegiate culture.[7]

I do not mean that there is not a commitment to an educated and diverse population, but rather that diversity based on principles of equality and equity easily gets ignored in meritocratic populations. Gated communities do not offer access to the poor except when they are service workers, manual laborers. Elite law schools feed not the rural poor (except in occasional *pro bono* cases, a term that confirms the *prima facie* evidence of the secondary nature of the poor) but rather the high-powered law firms. There are exceptions, but they seem to have been exceptions at a certain time, not the rule.

Efforts to create a public good were perhaps evidence of an exception in the post-World War II period, from the Brown decisions of 1954 and 1955 (which did not directly apply to higher education but had a decided impact on desegregation efforts among colleges and universities) to the 1958 National Defense Education Act to the 1965 Higher Education Act and ensuing reauthorizations. The shift from a public good, with the federal government awarding grants to students in financial need to heavily emphasizing loan programs and placing the expectation of success on individuals, a measure of the private good beginning in the 1980s, indicates a failure to make a difference. Political expectations starting in the 1980s reflected a different set of social expectations, and while the socioeconomic contract between institutions of higher education and their communities remained, they have come to rest on the shoulders of each person rather than the community because of loans for individuals. Curiously, however, such a presumable encouragement to succeed as an individual has not particularly altered college graduation rates, which have been fairly stable for well over a century.[8]

HOW WE THINK HISTORICALLY MATTERS FOR THE PAST AND THE PRESENT

In unsettling ways, unfortunately, historians of higher education have aided and abetted such problematic conditions by allowing assumptions about who belongs and why, and where. Often historians of higher education, including those who are deeply interested in communities with limited opportunities, write to the best-known institutions. A version of this appears in add-on history, a problem little different from similar approaches in contemporary scholarship. Rudolph's remarkable review of over 100 institutional histories (read a few, you may quickly learn why it is a remarkable effort) in 1962 offered atypical discussions of black higher education and the higher education of women; while those discussions were highly unusual at the time, nevertheless the white women and African Americans were added on, and that approach often continues to obtain. At the persistent risk of losing a narrative focus, I have attempted to write this work as a means for seeing the meanings of higher education across multiple and, in fact, shifting populations. What it means to be a woman at a women's college or a coeducational institution of higher education in the early 1900s is a very different construct of gender than in the early 2000s, with the recent substantial albeit incomplete increase of opportunities for careers yet still within the context of women as sexual (or asexual) objects who are not as good as men. The politics of knowledge also range across race and ethnicity as well as socioeconomic class.

Hence, while an admittedly awkwardly approach, I contrast my historical narrative with works that evidence a sweeping command of the passage of history in higher education but remain focused on research universities or add on white women and people of color. The U.S. college and university remains an institution of international envy—less so now that maybe 40 years ago, and still not of the reputation perhaps of, for example, Oxford and Cambridge but still a force to be acknowledged—and in great part because of the extraordinary output of research. At the same time, those institutions clearly evidence the problematic nature of selectivity. Adding on different groups experiencing exclusion or some form of stratification still centers the narrative on white men; in this book I have attempted to offer all institutions and participants as evidence of the development of U.S. higher education and, at times, to recenter the historical narrative in terms of the experiences of white women and people of color. Much remains to be written about the experiences of all people of color, as the historiography of higher education continues to shift into expanded discussion on the varied backgrounds and experiences of participants from a variety of Latin American and Asian nations. So too, historical examinations of the experiences of participants of varied sexual and gender identities and of participants with disabilities remains at a nascent stage. This book, I hope, is a mere first step toward an inclusive history of U.S. higher education.

In historiographical terms I find my context in a broad circle of colleagues (old and new) who have challenged the historiography we all inherited from Thwing, Veysey, and Rudolph, and we challenged it because we knew it. Linda Eisenmann and Jana Nidiffer have long investigated how women and gender shape higher education; note the direction of the relationship. Working from initially a very small group of historians of women in education, Linda and Jana have raised questions about how women entered higher education, experienced higher education, used higher education. While it is certain that higher education shaped women in many ways, it is critical to revise histories of higher education so that it is clear that resistance is a means of establishing space in a number of forms—physical, intellectual, social. Joy Ann Williamson and Marybeth Gasman have reminded us time and again that the role of African Americans in higher education is complex, facing oppression and marginalization while all the while maintaining a drive toward equality. The work of all four historians of higher education has led the way for me, and for a growing number of younger historians of higher education who no longer take the research university or the add-on approach as sufficient.

There is actually another basic message here. I cannot urge readers enough to take care and read as many of the works of as many historians as possible, in order to understand the complexities of what has come to be in U.S. colleges and universities. What all of these historians typically communicate—even those from decades ago—is that we are remiss if we do not know our complex histories. The research chapter in this book is an add-on chapter, deliberately, but it very much rests on the work of scholars who have centered that institution. And in that sense, there is use in broad knowledge of historical study, in knowing how history haunts us yet offers possibilities for growth. With historical knowledge, we can critique ourselves and move to new sets of remembrances of things past.

I see possibilities of growth beyond the meritocracy; this history shows the lives and accomplishments of so many groups that don't have the opportunities often afforded by elite institutions of higher education. A valued colleague, Jackie Blount, remarked to me that the current problem with historical examinations of gay and lesbian students and faculty members is that our representations are too often portraits of problems, research on the institutional investigations into the supposed deviant behavior of these human beings leading to negative outcomes. So, I turn to an individual example to call upon readers to think about what could be. Angela Davis, African American, was born and raised in Birmingham, Alabama, at the very time when white racists were bombing churches and killing African American girls. She went to Brandeis University (rooted in Jewish values), was elected to Phi Beta Kappa, and then went to Germany for graduate study with Hebert Marcuse, a highly insightful critic of our social behaviors. In 1969 she accepted a temporary teaching position at UCLA, where the governing board promptly dismissed her (encouraged by Governor Ronald Reagan) because she was a member of the Communist Party USA; the decision was overturned by a court, and the governing board fired her again for different reasons, this time her political statements. She remained an activist on several issues, especially the injustices of the U.S. penal system, and eventually in the 1980s became a professor again at San Francisco State University, later holding appointments at University of California, Santa Cruz and Rutgers University. Her scholarship has long addressed injustices in terms of prisons, gender, and race and ethnicity; a magazine, *Out*, identified her as a lesbian. She remained committed to her principles through all of the attempts to exclude her from academe and continues in the 2010s to speak and write about those principles. (In early 2019, a Birmingham civil rights organization rescinded an award for Angela Davis for her pro-Palestinian views and the resultant concerns about anti-Semitism, a reminder that diversity is complex.) The past can inform our hopes for the present and our expectations about the future.

In institutional terms, how one type of institution influences another ought to remind us that the forces are not simply downward. For example, it is not simply the "Harvard of [fill in the blank, i.e., the Midwest, Wisconsin, Alabama, wherever]" but also the reverse. Dr. Edward C. Clarke attempted to influence thinking about the higher education of women, but women academics responded, primarily through the efforts of the Association of Collegiate Alumnae (now the American Association of University Women), and successfully refuted his claims through the use of statistical analysis. In a broader sense, the repeated *de facto* segregationist efforts of Northern colleges and universities, much less the *de jure* ones of Southern and some Northern institutions of higher education, encountered the careful efforts of presidents of black colleges to ensure that students at their institutions learned that a college education meant applying principles of equality to activism, and those activists eventually had an effect on both Northern and Southern colleges and universities as they desegregated.[9] There is also the rapid switch to coeducation among all previously all-male northeastern colleges and universities in the 1970s or even later, in recent years reframing the meaning of gender on those campuses, although the experiences and values of students at four women's colleges suggest that the students adapted to meritocracy given that the students at the more selective institutions were indeed more likely to go to graduate or professional school. Knowing that the past does not have to be a constraint offers possibilities for the present and the future; it is also a knowledge that the past carries weight. Rather than accepting the apparent inherent value of the meritocracy, we might be better served by remembering that principles of equality and equity can be part of higher education whatever the institution by remembering that the past is not glorious and that the present holds challenges that we ought to recognize and address.

That said, I think historians have no business predicting the future; nor, for that matter, do any social scientists. Life changes in unexpected ways—the Great Recession of 2008 is an excellent example; on a personal level, in the spring of 1980 in a doctoral seminar I announced that sooner or later a research university faculty would unionize. In the fall of 1980 the U.S. Supreme Court issued the Yeshiva decision, arguing that faculty members at institutions with faculty responsibility for such matters as admission and curriculum were, in part, managers. So much for prediction when the Supreme Court overturns my efforts (insert a face emoticon with its tongue sticking out here). Or, put another more ironic way, the web page for my history of higher education course typically includes a quote from the history club at Carroll College (now Carroll University) in the early 1970s: Why study history, there is no future in it.

Of course, there is no future in history. There is most definitely a present, and history, for the better, can nicely muddle how we see it and how we try to construct the future. But while historians allow us to forget or ignore, historical thinking has the potential to allow us to see the forgotten or ignored. An assortment of examples makes my point. In an Anthony Bourdain travel show, he makes a convincing argument that grits came from Senegal. One of my students who read widely in such fields as architectural history told me that the charming ironwork fences of Charleston were often forged by enslaved Africans from West Africa and reflected some of their symbols. Historians have traced civil disobedience from Henry David Thoreau to white women in the suffrage movement to Mahatma Gandhi seeking freedom from colonizing Great Britain to the civil rights movement. The maintenance of cultures of origin evident in Latinx experiences and events serve as a reminder that that European white ethnic groups have long done the same. Richard Jackson, dismissed because he was perceived as homosexual, was adamant about the possibilities of higher education in a democracy. There is the potential for successful challenge in the roots of our pasts. Or as Willow said to me once, "In order for there to be a second generation, there has to be a first generation." As I have started saying to the students in my history of higher education classes at the end of the semester: Don't forget history.

DISCUSSION QUESTIONS

1. What did a segregated institution of higher education look like? What does it look like now?
2. Can we have equality and meritocracy?

NOTES

1   Philip Kotler and Patrick E. Murphy, "Strategic Planning for Higher Education," *Journal of Higher Education* 52, no. 5 (September/October 1981): 470–489.

2   Robert K. Merton, "The Unanticipated Consequences of Purposive Social Action," *American Sociological Review* 1, no. 6 (December 1936): 894–904.

3   W. Bruce Leslie, *Gentlemen and Scholars: College and Community in the Age of the University* (New York: Routledge, 2005); David Potts, *Wesleyan University, 1831–1910: Collegiate Enterprise in New England* (Middletown, CT: Wesleyan University Press, 1999 revised edition).

4   Michael Young, *The Rise of the Meritocracy, 1870–2033: An Essay on Education and Equality* (Baltimore: Penguin Books, 1958/1961).

5   Joseph F. Kett, *Merit: The History of a Founding Ideal from the American Revolution to the 21st Century* (Ithaca, NY: Cornell University Press, 2013).

6   Christopher P. Loss, *Between Citizens and the State: The Politics of American Higher Education in the 20th Century* (Princeton: Princeton University Press, 2012), 178.

7   Hugh Hawkins, "American Universities and the Inclusion of Professional Schools," *History of Higher Education Annual* 13 (1993): 53–68.

8   William G. Bowen, Matthew M. Chingos, and Michael S. McPherson, *Crossing the Finish Line: Completing College at America's Public Universities* (Princeton: Princeton University Press, 2009); Vincent Tinto, *Leaving College: Rethinking the Causes and Cures of Student Attrition*, 2nd ed. (Chicago: University of Chicago Press, 1993). Tinto made this observation in the first edition as well.

9   Philo Hutcheson, Marybeth Gasman, and Kijua Sanders-McMurtry, "Race and Equality in the Academy: Rethinking Higher Education Actors and the Struggle for Equality in the Post-World War II Period," *Journal of Higher Education* 82, no. 2 (March–April 2011): 121–153. Hence, the final endnote has Marybeth Gasman and one of my dissertation graduates whom Marybeth mentored.

INDEX

AAU *see* Association of American Universities

AAUP *see* American Association of University Professors

AAUW (American Association of University Women) 196

academic citation 2, 175

academic drift 2

academic freedom 78, 87, 102, 118–119, 121, 174, 205

academies 4

Academy of Saint Mary-of-the-Woods (Indiana) 54

ACE *see* American Council on Education

ACT 178, 191

activism 80, 120, 144, 146–148, 196, 197, 213

Addams, Jane 95n3

administrative Progressivism 70

AFDC (Aid to Famiies with Dependent Children) 88

African Americans 12; Black Power 146; civil rights 113–114, 144, 146–149; effect of war on 100–101, 112; literary societies 21; naming of 16–17n2; veterans 114; women 21, 38, 117, 187 *see also* African Americans in higher education; slavery

African Americans in higher education 211; 19th century 47, 51–53; 20th century 191, 212; after the Civil War 103–104; athletes 141–142; citations of 175; colonial period 21, 31; exclusion 2, 4, 21, 186; fraternities 151, 179; medical students 82–83; in research universities 166–167, 172, 179; sororities 151–152, 179; tenure 115; USAFI courses 111; women 56, 79, 152–153, 187 *see also* black colleges

AFT *see* American Federation of Teachers

Agnes Scott College (Decatur, Georgia) 140

agricultural and mechanical education 60

Aid to Famiies with Dependent Children (AFDC) 88

Alabama State Board of Education 193

Alaska 110

amateur history 5

AME (American Methodist Episcopal Church) 53

American Association for the Advancement of Science 165

American Association of University Professors (AAUP) 86–87, 106–107, 119, 121, 173, 195, 203

American Association of University Women (AAUW) 196

American Baptist Home Mission Society 123

American Council on Education (ACE) 89, 91, 92, 93, 109, 113, 131–132, 167, 178; Commission on the Education of Women 196

American Dietetic Association 187

American Federation of Labor 87

American Federation of Teachers (AFT) 87, 195

American Indian Wars 122

American Indians *see* Native Americans

American Legion 90

American Literary, Philosophical, and Military Academy (Norwich University) 59

American Medical Association 29

American Methodist Episcopal Church (AME) 53

American Revolution 101–102

An Apartment for Peggy (movie) 113

Anderson, James 104, 114–115, 172

Andover Theological Seminary 166

Angell, James B. 66–67

archives 5
Arkle, Thomas 69
Armed Forces Committee on Post-War Educational Opportunities for Service Personnel 92
Army Alpha Intelligence Test 107
Army Specialized Training Program (ASTP) 111
ASHE (Association for the Study of Higher Education) 3
Ashmun Institute *see* Lincoln University, Pennsylvania
Asian American students 116, 146–147
Association of American Colleges 121, 173
Association of American Law Schools 166
Association of American Universities (AAU) 120, 162–163, 165, 166, 169, 170, 179
Association of Collegiate Alumnae (*later* AAUW) 58, 213
ASTP (Army Specialized Training Program) 111
Atlanta Baptist Female Seminary 56

Bacone College (Oklahoma) 123
Baldwin, Abraham 22–23
Baptists 49
Bard College 79
Barnard College 69
Bascom, John A. 66
Bassi, Laura 26
Bates, Katherine 80
Baum, Frank 168
Beard, Charles 105, 119, 160
Becker, Carl 160
beer 137–138
Beloit College (Wisconsin) 47, 48–49, 50, 55, 159, 172, 203
Bennett College (Greensboro, North Carolina) 56, 144
Bennington College 79
Bethune, Mary McLeod 197
Bildungkultur 160
black colleges: 19th century 52–53, 104, 105–106; civil rights 144–145; funding 173, 197; status of 170, 186; student activities 141–142, 143; women 152–153
Black History Month 175
Black Mountain College 79, 172
Bledstein, Burton 77
Blount, Jackie 212
Bond, Horace Mann 173
Bonus March Camping Ground 90
boosterism 49, 50, 85, 187
Borst, Charlotte G. 82, 188
Bouman, Jeffrey 66, 189
Bourdain, Anthony 214

Bourdieu, Pierre 21
Brown, Francis J. 89, 91, 92, 109
Brown, H. Rap 148
Brown University *see* Rhode Island College
Brown v. Board of Education of Topeka (1954–1955) 127n38, 210
Brubacher, John S. 2, 44
Bryn Mawr College 80, 171, 176
Bush, Vannevar 109, 164
Bushnell, Jackson J. 48
business programs 63
Butler, Nicholas Murray 105, 177, 178

Cain, Timothy 69–70, 87
California public higher education 194, 195
California State University 142, 146
Caltech (California Institute of Technology) 133
Camp, Walter 139
Carleton College (Minnesota) 134, 135
Carnegie, Andrew 178
Carnegie Corporation 94
Carnegie Foundation for the Advancement of Teaching 81, 177, 178
Carroll College (University) 213
Carter, Jimmy 146
Catholic colleges 32, 54, 169–170
Central Intelligence Agency 150
Chamberlain, T.C. 48
Chapin, Aaron Lucius 48
Charles Drew Medical University (Los Angeles) 83
Cheyney University (Pennsylvania) 52
Church, Robert 39
Churchill, Ward 121–122
Citadel 103
citizenship 38, 103, 105, 113, 120
civil rights 89, 113–114, 144–145, 146–149, 175
Civil War 102–106
Clap, Thomas 32
Clark, Burton 194
Clark, Daniel 89
Clarke, Edward C. 11, 57–58, 212
classical curriculum 22–23, 34, 36, 40, 60, 105
Clifford, Geraldine 79, 152, 189
coeducation 47, 53–54, 56, 58, 64, 66, 134–135, 185, 188, 213; dormitories 152; societies 65; student services 68; women professors 26
Cohen, Michael David 105
Cold War 118–121
College Entrance Examination Board 177, 178
College of New Jersey (later Princeton) 22, 25, 28, 163
College of Philadelphia 28
College of William and Mary 28, 31, 122, 149, 208

colleges 4; sports 10; and their communities 7–9 *see also* colonial era colleges; midwestern colleges and universities

colonial era colleges 14, 20–21, 24–29; admission requirements 39; faculty lives 35–36; governing boards 22, 25, 27, 28; moral and economic purposes 28–35; presidents 27–28, 35; student life 32–34

Colorado College 187

Columbia University: academic freedom 118–119, 205; civil liberty 102; foundation 28; matriculation 177, 178; organization for gay men 145; role of the university 106; student societies 147–148; Teachers College 69; women professors 170–171

Columbus, Christopher 130, 200

commencement 30

Committee on Civil Rights 114, 115

Communism 119–120, 150, 212

community colleges 58, 172

Congregationalists 49, 50

Congress of Industrial Organizations 87

contingent faculty 174

Cornell, Ezra 62

Cornell University 62, 69, 151

Cremin, Lawrence 29, 78, 183

curriculum: classical curriculum 22–23, 34, 36, 40, 60, 105; Early Republic 40; liberal arts 25–26; women 40

dame schools 36, 38

Dartmouth College 23–24, 28, 31, 122, 208; Amos Tuck School of Administration and Finance 63; literary and debate society 65, 149, 150; political activism 144

Darwin, Charles 161

Davie, William 22

Davis, Allison 115

Davis, Angela 212

De Tocqueville, Alexis de 24

Dead Man on Campus (movie) 154

deans of men 69, 132

deans of women 69, 132, 135, 152–153

Declaration of Independence 29

democracy 77, 78, 88, 92–93, 112, 115–116

denominational institutions 27, 29, 32, 49–53, 102, 163, 184

Department of the Navy educational programs 110, 111

Dewey, John 70, 95n3, 193

Diamond, Nancy 165

Digest of Educational Statistics 117

Dilley, Patrick 136

diplomas 25

diversity in higher education 200–201, 209–210

divinity schools 166

Dixon v. Alabama (1961) 144

Dolan, Amy Well 153

Dorn, Charles 116

double consciousness 12–13

Double V 101, 115

Du Bois, W.E.B. 12, 104, 141

Dzuback, Mary Ann 9, 26, 80, 204

Early Republic: curriculum 40; faculty lives 35–36; institutions 20–24, 36–40; moral and economic purposes 28–35; student life 32, 33–34

Eaton, Nathaniel 32, 137

economics 176–177

Edmonds, Ronald R. 6

Educational Testing Service (ETS) 178

efficiency 77

Eisenhower, Dwight D. 113, 127n38

Eisenmann, Linda 196, 211

elective system 161–162, 203, 204

Elementary and Secondary Education Act (1965) 117

Eliot, Charles W. 67–68, 161, 162, 166, 178, 197, 203, 205–206, 209

elite institutions 14, 19, 22–24, 191, 192, 208

Ellison, Ralph 16, 200

Elmira College (New York) 54

Ely, Richard T. 78

Emancipation Proclamation (1863) 103

Emerson, Joseph 48

Emerson, Lizzie 137

Emmanuel College (Cambridge) 27

Emory University 169

endnotes 2, 5

engineering programs 37, 38, 40, 78, 105

Enlightenment 13, 20–21, 24, 33, 76, 94, 101

equality of opportunity 114, 208

Erskine, John 105

ethnicity *see* race and ethnicity

ETS (Educational Testing Service) 178

exclusion 14, 16, 19–20, 82–83, 183–184; institutional stratification 184, 186–189, 190, 192, 193–194; social stratification 185, 187–189, 190, 194–195

extension education programs 78

faculty lives 35–36, 168–169

faculty roles 195–196

faculty unions 75, 86–88

Fairweather, James 174–175

Farnham, Christie Anne 103

Faulkner, W. x
federal aid for education 111, 112, 113, 117, 120–121
Federal Bureau of Investigation 141, 142
Federal Educational Privacy and Rights Act (1983) 146
feminism 118, 175
Fisk University 120, 148
Flexner, Abraham 29–30, 75, 81–82, 84
Flexner report (1910) 178, 187, 189
football 138–143
footnotes 5
for-profit institutions 40, 81, 168, 206–207
Franklin, Benjamin 25, 37
fraternities 150–151, 152, 179
Freeman's Bureau 105
Friedan, Betty 117, 196
Friedman, Milton 177
Fund for Negro Students 115

Gaines v. Canada (1938) 173
Gallaudet University 145
Gandhi, Mahatma 214
Gasman, Marybeth 187, 197, 211
Geiger, Roger L. 3, 54, 139, 164–165, 168
gender 9, 39, 133–137; and Progressivism 79–80;
    and race 187, 188; and research 175; residential
    segregation 47; and socioeconomic class 64–67,
    152, 188; and student services 68–69 see also
    women
General Education Board (GEB) 89, 172, 173
Georgetown College 32
Georgia Tech 165
G.I. Bill 75–76, 89–93, 111, 112, 113, 191
Giles, Harriet 56
Gilman, Daniel Coit 166
Goldmark Report (1923) 83
Goldwater, Barry 176
the good old days 10
Gordon, Lynn D. 76, 134
Gouldner, Alvin 168
Graham, Hugh Davis 165
GRE (Graduate Record Examinations) 178
Great Recession (2008) 213

Hall, Lyman 29
Hamilton, Alexander 102
Hamilton College 185
Hamilton, Richard 176
Hampton Institute 122
Hansot, Elizabeth 93
Hargens, Lowell 176
Harlem Renaissance 135
Harper, William Rainey 84

Harris, Rufus C. 92
Harvard Annex 19–20
Harvard College: academic freedom 102; American
    Indians 31, 122; colonial era 35, 137, 138; Early
    Republic 35; elective system 161, 162, 203,
    204; establishment 27, 28–29; faculty lives 35;
    football 139; matriculation 177, 178; presidents
    205–206; same-sex relationships 135–136; science
    37; students 30, 33, 138, 177, 192, 208, 209;
    Unitarianism 166; wealth 67–68, 197
Harvard, John 27
Harvard Law School 63, 189–190
HASHE (historians at ASHE) 3
Haskins, Charles Homer 137n17
Hawkins, Hugh 93
Hevel, Michael 138, 153
higher education: as corporation 25; historiography
    of 204–207, 211; meanings of 2; as means to
    national defense 89; and Progressivism 93–94,
    167; terminology 25; utility and research 40,
    43n29
Higher Education Act (1965) 117, 165, 210
Higher Education Facilities Act (1963) 165
Higher Education for American Democracy 88, 89
Himstead, Ralph E. 173
Hispanics 12
historical evidence 6
historiography 1; of higher education 204–207, 211
    see also thinking historically
history 200–201; amateur history 5; professional
    history 5–6, 17n3; teaching 202 see also thinking
    historically
History of Education Society 3
Hofstadter, Richard 77, 204–205
Holden, Charles 141n27
Holley, Horace 51
Holmes, Hamilton 186
honors organizations 149
Hoover, Herbert 90
Hopkins, Mark 154
Horowitz, Helen 132, 202
House Un-American Activities Committee 120
Howard University 87, 152–153
Hunter-Gault, Charlayne 186

Idealism 160
Illinois College 65
Illinois State Normal University 65
in loco parentis 15, 32, 144
Indiana Unversity 151, 179
institutional racism 172–173, 186, 193, 210
institutional wealth 67–68

institutions of higher education 4; admission requirements 39; Early Republic 20–24, 36–40; reasons to study history of 11–13 *see also* research universities
intelligence tests 107
Iowa Wesleyan 49
Ivy League 140, 185, 192, 209

Jackson, Richard 136, 214
Jackson State University 148
James, William 168, 171
Japanese Americans 116
Jefferson, Thomas 19, 33, 79, 143, 162, 190, 207
Jesuit institutions 169–170
Jews and Judaism: discrimination against 47, 82–83, 106, 114, 146, 178, 187–188; fraternities 151, 152; in higher education 45; in training schools 193
Jim Crow laws 52, 61, 104, 105
Johns Hopkins University 81, 82, 161, 166, 167, 203
Johnson, Charles 120
Johnson, Lyndon Baines 117, 147, 165
Johnson, Mordecai 152
Joint Army and Navy Committee on Welfare and Recreation 109
Joliet High School 58, 84
Joliet Junior College (Illinois) 84
Jordan, Vernon 197
Journal of Negro History 175
Julius Rosenwald Fund 173
junior colleges 58, 84–86, 190
juntos (learning societies) 25

Kaiser, Sara 153
Karier, Clarence J. 95n3
Kean, Melissa 186
Kennedy, John F. 12, 196
Kent, Aratus 48
Kent State University 148
Kerber, Linda 101–102
Kerr, Clark 146
Kett, Joseph 209
Kilgore, Harvey 164
Kim, Dongbin 191
King's College *see* Columbia University
Kingsbury, Susan Myra 80
Kipling, Rudyard 46
Kirk (President of Columbia University) 148
Kirkland (President of Harvard) 162
Korean War 163
Kotler, Philip 202–203
Kovacs, Philip 176
Ku Klux Klan (KKK) 179

Ladd, Everett Carl 176
LaFollette, Bob 78, 88
Lagemann, Ellen 94
LaGrange Female Institute (Georgia) 53, 184–185
land grant institutions 10, 59, 60–62
Lane Seminary (Cincinnati, Ohio) 51
Laney, James T. 168
Latinx students 147, 187, 214
law schools 63, 166, 173, 185, 189–190
Lawrence College (Appleton, Wisconsin) 54
Lawrence Scientific School 37
leadership 23–24, 37, 38, 106, 188
Lehrfreiheit 86
Lerner, Gerda 17n3, 200
Leslie, Bruce 192, 200
liberal arts education 8–9, 36, 45, 60, 79; elite status 166, 183, 189, 192; medieval Europe 25–26; women 63, 66
Light, Donald 171
Lincoln, Abraham 29
Lincoln University (Pennsylvania) 52, 186
Lipset, Seymour 176
literary and debate societies 21, 25, 64–65, 135, 143, 149, 150
Locke, John 13, 20, 95n3
Loss, Christopher 107, 209
Lovejoy, Arthur O. 87
Lowell, A. Lawrence 135
Lowen, Rebecca 109

MacArthur, General Douglas 90
McCarthy, Joseph P. 119
manliness 141, 178
Marcuse, Herbert 212
Marshall, Thurgood 144
Martin, Caryl 140n24
Marx Brothers 143
Mary Sharpe College (Winchester, Tennessee) 54, 184–185
Massachusetts Bay Colony 27
Massachusetts: women's athletics 140
Matthew Effect 175
Mays, Benjamin 145
medical education 81–84, 114, 178, 185, 188
medieval universities 24–25; liberal arts curriculum 25–26; organizational control 26–27
memory as evidence 6
merit aid 195
meritocracy 19, 30, 172, 200–204, 207–210
Merton, Robert 175
Methodists 49
Mexican Americans 145–146, 147 *see also* Latinx students

Miami University 64

middle class: 19th century 62, 63, 66–67, 75; 20th century 89, 184; manliness 141; women 117, 151 *see also* Progressivism

Middlebury College 185

midwestern colleges and universities 14; 19th century 47–55, 58–59, 60–61, 65, 66–67, 68–69; administration 68; certification of secondary schools 58–59

military training 102–103, 106, 107–108

Mill, John Stuart 95n3

Miller, Patrick 142

Milwaukee Female Normal Institute and High School (Wisconsin) 54

Milwaukee Vocational School 195

missionary societies 56, 104

Mississippi State University 142

modern languages 38, 40, 105

Moffat, Michael 133n7

Moore, Kathryn 132

moral and economic purposes of higher education 28–35; faculty lives 35–36; institutions of the Early Republic 36–40

Morehouse College 145

Morehouse School of Medicine 83

Mormons 187

Morrill Land Grant Acts (1862; 1890) 4, 38, 46, 47, 59, 60, 61, 102, 103, 108, 111, 202

Mt. Holyoke Female Seminary 64

Murphy, Patrick 202–203

NAACP 113, 114, 144; Legal Defense Fund 173

Naismith, James 140

name-date-place 3–5, 201

naming 16–17n2, 42n15

Nash, Margaret A. 64, 136

Nast, Thomas 12

nation-building 23

National Academy of Sciences 165

National Association for College Women 153

National Association of Deans of Women 69, 153, 196

National Defense Education Act (1958) 117, 120, 165, 210

National Education Association 87, 195

National Endowment for the Arts 165

National Endowment for the Humanities 165

National Institutes of Mental Health 165

National Labor Relations Board 195

National Scholarship Service 115

National Science Foundation 109, 164, 165

National Student Association 150

National Teacher Examination 178

National Youth Administration 111–112

Native Americans 50; Cherokee 123; Choctaw Nation 122–123; doctors 81; in higher education 21, 30–31, 122–124; Moscogee Creek 123; naming 42n15; tribal colleges 122–124; Virginia colony college 59; wars 122

Navy College Training Program (V-12 Program) 111

Negro History Week 175

New Deal 88, 90, 111

New Light movement 32

New York Times 118–119, 193

New Yorker xiii, 204

Nicholson, Marjorie Hope 168

Nidiffer, Jana 66, 69–70, 132, 153, 189, 211

nineteenth century 44–47; gender and socioeconomic class 64–67; higher education institutional expansion 58–63; midwestern colleges 47–55; purpose of college 54–58; rise of wealth and administration 67–70

Nobel Prize winners 163, 175, 177

normal schools 4, 47, 65–66, 140, 185, 189, 192–193

North Carolina A&T University 148

Northwest Ordinance (1787) 59

Northwest Territories 59

Norwich University 37, 59

Nott, Eliphalet 206

nursing 63, 82, 83

Oberlin College 4, 51–52, 178

objectivism 160

Ogren, Christine A. 65–66

Ohio University 59

Olin Foundation 176

Olson, Keith 91

On the Origin of Species 161

oral histories 5–6

Out (magazine) 212

Oxford Female College 64

Oxford Female Institute 64

Oxford University 27, 29

Packard, Sophia 56

Palmieri, Patricia 80, 204

Parker, Francis 193

Parsons, Talcott 171

Payne, Daniel 53

Payne Theological Seminary 53

pedagogical Progressivism 70

pedagogy 36

Pedersen, Robert Patrick 84, 85

Pell Grants 195

Pepper, Claude 92

Peterson, Frederick Douglass 197

Phillips Exeter Academy 77

philology 159–160
philosophy 161
physical fitness 141
Player, Willa 144
Plessy v. Ferguson (1896) 61
political activism 120, 144–145
political engagement 88
Populism 60–61
Post-War Manpower Re-Adjustment Conference 91–92
Potts, David 49
Powell, Lewis 176, 177
Pratt, Scott 162
preparatory departments 48
Presbyterians 49, 51
presentism 9–10, 30, 61, 85
President's Commission on Higher Education (1947) 114, 115, 116, 191, 196
President's Commission on the Status of Women (1962–1963) 196
Princeton University 40, 48, 131, 139, 163–164, 177
Pritchett, Henry 81, 178
private institutions 23
private sphere 38
professional historians 5–6, 17n3
professions 29–30
professors 86; political attitudes 176; in research universities 171–177; tenure 173–174
Progressivism 14, 67, 74–81; administrative Progressivism 70; and gender 79–80; and higher education 93–94, 167; medical education 81–84; pedagogical Progressivism 70; political engagement 88
Protestantism 30, 45, 49–50, 187
psychology 161
public philosophy 76
public sphere 38
Puritans 27, 29

quadrivium 25–26
Queens College *see* Rutgers University

race and ethnicity 9, 12–13, 47; and gender 187, 188; institutional desegregation 115; *To Secure These Rights* (1947) 114; "separate but equal" 61; in sport 141–142
racism 103, 104, 106, 114, 179, 197; institutional racism 172–173, 186, 193, 210
Ramparts (magazine) 150
Rankin, John 111
rationality 76, 77, 95n3
Reagan, Ronald 212

Reeves, Floyd W. 91, 92
reflection 7
religion 28–29, 32, 45
religious seminaries 29
Rensselaer Polytechnical Institute 36, 37, 59, 161, 189, 206
research universities 3, 15, 63, 118, 159–161; contingent faculty 174; discrimination 170; elective system 161–162; faculty members 168–169; finance 163, 164–165; institutions 161–171; professional schools 166; professors 171–177; research focus 163; research goals 174; salaries 174–175; students 177–180; tenure 173–174; and undergraduate programs 168
Reserve Officer Training Corps (ROTC) 102, 108
revisionism 11
Rhode Island College 28
Ritterband, Paul 45
Rockefeller, John D. 56
Rockefeller, John D., Sr. 197
Rockford Female Seminary (Illinois) 54, 55, 64
Rollins College 79
Roman Catholicism 12, 32, 187
Roosevelt, Franklin D. 90, 109
Roosevelt, Theodore 88, 139
Rosenwald Fund 173
Rossiter, Margaret 79, 204
ROTC *see* Reserve Officer Training Corps
Rousseau, Jean Jacques 7
Rudolph, Frederick 2, 78, 210, 211
Rudy, Willis 2
Rury, John 107, 191
Rush, Benjamin 37
Rutgers University 28, 133, 139, 154, 185, 212

SACS (Southern Association of Colleges and Schools) 170
San Francisco State University 212
Sarah Lawrence College 79
SAT 178, 191
SATC *see* Student Army Training Corps
Schetlin, Eleanor M. 132
Schwartz, Robert 69, 132
science 37, 109, 118, 120
scientific agriculture 60
scientific inquiry 160
Second Great Awakening 143–144, 166
secondary content 2
secondary schools 48–49, 58–59
Sedlak, Michael 39
segregation 51, 61, 83, 85, 134, 142; desegregation 115, 186, 210; residential segregation 47

"separate but equal" 61
Serviceman's Readjustment Act (1944) *see* G.I. Bill
Seven Sister colleges 115, 187
sex and love 133–137, 145
sexual identity 56–57, 135–137, 145, 212, 214
Sheffield Scientific School 37
Sill, Anna Peck 55, 64
Silverman, Jennifer A.R. 136
Simon, William 176, 177
slavery 9–10, 20, 34, 38, 59; assistance to formerly
    enslaved 105; emancipation 103–104
Sloan, Douglas 95n3
Slowe, Lucy Diggs 152–153
Smith College 115
social relationships 54
social sciences 77, 78, 79–81, 175–176
social stratification 185, 187–189, 190, 194–195
societal problems 78
socioeconomic class 8–9, 46–47, 207; after World
    War II 111–112; and enrolment 179, 195; and
    gender 64–67, 152, 188, 189
socioeconomic contract 7–8
Solomon, Barbara 3, 101
sororities 150, 151–152, 179
South Carolina State 148
Southern Association of Colleges and Schools
    (SACS) 170
Southern Association of Schools 83
Southern University and A&M College 148
Southern women's colleges 54, 135, 188
Spelman College 56, 144
Spring Hill College (Mobile, Alabama) 115, 186
Sputnik 120
St. Louis College 32
St. Olaf College (Minnesota) 134–135
Stanford, Leland and Jane 67
Stanford University 66, 67, 109
state universities 62, 184, 186
State University of New York (SUNY) 187
Statement on Principles of Academic Freedom and
    Tenure (1940) 87, 173–174
Stone, Lucy 52, 57
stratification 16, 20; curricular divisions 192;
    elite institutions 14, 19, 22–24, 191, 192, 208;
    institutional stratification 185, 186–189, 190, 192,
    193–194; merit aid 195; social stratification 185,
    187–189, 190, 194–195; standardized testing 59,
    76–77, 82, 107, 178, 190–192 *see also* gender; race
    and ethnicity
student activities 15, 64–65, 85, 130–133; beer 137–138;
    dancing 134, 135; football 138–143; Harvard 33;
    literary and debate societies 21, 25, 64–65, 135,

143, 149, 150; other important activities 143–153;
    political activism 120, 144–145; yearbooks and
    newspapers 23
Student Army Training Corps (SATC) 106, 107–108
student assessment 107
student discipline 132–133
student government 66, 149–150, 153
student life 32, 33–34, 150–152
student riots 32, 137, 138, 143
student selectivity 6, 84, 104, 185, 190–192, 194,
    206, 208
student services 68–70, 112, 130–131, 144, 154
students: colonial era 30, 31–34; deaf students
    145; disabled students 146; diversity 209; Early
    Republic 32–34; equality of opportunity 114, 208;
    in research universities 177–180; sex and love
    133–137, 145 *see also* coeducation
subjectivity 160
SUNY (State University of New York) 187
Sweet Briar College (Virginia) 139

Talbott, Marion 58, 69
Taylor, Frederick Winslow 68, 70, 77
Templeton, John Newton 59
tenure 115, 173–174
Terman, Lewis 107
terrorism, war on 121–122
testing 207; and family income 191–192; standardized
    tests 59, 76–77, 82, 107, 178, 190–192
Thayer, Colonel Sylvanus 137
Thelin, John 2–3, 45, 68, 140–141
theology 159–160
theory 16
thinking historically 1–2, 41n5, 210–214; amateur
    history 5; endnotes 2, 5; name-date-place 3–5, 201;
    professional history 5–6; secondary content 2
Thomas, M. Cary 80
Thoreau, Henry David 214
Thwing, Charles Franklin 204, 211
Ticknor, George 162
To Secure These Rights (1947) 114
Transylvania University (Lexington, KY) 50–51, 134
Treaty of Dancing Rabbit Creek 123
tribal colleges 122–124
trivium 25
Troy Female Seminary (New York) 38–39, 54, 69
Troy University (Alabama) 193, 194
Truman, Harry S. 114
Tulane University 92, 186
Turner, Nat 31
Tuskegee Institute 187, 197
Tyack, David B. 70, 93

UNCF (United Negro College Fund) 197
Union College (New York) 150, 206
Union Seminary (Columbus, Ohio) 53
Unitarians 51, 166
United States Armed Forces Institute (USAFI)
    92–93, 110–111
University of Alabama 34, 103, 143, 186, 194
University of Alaska 62
University of Arkansas 48
University of Berlin 81, 159
University of California: Berkeley 62, 116, 139, 146,
    194, 205; Cal 139, 194; College of Commerce 63;
    communism 119; fraternities 150; Los Angeles
    120, 146, 212; loyalty oath 119; research 167; Santa
    Cruz 212
University of Cambridge 27
University of Chicago 58, 66, 69, 109, 115, 134, 164,
    167, 173, 176–177, 193
University of Colorado Boulder 121, 122
University of Columbia 164
University of Georgia 22–23, 28, 143, 165, 186
University of Göttingen 159–160
University of Halle 159–160
University of Hawai'i 62
University of Idaho 62
University of Illinois 65, 69, 148, 179
University of Iowa 179
University of Kansas 179
University of Kentucky 133–134
University of Maine 108
University of Michigan 66–67, 84, 150, 164, 167, 177
University of Minnesota 163, 179
University of Minnesota General College 79
University of Mississippi 166
University of Missouri 136, 145, 173
University of Montana 62
University of Nebraska 179
University of North Carolina 22, 28, 141
University of North Dakota 62
University of Notre Dame 142–143
University of Oregon 60
University of Paris 27, 35–36
University of Pennsylvania 150, 195; grading system
    33, 138, 202; Wharton School of Finance and
    Economy 63 see also College of Philadelphia
University of Tennessee 103
University of Texas 136
University of Virginia 33–34, 143, 149, 162, 185, 203
University of Washington 119
University of Wisconsin 62; admission criteria 179–180;
    Progressivism 77–78; research 48, 164, 167, 171,
    177; sexual identity 136; women 66, 179

U.S. Military Academy 36, 189
USAFI see United States Armed Forces Institute
USSR 119, 120, 121
utilitarian education 45, 59–60, 63

Van Hise, Charles 78
Vanderbilt University 166, 186
Vansina, Jan 6
Vassar College 54
Veblen, Thorstein 75, 86, 167
venture schools 40
Veysey, Laurence 2, 43n29, 48, 68, 86, 132, 133, 154,
    167, 205, 211
vice-presidents 69–70
Vietnam War 116–118, 124n1; anti-war protests 146,
    148; Selective Service exclusion 117
Vietnamese American students 147
Virginia Military Institute 60
Von Humboldt, Wilhelm 159

Waite, Cally 51, 178
Wallace, Henry 88
War Department educational programs 110, 111
war: effects on higher education 14–15, 88–89,
    100–101; American Revolution 101–102;
    assistance to veterans 105; Civil War 102–106;
    Cold War 118–121; effect on African Americans
    100–101, 112; effect on research 163–165; impact
    of G.I. Bill 75–76, 89–93, 112; Korean War 163;
    tribal colleges 122–124; Vietnam 116–118,
    124n1, 146, 148; war on terrorism 121–122;
    World War I 90, 106–108, 114, 178; World War II
    15, 88–89, 91, 100–101, 108–116, 121
War on Poverty 117, 165
Washington, Booker T. 104
Washington, George 22, 102
Weber, Max 30
Webster, Daniel 23
Wechsler, Harold 45, 152, 178
Wellesley College 80, 176, 189
Wells College 185
Wesleyan College (Macon, Georgia) 53, 54, 140
West Point 37, 59, 137
West Virginia 120
Western expansion 50
Western Female Seminary 64
White, Hayden xii
White, Walter 114
Wichita, Kansas 144
Wigglesworth, Edward 102
Wilberforce College (Ohio) 52–53, 186
Willard, Emma 38–39, 40, 54, 58

William Smith College 185
Williams College (Massachusetts) 154
Williamson, Joy Ann 148, 211
Willie, Charles V. 6
Willis, Rudy 44
Willow 214
Wilson, Logan 171
Wisconsin: land grants 59; normal schools 65–66, 140
Wisconsin Idea 77–78, 93
Wissenschaft 86, 160
Witherspoon, John 29
Wolfe, Thomas 134
women: African Americans 21, 38, 117, 187; in the American Revolution 101–102; Boston marriages 56–57; doctors 81, 83; historians 5, 17n3; role in society 38; same-sex relationships 56–57, 135–137; teachers 38–39, 103; during war 103, 108, 116; Wellesley marriages 57, 135
women in higher education 2, 3, 4, 10, 211; 19th century 47, 51–52, 53–58, 62, 63, 64, 65–66, 68–69, 184–185; 20th century 191, 196–197; African Americans 56, 79, 152–153, 187; athletics 139–140, 152; citations of 175–176; on coeducational campuses 134–135, 185; deans of women 69, 132, 135, 152–153; Early Republic 38–40; exclusion 20, 21, 26, 31, 39, 52, 179, 185; faculty members 79–80, 170–171; Harvard Annex 19–20; Irish women 193; Jewish women 193; law students 185; medical students 82, 185; normal schools 4, 47, 65, 185, 189, 192–193; purpose of college 54–58; in research universities 166–167, 170–171; socioeconomic class 188, 189;

sororities 150, 151–152, 179; venture schools 40; in World War II 116, 117
women's colleges 36, 53–54, 56, 79, 144, 184–185, 204; Southern colleges 54, 135, 188
women's rights 52, 117–118
Woodruff, Robert 168
Woodson, Cater G. 175
World Trade Center attacks 121–122
World War I 90, 106–108, 114, 178
World War II 15, 108–116; African Americans 100–101; attack on Pearl Harbor 121; educational programs for armed forces 109–111; higher education 89, 91, 109; veterans 88–89, 112, 114; women 116, 117
Wounded Knee 122
Wright, Bobby 30–31, 42n15

Yale College 27, 28, 37; curriculum 22, 36; doctorates 35, 161; football 139, 143; influence of 48; matriculation 177; president 32; wealth 68
Yale Laws (1745) 31, 133, 137
Yale Report (1828) 4, 20, 32, 34, 39, 40, 42n18, 102, 132, 188
Yerkes, Robert 107
Yeshiva University 195, 213
YMCA 145, 190
Young, Ella Flagg 57, 193
Young, Michael 19, 207

Zinn, Howard 6, 124n1, 201
Zook, George 89
Zuckerman, Harriet 175

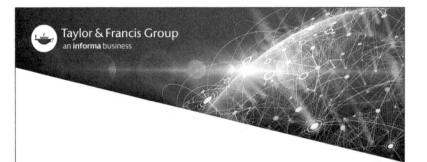